Digital Media Law

MW01078311

Digital Media Law offers a practical guide to the law of media and communication, focusing on digital channels, models, and technologies. It draws together the aspects of media law that are most critical for those engaged in the production and distribution of digital media, from traditional broadcasters and internet-based services to major internet platforms.

As an expert scholar and educator in media law, Christopher S. Reed brings considerable experience as an in-house lawyer for a U.S.-based media company with extensive news, sports, and entertainment operations. This blend of practical and scholarly insight delivers a textbook that packs foundational principles and concepts into the context of the digital environment, focusing on how those doctrines are applied in the face of rapidly evolving newsgathering, production, and distribution technologies.

Key features include:

- "In the News" sections that tie the legal principles to real-world events or situations
- An integrated fictional case study of a media enterprise
- Insights into digital media policy.

This accessible textbook is the ideal companion for advanced undergraduate and graduate students as well as practitioners interested in law, journalism, and media studies.

Christopher S. Reed is a lawyer in the entertainment industry focusing on intellectual property, First Amendment, antitrust, and general commercial litigation. He previously served as the head of global content protection at 21st Century Fox, the senior policy advisor to the U.S. Register of Copyrights, and a trial attorney for the Antitrust Division of the U.S. Department of Justice. He began his legal career as a law clerk to the Honorable Steven J. McAuliffe of the U.S. District Court for the District of New Hampshire. He holds a BS in economics from Lehigh University, and JD and LLM degrees from the Franklin Pierce School of Law at the University of New Hampshire, where he now serves as a professor of practice. His website is www.chrisreed.com.

Digital Media Law

A Practical Guide for the Media and Entertainment Industries

CHRISTOPHER S. REED

Routledge
Taylor & Francis Group

LONDON AND NEW YORK

Cover image: metamorworks /iStock/Getty Images Plus via Getty Images

First published 2023
by Routledge
4 Park Square, Milton Park, Abingdon, Oxon OX14 4RN

and by Routledge
605 Third Avenue, New York, NY 10158

Routledge is an imprint of the Taylor & Francis Group, an informa business

British Library Cataloguing-in-Publication Data
A catalogue record for this book is available from the British Library

Library of Congress Cataloging-in-Publication Data
Names: Reed, Christopher S., author.
Title: Digital media law : a practical guide for the media and entertainment
industries / Christopher S. Reed.
Description: Abingdon, Oxon ; New York, NY : Routledge, 2023. |
Includes bibliographical references and index. | Summary -- Provided by Publisher
Identifiers: LCCN 2022015260 | ISBN 9781032055312 (hardback) |
ISBN 9781032052304 (paperback) | ISBN 9781003197966 (ebook)
Subjects: LCSH: Digital media--Law and legislation--United States.
Classification: LCC KF2750 .R44 2023 | DDC 343.7309/9--dc23/eng/20220801
LC record available at https://lccn.loc.gov/2022015260

ISBN: 978-1-032-05531-2 (hbk)
ISBN: 978-1-032-05230-4 (pbk)
ISBN: 978-1-003-19796-6 (ebk)

DOI: 10.4324/9781003197966

Typeset in Bembo
by Deanta Global Publishing Services, Chennai, India

ABOUT THE AUTHOR

Christopher S. Reed is a lawyer in the entertainment industry focusing on intellectual property, First Amendment, antitrust, and general commercial litigation. He previously served as the head of global content protection at 21st Century Fox, the senior policy advisor to the U.S. Register of Copyrights, and a trial attorney for the Antitrust Division of the U.S. Department of Justice. He began his legal career as a law clerk to the Honorable Steven J. McAuliffe of the U.S. District Court for the District of New Hampshire.

Chris is the author of *The Unrealized Promise of the Next Great Copyright Act: U.S. Copyright Policy for the 21st Century* (2019) and *Copyright Workflow for Photographers* (2014).

He holds a BS in economics from Lehigh University, and JD and LLM degrees from the Franklin Pierce School of Law at the University of New Hampshire, where he now serves as a professor of practice.

Chris resides in Los Angeles. His website is www.chrisreed.com.

CONTENTS

Acknowledgments   ix
Preface   xi
Disclaimer   xiii

1   DEFINING DIGITAL MEDIA   1

2   LAW AND THE U.S. LEGAL SYSTEM   15

3   THE FIRST AMENDMENT   37

4   DEFAMATION   61

5   PRIVACY AND PUBLICITY   89

6   NEWSGATHERING   113

7   REPORTING ON THE GOVERNMENT   137

8   COMMERCIAL SPEECH AND ADVERTISING   159

9   RADIO AND TELEVISION   177

10 THE INTERNET   197

11 INTELLECTUAL PROPERTY: MEDIA AS IP USER   223

12 INTELLECTUAL PROPERTY: MEDIA AS PRODUCER   249

Case: Mountain One Media   259
Index   263

ACKNOWLEDGMENTS

Although the cover and title page identify only a single author, this book, as with most books, was the product of assistance, feedback, guidance, and support generously offered by others.

I am especially grateful to Jonathan T.D. Neil, founding director of the Center for Business and Management of the Arts at Claremont Graduate University, and Sarah Conley Odenkirk, its associate director at the time, for inviting me to develop a media business and law course for its arts management master's degree program. Developing and teaching that course was the impetus for creating much of the material that became the foundation of this book.

Similarly, thank you to University of New Hampshire Franklin Pierce School of Law dean Megan Carpenter, and executive director of the Franklin Pierce Center for Intellectual Property, Micky Minhas, for inviting me to teach a media law course at the school's summer intellectual property law institute, which gave me additional opportunities to further develop the material.

Most importantly, I am grateful to the students at both institutions who took my courses and whose feedback and input have been instrumental in making this book the best it can be.

Additional thanks to Greg Dina, Elizabeth Townsend Gard, Vivian Lee, Kathy Olson, and Maria Pallante. Also, a big thank you to the team that helped bring this book to fruition, including Naomi Round Cahalin, Terry Clague, Zoe Everitt, Jeremy North, and Lillian Woodall.

Finally, thank you to my partner Ryan, without whose support this book – or any of my other projects – would not be possible.

Notwithstanding the help and support of the people listed here, this book is principally my own work, and all errors, omissions, and the like are mine alone. The views expressed in this book are also mine alone and are not necessarily the views of any employer, client, customer, or other affiliated entity, past or present.

PREFACE

As the title implies, this book aims to be a practical guide to the legal issues confronted by those who are engaged in the production and distribution of digital media, ranging from traditional broadcasters and publishers to the major internet platforms and the new class of "media enterprises" that they have spawned such as YouTube influencers and TikTok stars.

I have written this book from the dual perspective of a practicing lawyer and an instructor. As a lawyer in the media and entertainment industry, I have worked with and helped defend numerous creative professionals as they practice their craft, and I have gained an understanding of the legal issues they regularly encounter and an appreciation for the context and environment in which those issues arise. As an instructor, I have had the opportunity to teach media law to budding lawyers in a law school environment, as well as media professionals in an arts management master's program.

This book is my attempt at bringing together the aspects of media law that I believe are most critical for journalists, producers, and the like, to understand. I begin with some foundational principles and concepts that underlie the law and the U.S. legal system generally, and then explore how those doctrines apply to the business of producing and distributing news, information, and entertainment for mass audiences. To help reinforce the concepts, each of the major substantive chapters in this book includes a brief "In the News" section that ties the legal principles featured in the chapter to a real-world event or situation, so you can see how media law issues play out in practice.

ORGANIZATION

I have attempted to organize this book in a logical fashion, beginning with Chapter 1's scoping discussion to identify what we mean by "digital media" and in what ways it is different from, or similar to, "traditional media." Chapter 2 offers a discussion of the general framework of U.S. law and the legal system, and Chapter 3 looks specifically at the First Amendment, which is the foundation of virtually every aspect of media law.

The subsequent chapters delve into a number of specific areas of media law that readers are most likely to encounter, beginning with Chapter 4's treatment of defamation, rights of privacy and publicity in Chapter 5, limitations and restrictions on newsgathering in Chapter 6, unique considerations of reporting on the government in Chapter 7, and commercial speech in Chapter 8. The next two chapters look at the specific regulatory environment of traditional radio and television broadcasting

(Chapter 9) and the internet (Chapter 10), with a particular emphasis on recent calls to increase oversight of the major internet platforms.

The final two topical chapters focus on the role of intellectual property in the media enterprise, with Chapter 11 considering the media enterprise as a "user" of intellectual property assets, while Chapter 12 considers the media enterprise as a creator and owner of intellectual property.

The last chapter of this book features a case involving a hypothetical media enterprise, Mountain One. The facts and circumstances presented in the case raise issues that are discussed throughout this book. You can use the case to check your own knowledge and understanding of the material, or as fodder for discussion in study groups, class discussions, and the like.

LIMITATIONS AND A WORD OF CAUTION

This book is principally about U.S. law and the U.S. legal system. Although there are some references to laws and legal systems outside of the United States, it is not the primary focus of the book. Moreover, this book is intended to be a broad survey of the areas of law applicable to the practice and craft of producing news, media, and entertainment, and provides exposure and familiarity to a broad range of areas that media professionals may encounter. It is not intended to be an in-depth treatise on any one topic, and in many cases, the topics discussed here are the subject of much more in-depth resources that I encourage you to review for a more detailed discussion.

In that same vein, although this book is about law and law-related topics, it is not intended to be legal advice, or a substitute for such advice. For that, you should consult a lawyer, experienced in media law issues, who is duly licensed and authorized to practice in your jurisdiction. If you are employed by a media enterprise, you will very likely have a procedure in place to escalate legal questions and issues to your colleagues who are best suited to help navigate them.

DISCLAIMER

This book is intended for educational purposes only. No portion may be construed as rendering legal advice for specific cases, or as creating an attorney-client relationship between the reader and the author. The opinions expressed in this book are solely those of the author and are not purported to be those of any employer, client, customer, or other affiliated entity, past or present.

1

CHAPTER 1
DEFINING DIGITAL MEDIA

Before we jump into the law of digital media, it is helpful to define what "digital media" means and in what ways it is similar to, and distinct from "traditional media." This chapter considers how advances in technology have led to changes to the way content is created, distributed, and consumed, and examines in what ways the law of traditional media is the same for digital media and where digital distribution has given rise to new legal doctrines.

INTRODUCTION

Ask someone of a certain age what "the media" means, and they might tell you that it refers to newspapers, television and radio stations, magazines, and books. Ask the same question of someone of a different (read: younger) age, and they might tell you that "the media" comprises services such as Facebook, Twitter, or TikTok, or they might mention various streaming platforms such as Netflix, Amazon Prime Video, and Hulu, or they might discuss the latest true crime podcast they just listened to.

They're both right.

There is a common theme among what those across various generations describe as "the media": all of the media outlets listed above are principally aimed at communicating something to the public on a mass scale. As we will see throughout this book, the nature of media has changed in recent years, owing largely to corresponding changes in technology that have changed the way media is produced, distributed, and consumed.

For the purposes of this chapter, we will consider media as falling into two categories: (1) "legacy" or "traditional" media, such as newspapers, television, and radio; and (2) "digital" media, which comprises that which is distributed primarily by the internet.

We will see that in some cases, the legal and regulatory framework that applies to traditional media applies equally to the digital landscape, yet, in other cases, the digital media regulatory environment is very different.

Two other definitions of note: we will use the term "media enterprise" to mean those who are engaged in the activity of producing, packaging, or distributing content with the intent to distribute it to other people to consume (watch, read, listen to), and we will use the term "media product" or "media property" to refer to a media enterprise's output – the content that is distributed in packaged form, such as books, films, articles, television, shows, podcasts, and so on.

DOI: 10.4324/9781003197966-1

CHARACTERISTICS OF TRADITIONAL MEDIA

One of the defining characteristics of traditional media enterprises is that they generally required significant capital investment to enter the market. To start a newspaper, book, or magazine publishing company, one had to build or at least secure access to printing facilities and a distribution mechanism to get the finished products into newsstands, bookstores, and other places where people typically acquired or consumed such material. Similarly, record labels required studios with expensive, complex equipment, and facilities to manufacture vinyl discs, cassette tapes, and eventually compact discs; they too needed to establish a distribution network to get those physical copies into the hands of consumers. Running television and radio stations required not only a significant investment in equipment – studios, transmitters, antennas, and the like – but also a license from the government to use a portion of the limited public electromagnetic spectrum (discussed more fully in Chapter 9).

We can boil all this down into one overarching principle of traditional media, which is simply that only a few people get to do it. Because of the scale and investment required, the media landscape is largely dominated by a handful of major players in each industry: there are five major book publishers (Penguin Random House, Hachette, HarperCollins, Macmillan, and Simon and Schuster), five major film and TV studios (Disney, Netflix, Paramount, Sony Pictures, and Warner Media), four broadcast television networks (ABC, CBS, FOX, and NBC), three major radio broadcasters (iHeartMedia, Cumulus, and Audacy), four major television broadcasters (Nexstar, Sinclair, Tegna, and Gray), three major record labels (Universal, Sony, and Warner), and three major newspaper chains (Gannett, Media News Group, McClatchy), and, of course, several dominant newspapers with national reach, such as *The Washington Post* (owned by Amazon.com founder Jeff Bezos), *The New York Times*, *USA Today* (Gannett), and *The Wall Street Journal* (News Corp., which also owns book publisher HarperCollins).

To be sure, despite the apparent consolidation among media enterprises, there is no shortage of creative professionals eager to write the next great American novel, produce the next hit television series, or write a multi-part investigative piece about government corruption, but in the world of traditional media, those people must be hired by media enterprises, who agree to take on their projects, and take on the financial risk of doing so. This dynamic makes sense, because the cost of producing and distributing content in the traditional media environment is so high. It would be economically inefficient, and likely cost prohibitive, for most individuals to assemble the infrastructure necessary to produce and distribute traditional media products, so it requires large, well-resourced companies to take risks on deciding which movies to produce, albums to release, or books to publish.

The economics of producing media products can be described by the **Pareto principle**, which suggests that, on average, about 80% of the revenue will be generated from about 20% of a media enterprise's catalog. That essentially means that for every major hit, there may be dozens of failures. Larger, well-resourced companies have the ability to spread that risk out across dozens of products, allowing the runaway hits to essentially fund the failures. Creating this broad portfolio of content requires a significant investment beyond the capital investment in production and distribution infrastructure discussed previously, and because it is difficult to know in advance which media products will be successful, only large, well-resourced enterprises are capable of making the investments and taking risks at the scale required of the traditional media industry.

Another key characteristic of traditional media is that in most cases, a media enterprise has no direct connection to its consumers, because the end product reaches them through a complex network of distribution intermediaries. Publishers, for instance, sell their books, magazines, and newspapers to a distributor, who in turn, sells them to bookstores and newsstands, which ultimately sell them to consumers. The same is true for music, which goes from record labels to distributors and then into music stores. Most U.S. households get their broadcast television through a cable provider such as Comcast Xfinity or Spectrum.

Accordingly, many media enterprises relied on proxies to determine how the public engaged with their products. Perhaps the best example comes from the broadcasting industries, where television and radio stations rely on ratings data compiled by third-party services that aim to estimate the number of people in the audience. As we will see later in this chapter, the lack of a direct connection to their audiences, and the related lack of information about how their audiences engage with their content, has put traditional media enterprises at a disadvantage with respect to their digital media counterparts.

CHARACTERISTICS OF DIGITAL MEDIA

As you have probably guessed, if for no other reason than some of the examples in the section above now seem quaint, the rise of digital media has dramatically changed the media landscape.

The "digital" in "digital media" is essentially a shorthand way to represent a series of advances in technology that have led to significant changes in the way media enterprises create media products and how they are distributed to consumers.

As noted, media production used to require a significant investment in expensive, professional equipment. Filming a movie, for example, required large, heavy cameras and sophisticated editing equipment. Today, a budding filmmaker can easily shoot, edit, and upload a video from a cell phone that fits in his or her pocket. A singer/songwriter can easily record, mix, and distribute a song or a collection of songs (what we once called an "album") with a relatively inexpensive microphone and a laptop, as opposed to renting an expensive recording studio or being forced to sign an exclusive deal with a record label to get access to one. In short, technology has advanced, and the price of that technology has fallen so precipitously, such that virtually anyone can create professional quality media without the considerable investment that was once required.

Technology has also changed the way that media products are distributed to consumers, and the way consumers interact with them. The rise of nearly ubiquitous high-speed internet connectivity, either through wireline connections in homes and businesses or through increasingly fast cellular networks, coupled with the proliferation of mobile devices, has given consumers more ways to obtain and consume content than ever before. The notion of "watching television" or "seeing a movie" has been transformed into a single experience involving "watching content on a screen," which might mean a traditional large screen in a someone's living room, a laptop, or a mobile device such as a smartphone or tablet. Books can now be consumed on virtually any device, including those built specifically for buying and reading books, such as Amazon's Kindle line of devices.

These advances lay the foundation for new forms of entertainment and media to spring to life. Netflix, for example, which began as an internet-based DVD rental outfit that mailed physical discs to its customers, harnessed the power of the evolving internet and launched the streaming video content service that it has become best known for. Today, Netflix is the functional equivalent of a traditional television station or network, offering viewers a vast library of content. The difference? It's all available on demand and asynchronously, as Netflix can distribute specific content to specific users, as opposed to a traditional broadcaster, which offers a single slate of programming to everybody.

The technological environment that spawned Netflix has also allowed independent creators to distribute their content without the need for a large media enterprise to serve as an intermediary because the investment required to distribute on the internet is negligible compared with the investments required to distribute through traditional channels. Thanks to platforms such as YouTube and Soundcloud, virtually anyone can distribute their videos, music, and written works to the world for free. That has not only given creative professionals new opportunities to create their own works, but also changed the competitive landscape for the entire media industry, as traditional players now find themselves competing against independent creators.

Traditional media companies have not ignored the shift to digital (though some would argue they have been a bit slow at adapting). There is no one path to the digital environment, with different companies in different sectors of the media industry taking different tacks.

In the television and film industries, many of the traditional studios and broadcasters have launched their own streaming platforms, such as Disney+ (The

Walt Disney Company, and its suite of brands, including Disney, Marvel, National Geographic, and Twentieth Century Fox), Paramount+ (Paramount, which includes popular networks such as CBS, MTV, and Nickelodeon), Discovery+ (including the Discovery Channel, TLC, HGTV, and numerous other lifestyle networks), HBO Max (Warner Brothers Discovery, including the popular suite of Discovery networks and the historic Warner Brothers film and television library), and Peacock (NBC Universal, including NBC, Bravo, and Lifetime). Many local TV stations stream local news broadcasts on their websites and make them available through smartphone and tablet apps. Although each company has adopted a slightly different strategy, broadly speaking, most of these services offer a library of programming that is (or was at some point) also available on the traditional networks, but also some original programming, available only on the streaming platform. These "streaming originals" are intended to stimulate consumer demand, leading to new subscribers.

In other segments, the traditional players distribute through digital aggregators rather than their own platforms. In music, for example, rather than establish their own proprietary streaming services, most record labels have coalesced around making their works available on platforms such as Spotify, Apple Music, and Tidal; in the book industry, the major publishers sell their electronic books through online retailers such as Amazon, but also the online versions of traditional retailers such as Barnes & Noble's BN.com.

In the radio industry, many of the nation's leading broadcasters have launched apps, such as iHeartMedia's iHeartRadio App, or Audacy's eponymous app, which allow users to listen to their broadcast stations, but also assemble playlists of their favorite content. The radio industry also offers a good example of where modern advances in technology have allowed creators to re-deploy older technologies to reach new audiences. Podcasts have grown significantly in popularity in recent years, yet the technology that underlies them is relatively simple and well established. From a technical perspective, podcasts are little more than recorded audio, which the radio industry has been producing for decades. From a creative perspective, most podcasts feature some version of what radio has been doing since its inception: interviews, music, news reporting, in-depth documentaries, and so on.

What distinguishes podcasts from traditional radio programming is the delivery mechanism. Podcasts are delivered asynchronously – that is, they are downloaded, stored, and listened to at a time that is convenient for the listener – in contrast to traditional radio broadcasting, which is ephemeral, and the audience must be listening at a particular time to hear it or they miss it. Podcasts, on the other hand, are generally available for months or years after they are first released, and often find audiences well past their initial launch date. Moreover, because the cost of producing a podcast is lower than the cost of operating a radio station or radio network, podcasters have more freedom to take risks and experiment with innovative forms of programming.

Finally, one significant feature of digital distribution is that it is much easier to forge a direct connection with the audience than it has been in the traditional media environment. As noted previously, traditional media enterprises distribute their products through myriad channels, and content often works its way through a number of intermediary distributors who ultimately develop the relationship with the consumer. In the digital environment, platforms get a wealth of data back about how consumers interact with their content. Netflix, for instance, knows exactly how many people have watched a particular title, or how many episodes of a series people watch before abandoning it. It also has the ability to scan its data – derived from the viewing habits of more than 200 million worldwide users – to look for patterns, identify trends, and predict demand for new programming.

Access to such data, and perhaps more importantly, the ability to analyze it critically and develop programming and business strategies around insights developed from that data, is quickly becoming a key driver of competitive advantage in the digital media environment. That is why many traditional media enterprises have been investing heavily in building their own streaming platforms, allowing them to capture the audience data for themselves, rather than allowing an intermediary such as Netflix to capture it and use it to ultimately compete with them by using that data as a basis to launch its own original programming.

The pressure on traditional media companies in the television and film space to build large content libraries to support new streaming services has led to a wave of industry consolidation in recent years.

In March of 2019, The Walt Disney Company acquired most of 21st Century Fox, including the legendary Twentieth Century Fox studio, and dozens of television networks, including FX and National Geographic, and it gave the combined company a controlling interest in the popular streaming service Hulu. Disney+ launched several months later, featuring much of the content it had acquired from Fox. Soon after, CBS and Viacom merged and launched Paramount+. In 2022, WarnerMedia, including the Warner Brothers film and television studio and a number of cable networks, such as HBO and CNN, merged with Discovery Communications, which operates popular cable networks such as The Discovery Channel, TLC, and HGTV. Eventually, the two are expected to combine their streaming services, HBO Max and Discovery+ into a single platform. In late May 2020, Amazon announced it would acquire MGM, bringing with it the popular *James Bond* and *Rocky* franchises, as well as popular television and streaming series such as *The Handmaid's Tale* (originally distributed by Hulu) and *Fargo* (FX).

In sum, digital media technology, and the evolution of the media business that has resulted, has changed the media landscape significantly by expanding access to new players, but also triggering significant consolidation among existing players looking to compete in an increasingly crowded marketplace.

THE MORE THINGS CHANGE...

There is an old proverb that states that the more things change, the more they stay the same, and that is especially true with respect to three key features of the media industry as it evolves from its traditional roots into the digital era.

THE GAME IS STILL ABOUT BUILDING AUDIENCE

Fundamentally, for the success of media, a product requires that there is an audience willing to invest its time and money into consuming it. That means the practice of operating a media enterprise is fundamentally the same, whether it's traditional, digital, or a combination of the two.

The media industry has always operated with two principal business models: one where consumers pay directly for access to certain content, such as buying a CD or book at the store or subscribing to a premium cable channel such as HBO for a monthly fee, and one that is indirectly funded through the sale of advertising. In ad-supported models, the media enterprise essentially provides the content to its audience for "free" in exchange for the audience's commitment to watch advertising. At its core, the ad-supported model involves aggregating an audience, and then "leasing" the audience's attention to advertisers for discrete portions of time. The media enterprise generates its revenue from advertisers.

The rise of digital technology has led some media enterprises to experiment with new models, such as offering ad-free versions of traditionally ad-supported content in exchange for a monthly fee paid directly by the audience, or a commitment to watch fewer, but more targeted (or longer) commercial announcements.

Regardless of the distribution mechanism or the business model underlying it, producing and distributing media requires that someone consumes it.

IT STILL COSTS MONEY TO MAKE MEDIA

There is a fallacy among some consumers that because the cost of digital media production and distribution has decreased dramatically in recent years, the price for such media should decline significantly, or as some extremists believe, it should become free. But that view ignores the fact that despite the changes in the cost of media technologies, the cost of human inputs remains largely unchanged.

It is true that the cost to distribute content digitally – a film or an episode of television on a streaming service or a downloadable e-book, for example – has fallen substantially below what it costs to distribute that same content in hardcopy form, but the people associated with bringing that content to fruition must still be paid. Although distributing a book may no longer incur costs for paper, ink, and shipping, the writers, editors, and designers who create the book must still be compensated. Similarly, a budding filmmaker may now be able to distribute her film to the masses for free using YouTube, however, the writers, directors, producers, actors, and others who bring that film from idea to finished product still have to earn a living.

In that respect, then, a digital media enterprise is not that dissimilar to a traditional media enterprise. Although the cost structure has changed somewhat, it does not mean that media products will become costless.

THE GATEKEEPERS HAVE NOT GONE ANYWHERE

One of the celebrated virtues of digital media is that the lower costs of distribution mean that virtually anyone can now create content and distribute it widely, and instantly, at the push of a button. No longer must a would-be creative professional convince a studio, publisher, record label, newspaper, or another traditional media enterprise to invest in developing and distributing their work. Instead, they can simply upload it to YouTube, Soundcloud, Kindle Direct Publishing (formerly CreateSpace), WordPress, or any number of other (and ever-growing and evolving) platforms, and it's instantly accessible to the world. Traditional media enterprises and their complex distribution chains no longer serve as gatekeepers of creative content.

That, of course, offers significant positive benefits because it makes it easier for new content creators to enter the market, which, in turn, offers opportunities for new voices. Similarly, media consumers now have a wealth of information and entertainment options at their fingertips, and owing to mobile technology, that content is available nearly everywhere, on a device that, at least for most people, goes with them everywhere.

But the downside to this ubiquitous and seemingly eternal fount of content is that as the number of choices increases, it becomes more difficult for media products to be discovered, and media consumers may become paralyzed by the **paradox of choice** – a principle that suggests that it becomes more difficult to choose among a number of options as the number of available options increases. In media circles, this problem is often referred to as the **discovery problem**.

In the traditional media environment, the discovery problem was not as significant because there were fewer sources of content, the distribution channels were relatively limited, and media enterprises committed considerable resources to marketing their products. But now that essentially anyone can become a media enterprise, producing and distributing content using little more than a laptop or smartphone, finding the content worth consuming has become much more challenging.

Enter the new gatekeepers.

Whereas in the traditional media landscape it was film and television studios, record labels, and publishers that made decisions about what gets produced, distributed, and marketed, today it is the companies that operate the well-known platforms on which creatives host their works, such as YouTube (videos), Soundcloud (music), Medium (short-form articles), Stitcher (podcasts), and Apple (podcasts, apps) that hold much of the power. And that means that digital media is now beholden to algorithms – the black box calculus that determines the next video "you also might like" after watching something on YouTube, or that guides you to a similar track after listening to a song on Soundcloud. The algorithm decides who gets served what, and when, and it decides, in part, what content gets featured on the platform's homepage.

Of course, if a user goes to one of these platforms and searches for a specific title, it's easy enough to find it, but that requires that the user has already been exposed to the content or is at least aware of it. For content discovery – exposing media products to new audiences – getting the algorithm on your side is key.

Take podcasts as an example.

A recent study determined that there are over two million podcasts in production today, comprising about 48 million episodes.[1] Many of those podcasts are produced by traditional media organizations, such as National Public Radio (NPR) and *The New York Times*, and are relatively well known and sought after. But how will somebody discover one of the less familiar podcasts or a new podcast that doesn't have much traction yet? The answer lies in the algorithm.

If you have ever listened to a podcast, you have almost certainly heard the host implore you to "subscribe wherever you get your podcasts" and to leave a positive review. That's because the number of positive reviews, subscriber counts, and whether the subscriber counts continue to increase over time are all thought to be criteria that go into most major platforms' calculations as to which podcasts get featured on the platform's most prominent screen real estate or referred to users after they finish other titles.

Many of the heavyweights in the space are also among the most prolific traditional media brands, and some even have their own platforms, such as NPR, iHeartRadio, and Audacy. And, of course, where a media enterprise controls its own platform, it remains the gatekeeper of the content – for example, NPR is the gatekeeper of the content that is broadcast on its traditional radio network, as well as over its podcast platform, just as Disney is the gatekeeper for content that appears on its traditional platforms (the ABC network) as well as its Disney+ streaming platform.

But in the great expanse of the internet, those traditional brands must now compete with content on myriad other platforms that they do not control, all of which are

---

1 Podcast Insights, https://www.podcastinsights.com/podcast-statistics (accessed February 5, 2022).

competing for the audience's attention in the same basic media ecosystem. And even those enterprises that operate their own platforms are still beholden to a small number of tech giants because the apps through which those platforms are most commonly accessed must be downloaded and installed from "app stores" controlled by the likes of Apple and Google.

All of this is to say that although the media industry has changed dramatically in recent years, and the advent of digital technology has led to a raft of new players competing alongside the digital offerings of traditional media players, many of the fundamental dynamics that characterize the industry remain the same.

SOCIAL MEDIA

There is a subcategory of digital media that bears mentioning here. You have very likely heard the term "social media," and indeed, there is a strong chance that you are a participant in the social media landscape. Social media refers to internet-based platforms that facilitate communication and engagement between multiple users. Perhaps the most widely known example is Facebook, a platform founded by several Harvard students in the mid-2000s as a way to connect friends together online. Since its founding, Facebook has become a behemoth in the space, with 2.8 billion monthly active users at the end of 2020.

The precise definition of "social media" is elusive, due in large part to the fact that the technologies that underlie it, and the platforms that market themselves as social media services, evolve rapidly. Wikipedia describes social media as "interactive technologies that allow the creation or sharing/exchanging of information, ideas, career interests, and other forms of expression via virtual communities and networks."[2] It goes on to acknowledge that while there is room to quibble over the definition, there are some common characteristics of social media platforms, including (1) user interactivity; (2) the exchange of user-generated content such as photos and videos; (3) user-created "profiles" or homepages that are specific to each social media service; and (4) they develop networks of people with similar backgrounds and interests.

Some services focus more heavily on certain aspects than others. LinkedIn, for example, a professional networking site, emphasizes connections based on educational background, work experience, and related credentials, and users tend to post more written work than photos or images. Twitter's forte is short, pithy text exchanges of no more than 280 characters (though the service does allow users to post images and videos as well). Instagram, acquired by Facebook in 2012, is primarily for sharing images, while TikTok is a video-centric platform. Facebook is arguably the most

---

2 Wikipedia, Social Media, https://en.wikipedia.org/wiki/Social_media (accessed May 22, 2021).

general, "mass appeal" social media service, emphasizing text, images, and video, more or less equally.

IS EVERYONE A MEDIA ENTERPRISE?

So if digital media, and social media in particular, make it such that anyone with a connection to the internet can produce, package, or distribute content with the intent to distribute it to other people to consume – our definition of a "media enterprise" from earlier in this chapter – does that mean that, in the digital media environment, everyone is a "media enterprise?"

In a word, yes.

Perhaps the most critical feature of digital media, and in particular social media, is that quite literally anyone can produce it, and therefore, anyone can be a media enterprise, or at least serve the general function of one. Long gone are the days when to communicate a message one had to find a publisher or broadcaster willing to disseminate it. Now, all one needs is a social media account and the requisite app installed on their mobile phone and something to say.

Of course, social media is a relatively unsophisticated form of communication, but as we saw earlier in this chapter, even the more polished forms of media are now more accessible than they ever have been before.

WHAT DOES THIS HAVE TO DO WITH THE LAW?

So if anyone with an internet connection is a media enterprise, or at least capable of being one, does that mean that media law – the doctrines that comprise the bulk of this book – apply to everyone?

Again, in a word, yes.

The devil is in the details, as they say, but the reason media law has become so important to understand is that large portions of it are applicable to virtually all of us who engage in something as simple as posting an update on Facebook or writing an article on Medium.

Indeed, as you proceed through the book, you will see that the regulatory environment of media is largely driven by the nature of the distribution mechanism. Said differently, there are central principles of media law that apply equally to traditional and digital media enterprises, while there are others that apply solely to traditional or solely to digital enterprises.

The distinction between *traditional* media law and *digital* media law is really at the margins, in those pockets of the law that pertain specifically to methods or mechanisms of distribution. Understanding those distinctions, and knowing when to apply them, is essential to anyone working in a modern media enterprise, nearly all of which are multimodal, meaning they produce media products intended for distribution over both traditional and digital platforms.

Podcasting again offers a useful example.

As noted earlier, podcasting essentially represents the digital-era evolution of what we used to know as radio broadcasting: both podcasting and radio broadcasting involve the production and dissemination of audio-only programming. The difference lies mainly in the distribution mechanism. Radio broadcasts are ephemeral and require the use of the electromagnetic spectrum that is owned by the public and administered by the government (more on that in Chapter 9), while podcasts are available on demand, distributed over the internet, and either streamed from a server or downloaded onto a device such as a mobile phone and listened to at the users' convenience.

Despite the differences in distribution, many of the basic legal principles that apply to radio would apply to podcasts as well. For example, it would be unlawful for the host of a podcast to make defamatory statements about a third party, just as it would be unlawful to make such a statement on a radio broadcast. As sports law professor and legal commentator Michael McCann noted in a recent interview about a defamation case against a popular sports podcast, "[t]he setting [of a podcast interview] is so different, it makes people feel relaxed … but it's still a public record, and defamation doesn't … check out of the room in a podcast studio."[3]

But at the same time, there are certain rules that apply only to radio broadcasting because, as we will see later in this book, it is afforded a lesser degree of protection under the First Amendment, and therefore subject to more regulation. For example, it would be legal to include profane language in a podcast, but if that same program aired on a radio station, it might subject the station to fines if it is broadcast during certain hours.

So, while the law applicable to the *production* of media is largely the same regardless of whether the media is ultimately distributed via traditional or digital means, the nature of the *distribution* may result in differences in the applicable law. Understanding the distinctions, and how they apply in the contemporary media environment, is an important skill for any media industry professional, especially now that most traditional media enterprises have expanded to include digital offerings.

---

3 University of New Hampshire School of Law, *The Legal Impact, Podcasts, Baseball and Defamation*, April 15, 2021, https://www.podbean.com/site/EpisodeDownload/PB100CC02KFTAR (interview with Prof. Michael McCann).

Learning how to navigate those distinctions, and understand which doctrines and legal principles apply under what circumstances, is the focus of the rest of this book.

KEY POINTS AND TAKEAWAYS

1. Traditional media is characterized by scarcity – limited producers, distributors, access points, and mechanisms for consumption – while digital media is characterized by abundance and ubiquity.
2. Abundance and ubiquity led to the discovery problem, that is, when it becomes possible for virtually anyone to create and distribute media, it becomes more difficult to separate the wheat from the chaff, which has given rise to a new class of gatekeepers – the "big tech" internet platforms and the algorithms they use and control that guide users to content.
3. Notwithstanding changes in technology and attendant business models, the fundamental objective of creating and distributing media remains the same as it always has been – to gather audiences.
4. The law is more or less the same, too. The basic legal doctrines that apply to the production of traditional media apply equally, in most cases, to the production of digital media. The laws that apply to the manner of distribution, however, are quite different, as traditional media distributors are generally responsible for the content they distribute, while many digital distributors are characterized as "platforms" and are often insulated from liability.
5. The modern media enterprise is rarely focused on a traditional distribution modality. Instead, they seek to produce content that is susceptible to deployment across a variety of platforms, which thus exposes them to different regulatory schemes.

QUESTIONS FOR DISCUSSION

1. Think about the media that you consume on a regular basis. Who produces it? How do you access it? Do you use traditional mechanisms (e.g., radio, television, newspapers) or "digital" mechanisms such as streaming services? How do the two differ? How are they the same?
2. What are some of the key characteristics of traditional media? Of digital media? How are the two similar, and in what ways are they different?
3. What was the last movie you saw? Where did you see it? How did you access it? Think about the people or roles involved with getting that movie to you (e.g., writer, director, producer, studio, streaming service, theater staff). Which are necessary to create the movie? Which are necessary to distribute it? Which roles have changed with the advent of digital technology? Are there any that are no longer necessary in the digital environment? Has the digital environment given rise to new roles?
4. How do you use social media? Are you primarily a consumer of information, or do you post your own content regularly? What kind of content do you post? Who is your intended audience?

2

CHAPTER 2
LAW AND THE U.S.
LEGAL SYSTEM

With the basic parameters of the media environment established, we can move toward understanding how the law fits in. But before we get into media law issues specifically, it will be helpful to understand the basic structure of the U.S. legal system so we can better understand how Congress and the courts have helped shape media law over time.

What is the basic structure of the legal system in the United States? How do the three branches of government fit together and what role do the courts play in evaluating the constitutionality of laws and government actions? How do we find statutes, case law, and other resources necessary to understand the metes and bounds of the law? In this chapter, we will define the broad contours of the legal environment in which digital media professionals work.

THE CONSTITUTION OF THE UNITED STATES

You likely remember from your grade school civics education that the Constitution is among several documents that are considered foundational to the United States. The **Constitution**, together with its first ten amendments, known as the **Bill of Rights**, establish the basic structure of the United States government, and serve as essentially a contract between the people of the country and its government, granting limited power to the federal government, and reserving the rest for the states and their citizens. In what would become one of the most quoted speeches in U.S. history, President Abraham Lincoln later characterized the government structure as one that is "of the people, by the people, and for the people." The Constitution was drafted by a committee, the Constitutional Convention, the members of which are referred to as the country's Founding Fathers, or the framers of the Constitution.

Given its far-reaching implications, the Constitution is surprisingly short – just over 4,500 words – but it contains some concepts that have become cornerstones of our modern system of governance.

SEPARATION OF POWERS

The Constitutional powers of the federal government are spread across three separate branches: the **legislative**, the **executive**, and the **judicial**. The power and authority of each branch are spelled out by the Constitution in detail, but critically, the framers built a system of checks and balances among the three branches so that none would

DOI: 10.4324/9781003197966-2

independently become more important or powerful. Such a system was designed to avoid what the framers saw as tyranny of the monarchy in England, from which they fled.

Broadly, under the U.S. Constitution, the legislative branch is responsible for making laws, the executive branch is responsible for enforcing those laws, and the judicial branch is responsible for interpreting the laws, and the actions taken pursuant to those laws, to ensure they comport with the Constitution.

THE LEGISLATIVE BRANCH

The federal legislature is composed of two deliberative bodies, the **House of Representatives** and the **Senate**. The House has 435 members apportioned by population with larger states having more representatives than smaller states, while the Senate has 50 members, one from each state. The House and Senate each have a number of subject-specific committees that consider issues and proposed legislation specific to certain content domains.

A proposal for a new law, called a **bill**, may be introduced in either of the two chambers of Congress but must pass each by a majority vote before it is sent to the President for his or her signature. Only after the president signs the bill does it become enforceable law. A president may decline to sign, or **veto** a bill, essentially sending it back to Congress, if he or she disagrees with it, but Congress may override a presidential veto by a two-thirds vote (as opposed to a simple majority vote) in both the House and Senate.

THE EXECUTIVE BRANCH

The executive branch is headed by the **President** and comprises the various offices and functions that make up **The White House**, but also various administrative agencies, such as the Departments of Justice, Defense, Homeland Security, Education, Labor, State, and Commerce. Collectively, the executive branch is often called **the Administration**.

As described earlier, the President must sign bills for them to become law, but once laws have been enacted, it is up to the various agencies that comprise the administration to enforce them. Perhaps the most prominent enforcement agency is the Department of Justice, which includes the Federal Bureau of Investigation, the Drug Enforcement Administration, and the Bureau of Alcohol, Tobacco, and Firearms, among many others.

THE JUDICIAL BRANCH

The role of the judicial branch is to interpret the laws passed by the legislative branch and enforced by the executive branch. The Supreme Court, which sits atop the judicial system (the structure of which is discussed more fully in the following sections) has the ultimate authority to determine whether laws comport with the Constitution, and to strike those laws, or portions of those laws, that do not. We discuss the judicial branch in much more detail later in this chapter.

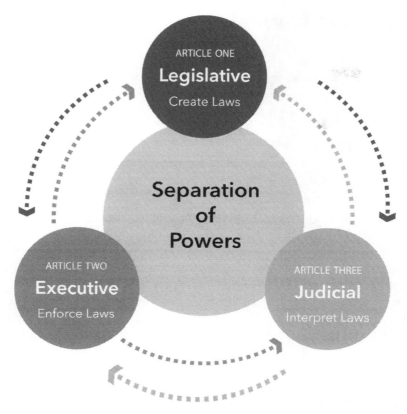

Figure 2.1 The federal separation of powers.

FEDERALISM AND STATE GOVERNMENTS

Federalism is the principle that certain powers are centralized in a federal government, while others are exercised by the states. The U.S. Constitution provides that all those powers not expressly granted to the federal government are reserved for the states, and those not exercised by the states are granted to the citizens. Because of federalism, citizens of the United States are subject to two distinct legal systems: the federal system, as described previously, and also a state system. Most state governments closely mimic the structure and functions of the federal government.

Historically, certain areas of law have been left to the states, such as personal injury and contract law, while others, such as communication law, and other areas that generally involve dealings among multiple states, are governed by federal law. If there is ever a conflict between state and federal law on a particular point, the **supremacy clause** of the Constitution provides that federal law controls, unless the state law is more protective of its citizens.

Regardless of whether a law originates at the federal or state level, it must comport with the U.S. Constitution, which serves as the ultimate backstop.

SOURCES OF LAW

When we think of "the law" we often think of the large, stately volumes that adorn lawyers' offices on television or in the movies, but the reality is that those books contain just a portion of the rules, policies, and procedures that comprise "the law." Law actually originates from a number of different sources.

CONSTITUTIONS

As noted in the previous section, the U.S. Constitution serves as the foundation for the entire U.S. legal system. In addition to the federal constitution, each U.S. state has its own constitution that prescribes the structure of each state's government and defines the powers and duties of the state government. Unlike the federal constitution, which is written so broadly that it serves effectively as a series of guiding principles for the government, many state constitutions are more detailed and provide more direct guidance to the state government and its citizens. For example, in California, the reporters' shield law, a narrow but critically important doctrine of importance to members of the media, finds its origins in the state constitution. We discuss shield laws in more detail later in this book.

Note, though, that because of the principles of federalism and supremacy discussed in the prior section, although states are free to have their own constitutions, and engage in legislative and enforcement activity consistent within the bounds of the state's constitutional framework, state action may never be inconsistent with the U.S. Constitution.

STATUTES

Statutes are the laws that are passed by the legislative branch and signed into law by the head of the executive branch – the president in the federal system or the governor in a state system. Those laws are generally organized into collections called **codes**. Federal statutes make their way into **United States Code** (abbreviated USC), which is organized into 53 topical categories called **titles**, within which the laws are organized into parts, chapters, and sections. Each title covers a broad topic, such as Title 18 which contains the federal criminal code, or Title 47 which contains the communications law.

Each state has its own code, many of which closely resemble the federal code's organizational scheme, while others, like California, divide their law into separate topical codes, such as the California Business and Professions Code or the California Penal Code.

REGULATIONS (ADMINISTRATIVE LAW)

Regulations are similar to statutes in that they are organized by subject area and are typically published in comprehensive codes. Unlike statutes, however, regulations are not voted on by the legislature and signed into law by the executive. Rather, regulations are **promulgated** by executive branch agencies and are usually much more granular and specific than the U.S. Code.

For example, the Communications Act of 1934, codified in Title 47 of the U.S. Code created the Federal Communications Commission (FCC) and authorized it to perform certain regulatory functions pertaining to radio and wireline communication. Under the authority granted by Congress, the FCC has developed regulations that pertain to specific aspects of communication, such as radio, television, cable, cellular telephone, wireline telephone, and so on.

Federal regulations are codified in the **Code of Federal Regulations**. State regulations are typically codified similarly.

EXECUTIVE ORDERS

Executive orders are issued by the President and have the force of law, despite the fact that they did not originate in the legislative branch. They are, however, subject to judicial review and can be struck by the courts if they are found to violate the Constitution or other laws. Similarly, Congress can effectively overturn an executive order by passing legislation that overrides it, but since legislation must be signed by the president to become law, or overcome a veto with a two-thirds majority in both houses of Congress, such actions are difficult and rare.

The Constitution does not expressly grant the president the authority to issue executive orders; rather, the authority flows from various other constitutional provisions that authorized the president to take certain actions, or from federal statutes, enacted by the legislature, effectively delegating such authority to the president.

Issuing new executive orders and striking the past president's executive orders is often done in the early days of a new presidential administration, as it is a quick and effective way to implement important policy changes. President Biden issued more executive orders during his first 100 days in office than any president since Harry Truman.[1]

In most states, governors have similar authority to issue executive orders, but they are of course binding only within the state.

COMMON LAW (CASE LAW)

The legal system in the United States is referred to as a **common law** system, which means that the law primarily flows not from statutes and regulations, but from

---

1 Jason Breslow, *Biden's 1st 100 Days: A Look by the Numbers*, NPR, April 27, 2021, https://www.npr.org /2021/04/27/988822340/bidens-1st-100-days-a-look-by-the-numbers.

decisions by courts that, over time, establish clear principles and rules that become recognized as having binding legal effect. This works because our judicial system follows the principle of **stare decisis**, Latin for "let the decision stand," which means we treat similar cases similarly, drawing distinctions where appropriate. Over time, as more and more cases are decided about particular issues, the law develops into a series of clearly articulated and regularly applied rules. Such law is called either **common law**, **case law**, or sometimes **judge-made law**. If Congress or a state legislature grows unhappy with the direction courts take the law, they are free to enact legislation to change the common law, essentially replacing it with statutory law.

RESTATEMENTS

Because studying decades of case law from different courts and jurisdictions can be daunting and onerous, legal scholars have attempted to synthesize the common law into what are called **restatements**. The restatements are not themselves the law, and have no binding effect, but they are useful guides to understanding the general elements of particular legal principles. Lawyers sometimes refer to the restatements' legal principles as **black letter law**, because the restatements present fundamental principles of the law in boldface type.

TYPES OF LAW

Broadly speaking, laws – both federal and state laws – fall into one of two categories: civil or criminal.

CRIMINAL LAWS

Criminal laws are enforced by the government on behalf of its citizens. Violations of criminal law are offenses against society or the people of the community in which the crime took place. For that reason, many states style criminal prosecutions as "the people" versus the defendant, such as the famous case against football star O.J. Simpson, accused (and subsequently acquitted) of murdering his ex-wife and her friend, known as *The People of the State of California v. Orenthal James Simpson*. In other jurisdictions, the case is brought by the state or government, such as *State of Minnesota v. Derek Michael Chauvin*, the case brought against a Minneapolis police officer accused (and subsequently convicted) of murdering George Floyd during an attempted arrest.

In addition to the "state" or the "people," the government is also sometimes referred to as the **prosecution**. The person against whom the criminal allegations or **charges** are brought is the **defendant**.

The subject matter of criminal laws is wide ranging and far reaching, including everything from violent crimes against people such as murder, kidnapping, or sexual assault, to crimes against property, such as burglary, arson, and theft, to conduct crimes such as driving under the influence of alcohol or drugs. Other criminal statutes target specific types of conduct, such as the Computer Fraud and Abuse Act, which renders it a crime to access certain computer systems without authorization.

Penalties for violating criminal laws are also wide ranging, depending on the severity of the crime. Serious crimes are generally punishable by incarceration in jail or prison, while others result in fines or probation. In some jurisdictions, certain very serious crimes, such as murder, are punishable by death.

CIVIL LAWS

Civil litigation is similar, but also quite different than criminal prosecution. For starters, although the government can bring civil litigation (and can be sued), it is more common for civil litigation to be between two or more private parties.

In a civil case, we call the party bringing the lawsuit the **plaintiff**, which alleges one or more **causes of action** or **claims** – that is, legally recognized facts or circumstances that may give rise to legal liability – against another party. As in criminal cases, the party against which the suit is brought is the **defendant**.

The defendant in a civil case is either **liable** or **not liable**, as opposed to guilty or not guilty, and the remedy for wrongdoing is generally **money damages, injunctive relief**, or a combination of the two. Money damages are exactly what they sound like – damages paid to the defendant to compensate for losses suffered as a result of the plaintiff's conduct. A court may also award **punitive damages**, which are money damages paid to the plaintiff beyond its calculable losses, to punish the defendant for misconduct, and to serve as a deterrent to others engaging in the same conduct.

Injunctive relief is an equitable remedy in which the court issues a judgment ordering the defendant engage in certain conduct. For example, a court might issue an injunction ordering a defendant to stop trespassing on the plaintiff's land, or ordering a defendant to destroy all infringing copies of the plaintiff's copyrighted work.

Civil claims can arise out of a wide range of substantive legal areas, including contract law, which governs voluntary, enforceable relationships between two or more parties, and tort law, which pertains to unintentional interactions between two or more parties that generally result in some injury (e.g., negligent acts). Civil claims can also arise out of statutes and regulations, such as copyright infringement, which vests in copyright owners certain rights that may be enforced in court.

Many of the claims we will discuss in the coming chapters, such as defamation and invasion of privacy, are considered torts.

CRIMINAL PROSECUTION PROCESS

The most common way a criminal case begins is by an **arrest** of a person accused of committing a crime. Typically, the defendant will be taken into custody and held in jail until his or her **initial court appearance**. During the initial appearance, a judge will determine whether there is sufficient evidence to charge the defendant with a crime and will remind the defendant of his or her Constitutional rights, such as the right to remain silent and the right to be represented by counsel. If the defendant cannot afford a lawyer, the court will appoint one.

The judge will also evaluate whether the defendant may be granted **pre-trial release**, that is, whether they may be released from jail while the charges are pending. In cases where the prosecution demonstrates the defendant is a danger to the community, or that the defendant is likely to abscond to avoid trial, a judge is less likely to release the defendant.

Soon after the initial appearance comes an **arraignment**, where the state presents its formal charges, and where the defendant must enter a **plea**, declaring whether they are **guilty** or **not guilty** of each of the charges against them. If the defendant pleads not guilty on at least one of the charges, the case will proceed to trial. Sometimes the prosecution will negotiate with the defendant and come to a **plea agreement**, which is where the defendant agrees to plead guilty to certain charges in exchange for others being dropped or a more lenient sentence.

If the defendant pleads guilty, the court will schedule a **sentencing hearing**. If the defendant pleads not guilty, the case proceeds to **discovery**, which is where the prosecution must provide all of the evidence it has against the defendant. Defendant's counsel will also conduct his or her own investigation into the facts and circumstances surrounding the crime and, in consultation with the defendant, will develop a defensive strategy. Discussions between the prosecution and defense counsel often continue during this period and it is not uncommon for the parties to reach a plea agreement as each side learns more about the other's case.

If the defendant does not reach a plea agreement with the prosecution during the discovery phase, the case will proceed to **trial** where the defendant's guilt or innocence will be determined by either a judge or jury. Under the Constitution, a criminal defendant is entitled to a trial by jury, where the jury decides whose version of the facts is true and determines whether the defendant is guilty or not. In a jury trial, the judge presides over the proceedings, answers legal questions, and interprets the law, as necessary.

After each side presents its evidence and makes its arguments, the jury will **deliberate** until they reach a decision which is called a **verdict**. In federal court, and in most states, the jury in a criminal trial must be unanimous. If the jury is unable to reach consensus, it is called a **hung jury**, and the judge may implore the jury to try again or may declare a **mistrial**.

Assuming the jury returns a verdict, the defendant will be determined to be either **guilty** or **not guilty** (note that courts – judges or juries – are not empowered to declare someone "innocent," only "not guilty"). If the defendant is found not guilty, then typically he or she is free to leave. If the defendant is found guilty, then the court will schedule a **sentencing hearing** to take place usually within several months. In cases where the defendant had been released pending the outcome of the trial, the judge will reevaluate whether to allow the defendant to remain free pending sentencing or whether they should be taken into custody to await sentencing in jail. Where a convicted defendant is facing jail or prison time, it is likely that the court will require the defendant to be held in custody until sentencing.

At the sentencing hearing, the judge will consider arguments from each side as to the appropriate sentence. In federal court, and in some state courts, the victims of the crime are given an opportunity to give a statement. After hearing the arguments and statements, the judge will impose a sentence.

After sentencing, the defendant may **appeal** the conviction, the sentence, or both, to an appellate court. The most common arguments made on appeal are that the defendant's trial counsel was ineffective, or that the jury was not impartial, meaning that it was predisposed to convict the defendant.

CIVIL LITIGATION PROCESS

The civil litigation process begins when a **plaintiff** files a **complaint** with the court, which it must formally **serve** on the **defendant**. Once served, a defendant must file a response within 20–30 days, depending on where the case has been filed. Generally, a defendant will respond by filing an **answer**, a point-by-point response to every allegation made in the complaint. A defendant may also file a **motion to dismiss**, asking the court to close the case because the plaintiff failed to establish a legal cause of action.

If the court denies the motion to dismiss, then the case proceeds to discovery, which is similar to the discovery period in a criminal case. During discovery, each side provides the other with the evidence that it intends to use in the course of providing its claims or defenses, and each side has the opportunity to take formal, documented interviews, called **depositions**, of key witnesses.

After discovery, but before trial, each side may file a **motion for summary judgment**, which seeks to convince the court that, in light of the evidence gathered in discovery, there is no dispute about the facts of the case, and that the issues can be decided as a matter of law by the court, without the need for a jury to make findings of fact. If neither side brings such a motion, or the court denies it, then the case proceeds to trial.

As in criminal cases, litigants may opt for a jury or a bench trial. Unlike in criminal cases, however, jury verdicts generally do not have to be unanimous in a civil setting; often, a simple majority is sufficient to decide the case. If the plaintiff sought money damages, often the jury will determine the damages award at the same time it determines whether the defendant is liable. Sometimes, usually for more complex trials, the court will bifurcate the case, and wait for a determination on liability before hearing evidence on damages.

If a prevailing plaintiff sought injunctive relief, the judge, as opposed to the jury, will determine whether such relief is appropriate. If so, she will craft an appropriate injunction given the facts of the case.

A litigant unhappy with the determination of a trial court may appeal to an appropriate appellate court once a final judgment has been entered.

BURDENS OF PROOF

In both civil and criminal law, the party bringing the lawsuit or criminal charges bears the **burden of proof** to establish that the defendant engaged in the unlawful conduct set forth in the criminal charges or civil complaint.

Most crimes and civil claims can be divided into several discrete **elements**. For example, in most states, to find a defendant guilty of burglary, the prosecution must establish that the defendant (1) entered into a building or structure; (2) without permission of the owner; (3) with intent to commit a crime. If the prosecution fails to prove any one of those four elements, the defendant cannot be convicted.

Most civil claims have elements as well. For example, to establish that a business owner is responsible for a patron slipping and falling on the business's premises, the plaintiff must establish that the business owner (1) had a duty to keep the premises safe; (2) he or she failed to satisfy that duty, which; (3) caused a cognizable injury to the plaintiff. If the plaintiff fails to establish any one of those elements, the defendant cannot be found liable.

The amount or **standard of proof** required to prevail depends on whether the matter is criminal or civil in nature. To convict someone on a criminal charge, the jury or judge must conclude that the prosecution has shown the presence of each element of the charge beyond a **reasonable doubt**. That means that if they have even the slightest doubt that the defendant committed the crime, they must vote to acquit. This high standard is often known informally by the axiom that it is better to let a guilty person go free, than it is to convict an innocent person.

To overcome the prosecution's case in a criminal matter, then, a defendant does not need to establish his or her innocence, only that the government has failed to prove its case beyond a reasonable doubt. Put differently, a criminal defendant need not put forth any evidence of innocence, or even rebut the prosecution's evidence. Rather, a defendant need only introduce enough uncertainty that a jury cannot conclude, beyond a reasonable doubt, that the defendant did not commit the crime.

By contrast, in a civil case, a plaintiff may prevail by showing only by a **preponderance of the evidence** – that it is more likely than not – that each element of the claim has been satisfied. This standard is less stringent than the criminal "reasonable doubt" standard because there is generally less at stake in a civil matter (a losing defendant will not potentially lose his or her liberty as they might in a criminal proceeding). Accordingly, to prevail over a plaintiff's claims, a civil defendant needs to show that the plaintiff failed to establish at least one of the elements of each claim brought against them.

In both criminal and civil cases, a defendant may assert an **affirmative defense**, which means that rather than attempt to discredit the claims or charges brought against them, the defendant admits to the conduct, but claims that it was legally excusable.

For example, a defendant charged with criminal trespass might assert the affirmative defense of "necessity," arguing that the trespass was necessary to avoid a more serious public harm. In the civil arena, a copyright infringement defendant might admit to making unauthorized copies of the plaintiff's work but assert that it is a legally acceptable "fair use" as described by the Copyright Act (and discussed more fully in Chapter 11).

STRUCTURE OF THE FEDERAL COURTS

The federal judicial system in the United States is divided into three levels: district courts, circuit courts, and the Supreme Court.

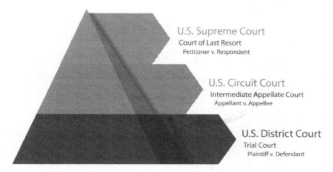

Figure 2.2 Hierarchy of the U.S. court system.

DISTRICT COURTS

The district courts are trial courts, which is where every case in the federal system begins. When someone files a lawsuit that raises a federal issue (and in certain
other cases where certain procedural requirements are satisfied), or when someone is
charged with violating a federal statute, their case will be heard in an appropriate U.S.
District Court.

The United States is divided into 94 judicial districts. Smaller or less densely populated states have only one judicial district, while larger more densely populated states
are divided into multiple geographic districts. For example, New Hampshire is a
single federal judicial district, the District of New Hampshire, while California is
divided into four: the Northern District (which includes San Francisco), the Eastern
District (which includes Sacramento), the Central District (which includes Los
Angeles), and the Southern District (which includes San Diego).

A complex set of rules governs where a plaintiff may bring a lawsuit, but generally
it will be where any one of the defendants resides, or where the conduct that is the
subject of the lawsuit took place. Criminal cases are typically brought in the district
where the alleged crime took place, although in some cases the court may change the
venue of the proceedings to avoid the publicity that may make it difficult to find an
impartial jury, and therefore making it difficult for the defendant to get a fair trial, as
required by the Constitution.

The principal job of the trial court is to determine the facts of a case and apply the
law appropriately. In the case of jury trials, it is the jury that serves as the arbiter of
the facts, while the judge applies the law. In bench trials, the judge also serves as the
finder of fact.

Decisions made by district courts are not binding on other courts but may be looked
to as **persuasive authority** by other judges sitting on the same court, or by courts in
other judicial districts.

CIRCUIT COURTS OF APPEAL

If a litigant believes that the district court made an error or improperly applied the
law to the facts, they may appeal the decision to a **circuit court of appeal**. The
party that seeks to overturn the district court decision is the **appellant**, and the party
who prevailed at the district court is the **appellee**.

There are 13 circuit courts of appeal, 12 of which are divided by geographic region,
which hear appeals from the various district courts within that region. For example, an appeal of a decision from the Central District of California would be heard
by the Ninth Circuit Court of Appeals, while a decision from the Middle District
of Tennessee would be heard by the Sixth Circuit Court of Appeals. Certain types

of cases, such as patent matters, or cases involving veteran's affairs are heard by the Court of Appeals for the Federal Circuit in Washington, DC, regardless of where the case originated geographically.

Most appeals are heard by a panel of three judges randomly chosen from among all those judges sitting on the court. In cases where the court is confronted with a matter of significant importance, the court will opt for an *en banc* **hearing**, where the case is heard before all of the sitting judges. A party that does not prevail before the three-judge panel will sometimes request an *en banc* rehearing of the case, but the decision to grant such a rehearing is entirely up to the court. A party that does not prevail at the appellate court may take the case to the Supreme Court.

Decisions made by the appellate courts are binding on all of the lower courts in the circuit, but not courts outside of that circuit, or on other circuit courts, though circuit courts are free to look to each other's opinions as persuasive authority. For example, if the Ninth Circuit articulates an interpretation of a particular federal statute, that interpretation must be followed by all of the federal district courts in Arizona, California, Idaho, Montana, Nevada, Oregon, and Washington. When confronted with the same issue, the Eleventh Circuit is free to adopt the Ninth Circuit's view of the statute, but it might also come up with its own view, and if it does, that view would be binding only on the federal district courts in Alabama, Florida, and Georgia.

Although cases of relevance to the media industry can come up all over the country, the Second and Ninth circuits tend to produce case law of most significance to media lawyers because the media industry is predominantly based in New York, which sits in the Second Circuit, and Los Angeles, which sits in the Ninth.

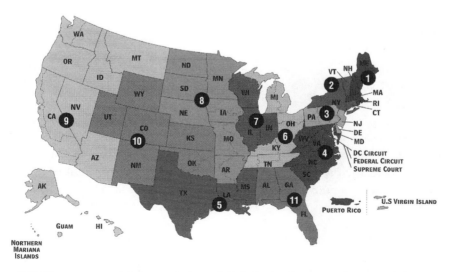

Figure 2.3 The geographic boundaries of U.S. federal courts. Source: Administrative Office of the United States Courts.

THE SUPREME COURT

The Supreme Court is the highest court in the United States, and as such, it is often referred to as the court of last resort. Unlike the district and circuit courts, the Supreme Court enjoys discretionary jurisdiction, which means that most of the time, it can pick and choose which cases to hear. The majority of cases heard by the Supreme Court get there by way of a **petition for a *writ of certiorari***, which is essentially a request for the Supreme Court to hear the case. The party that seeks Supreme Court review is the **petitioner**, while the responding party is the **respondent**.

Getting a case heard by the Supreme Court is difficult. Historically, the Court has agreed to hear just about 3% of the cases brought before it. Typically, the Court only takes cases that raise policy issues of significant national importance, or cases where a **circuit split** has emerged, that is, where two or more appellate circuits have reached diverging viewpoints as to a particular point of law, as in the example earlier involving the Ninth and Eleventh Circuits. The Supreme Court's role in such cases is to provide clarity and national uniformity.

The Supreme Court is perhaps best known for its role as the ultimate authority on whether a particular law or government action is Constitutional. You will recall from earlier in this chapter that the three branches of government serve as a check on the other branches' power, and the ability to strike laws as unconstitutional, and therefore unenforceable, is one way the judiciary exercises its oversight over the legislative branch, which makes the laws, and the executive branch, which enforces them.

Because of the Supreme Court's role in determining the constitutionality of certain laws, its decisions play a key role in role in media law, where courts must routinely balance the constitutional rights of citizens, flowing primarily from the First Amendment, with the government's attempts to maintain an orderly, well-functioning society, which sometimes requires it to regulate speech and other expressive conduct.

JUDICIAL APPOINTMENTS

Judges at all three levels of the federal judiciary are nominated by the President and confirmed by the Senate, and, if successfully appointed, serve for life, unless they voluntarily resign or are impeached and removed from office. The appointment process is another way the three branches of government act as checks on each other: the executive branch appoints judges to the judicial branch, the legislative branch approves them, and has the power to remove judges by virtue of its impeachment power.

District and Circuit Court nominees generally receive little public attention, while nominees for the Supreme Court typically result in significant publicity and closely watched hearings, given the importance of the Supreme Court and the far-reaching impact of its decisions.

STRUCTURE OF THE STATE COURTS

Most state judicial systems closely mimic the federal system, featuring a state supreme court, an intermediate appellate court system, and the trial courts, often established on a county-by-county basis. Many states also have specialized court systems or divisions of their trial courts staffed by experts that focus on specific areas of law. For example, many states have a separate family court system with judges who are experienced in handling divorces and child custody matters. Many states in the arid western United States have specialized water courts that deal exclusively with disputes over water rights. Delaware has a special court system designated solely for corporate matters, which is one of the reasons why so many companies, especially those that are publicly traded, choose to incorporate their business in Delaware, even if they primarily operate in another state.

Each state has a different naming convention for their court system. In many states, the trial courts are called district courts, as in the federal system, but also sometimes the superior court, or a court of common pleas. Notably, and somewhat confusingly, in New York, the trial courts are called "supreme courts" while the Court of Appeals is the state's equivalent of most states' supreme court. The intermediate appellate court is the Appellate Division of the Supreme Court. In Florida, the trial courts are referred to as "circuit courts," which is the name of the intermediate appellate courts in the federal system. Several states, primarily smaller, less densely populated states, such as Montana and New Hampshire, have no intermediate appellate court. In these states, decisions of the trial court are appealed directly to the state supreme court.

State supreme courts serve the same function to each state's law and constitution as the federal Supreme Court does to federal law and the U.S. Constitution: they are the ultimate authority on the interpretation of state law, and the ultimate arbiter as to whether a particular law or government practice comports with the state constitution. State laws that are upheld by state courts are still subject to review by the federal courts, including the U.S. Supreme Court, to ensure they are consistent with the federal constitution. As noted previously, the supremacy clause of the U.S. Constitution provides that states are free to legislate as they desire and may pass laws that are more protective of citizens than federal laws may be, but no law may ever violate the U.S. Constitution.

Indeed, many of the cases discussed throughout this book ended up before the U.S. Supreme Court because a state enforced one of its laws, and the person or entity against whom it was enforced challenged the constitutionality of that law under the federal Constitution.

FINDING AND RESEARCHING THE LAW

Earlier in this chapter we discussed the various sources of U.S. law, which included constitutions, statutes, regulations, executive orders, and case law, all of which are relatively easy to find if you ever need to. Here's how to do it.

CONSTITUTIONS, STATUTES, REGULATIONS, AND EXECUTIVE ORDERS

Constitutions, statutes, regulations, and executive orders are all relatively easy to find on the internet. The U.S. Constitution is on the official website of the U.S. Congress, https://constitution.congress.gov/constitution, and federal executive orders are posted on the website of the Federal Register, the official daily journal of the federal government, at www.federalregister.gov/presidential-documents/executive-orders. Similarly, the Government Printing Office, the agency responsible for publishing the official versions of the United States Code and the Code of Federal Regulations, offers websites for each, at www.uscode.gov and www.ecfr.gov, respectively.

State constitutions, statutes, regulations, and executive orders are also generally easy to find, though there is no standard organizational scheme across states. For example, in California, the constitution and the state codes are available from the same source, the California Legislative Information website at https://leginfo.legislature.ca.gov/faces/codes.xhtml, and the Code of California Regulations is available from the state's Office of Administrative Law at https://oal.ca.gov/publications/ccr/.

CASE LAW

Recall from earlier that much of the law in the United States derives from court cases that interpret and apply the law. Over time, courts develop and expand the law, as judges apply existing doctrines where applicable, and advance or adjust them from time to time as new fact patterns emerge, requiring small expansions or changes to the law. Because so much U.S. law comes from cases, it is important to understand how court decisions are published and reported.

As a practical matter, most courts today publish written opinions on their websites, which works well if you know which courts have considered a particular legal issue of interest. But in most cases, when performing legal research, you know the issue that you're looking for, but don't necessarily know which courts have considered it.

For that reason, written opinions from courts are aggregated and published sequentially in **case reporters** that are indexed by subject area, allowing a researcher to easily identify cases of interest from various courts. U.S. Supreme Court decisions appear in the **Supreme Court Reporter**, while federal appellate decisions appear in the **Federal Reporter**. District court opinions are published in the **Federal Supplement**. State court decisions appear in various state-specific reporters, but also one of seven regional reporters, that aggregate state cases from each geographic region of the United States. Because these reporters, and the organizational scheme, were first developed by West Publishing, these series are sometimes referred to as **West Reporters** or **national reporters**.

Historically, the reporters were large sets of print volumes that took up a significant amount of space and took a significant amount of time to comb through trying to find all of the case law that pertains to a particular issue in a particular jurisdiction. Today, of course, legal research has become much easier thanks to online research services, such as Westlaw, LexisNexis, and Bloomberg Law, that carry similar resources and offer robust search functions, making the old print reporters, and the laborious research methods that went with them, largely obsolete.

Although the online services have overtaken the traditional print books as the primary mechanism by which legal professionals conduct research, the organizational scheme persists, and legal professionals still refer to cases by citations that refer to the traditional reporter framework.

UNDERSTANDING CITATIONS

To identify the source of particular cases and other types of legal authority, legal professionals refer to a **citation** (sometimes referred to as a **cite** as a shorthand), which serves to help locate it, but also to indicate the extent to which the authority is persuasive or binding.

STATUTES AND REGULATIONS

The standard citation form for the U.S. Code, for instance, begins with the title number, followed by the abbreviation "USC," the "section" symbol, and the specific section of the code within the specified title. So the citation 17 USC § 107 refers to section 107 of title 17 of the United States Code. The Code of Federal Regulations citation form is essentially the same, except the abbreviation is "CFR." A citation to 47 CFR § 73.1212 refers to section 73.1212 of title 47 of the Code of Federal Regulations.

As you become more familiar with the law, you will begin to recognize commonly referenced statutes or regulations, or at least the titles from which they come, and based on that, will be able to identify at least the general area of law to which the citation refers, if not the particular law. For example, most media lawyers would recognize the USC citation earlier as referring to the provision of the Copyright Act dealing with "fair use" of copyrighted materials, and the CFR citation as referring to the Federal Communications Commission's rule about sponsorship disclosure on radio and television stations.

FEDERAL CASES

Case cites look similar but have some additional information that identifies the location and relative level of the court that rendered the decision.

Take, for example, this Supreme Court case citation: 510 U.S. 569 (1994).

The first feature to note is the acronym "U.S." which is the abbreviation used for the U.S. Supreme Court reporter. That tells us immediately that the citation refers to a federal Supreme Court case. The number just before, 510, refers to the volume in which the case appears. When reporters were published in print form, the volume referred to just that – a single physical volume – so the reader would know to go look for volume 510 on the shelf. Today, with electronic research, the volume number is less relevant, but because the organizational scheme persists, it is still used to identify cases.

The number following the "U.S." designation, 569, is the page number, within volume 510, on which the case starts. The date in parenthesis is the date the decision was rendered.

Sometimes you might see a number after the initial page number, such as 510 U.S. 569, 572 (1994). That second number, here 572, is known as a **pin citation** or **pin cite**. The pin cite indicates to the reader that the particular statement or legal proposition to which the cite refers appears on a certain page within the reporter.

Citations for appellate courts look similar but have additional information to help identify the court that rendered the decision (unnecessary with Supreme Court citations since there is only one Supreme Court).

Recall that federal circuit court opinions appear in the Federal Reporter, which has been divided into several series over the years, identified in citation form as F., F.2d, F.3d, and F.4th. For example, the citation for *Maloney v. T3Media, Inc.* is 853 F.3d 1004 (9th Cir. 2017). The citation tells us that the case is in volume 853 of the Federal Reporter, Third Series, that it begins on page 1004, and that the Ninth Circuit Court of Appeals issued its decision in 2017.

Federal district court opinions are published in the Federal Supplement, of which there are three series, abbreviated F. Supp., F. Supp. 2d, and F. Supp. 3d. The citation format is essentially the same as for circuit court citations, except that the court designations are a bit more complex owing to the fact there are more courts. For example, the Central District of California would be abbreviated as CD Cal., while the Northern District of Illinois would be ND Ill., and so on.

STATE CASES

State cases are typically reported in state-specific reporters published by various companies, but also in West Publishing's **regional reporters** that aggregate state cases from nine geographic regions of the United States. For example, the Atlantic Reporter, abbreviated A., A.2d., or A.3d, depending on the series, includes cases from Connecticut, Delaware, the District of Columbia, Maine, Maryland, New Hampshire, New Jersey, Pennsylvania, Rhode Island, and Vermont, while the Southern Reporter, abbreviated So. Or So.2d, covers Alabama, Florida, Louisiana, and Mississippi. Because the volume of cases is so high, relative to other states, New York and California each have their own dedicated "regional" reporters.

KEY POINTS AND TAKEAWAYS

1. US law is organized as a hierarchy, with the Constitution at the top, followed by federal law, and then state law. State law may not be inconsistent with federal law but may afford state citizens more protections than federal law. All laws must comport with the U.S. Constitution.
2. Courts are similarly organized in a hierarchy, with the U.S. Supreme Court at the top, the circuit courts of appeal in the middle, and the district courts below. Litigation or criminal matters begin in the trial courts and are appealed to the circuit courts, whose decisions are binding on all the trial courts falling within the circuit court's geographic region. Supreme Court cases are binding on all federal courts. Although the naming conventions differ by state, most state court systems closely follow the structure of the federal judiciary.
3. Laws originate from various sources, including the federal and state constitutions, statutes passed by Congress or state legislatures, regulations promulgated by administrative agencies, executive orders issued by the President or state governors, and common (case) law.
4. Civil litigation involves a plaintiff bringing a lawsuit against a defendant, who is found by a trier of fact – either a jury or a judge – either liable or not liable. A defendant found liable may be forced to pay money damages to the plaintiff, or may have an injunction issued against them, which is a court order mandating they either engage or refrain from engaging in certain conduct.
5. Criminal prosecution involves the state, by way of a prosecutor, bringing criminal charges against a defendant, who is found either guilty or not guilty by a trier of fact – either a jury or a judge, in the case of a bench trial – if the facts show beyond a reasonable doubt that the defendant committed the act(s) of which they are accused. A guilty defendant may be punished by imprisonment, the imposition of fines, or both.

QUESTIONS FOR DISCUSSION

1. What are the names of the statutory and regulatory codes in your state? For example, in Colorado, the statutory code is the Colorado Revised Statutes and the regulations are codified in the Code of Colorado Regulations; in Pennsylvania, the

statutory code is called the Pennsylvania Consolidated Statutes and the regulatory code is simply the Pennsylvania Code.

2. Where can you find the statutory and regulatory code in your state? Most states have websites where the codes are freely available.

3. What is the structure of the court system in your state? How are the courts organized and what is each level (trial, intermedia appellate, and last resort) called?

3

CHAPTER 3
THE FIRST AMENDMENT

What is the First Amendment and what rights does it afford citizens? Does it provide special guarantees to the press? What are the boundaries of the First Amendment and how do courts resolve tensions between First Amendment rights and other important constitutional values?

In the previous chapter, we established the broad contours of the law. In this chapter, we will orient ourselves within that broad universe by examining the spectrum of protection that First Amendment law has developed over the years and how it affects the media industry. Among other things, this chapter will examine distinctions between highly protected speech, such as political statements, and unprotected speech, such as obscenity.

FUNDAMENTAL FREEDOMS

The First Amendment to the U.S. Constitution provides that:

> Congress shall make no law respecting an establishment of religion, or prohibiting the free exercise thereof; or abridging the freedom of speech, or of the press; or the right of the people peaceably to assemble, and to petition the government for a redress of grievances.

In that single sentence, comprising only 45 words, the framers of the Constitution established a framework for what have become some of the most sacrosanct rights of U.S. citizens: the right to freely practice religious beliefs and be free from government attempts at establishing a national religion; the right to assemble peaceably, which enables the protests, demonstrations, and marches that have, throughout our history, led to momentous legal and cultural changes; the right to complain to the government and ask for changes to laws and policies; and the freedom to speak openly and freely, and the right of the press to report on government affairs and other matters of public importance.

The rights set forth in the First Amendment represent the framers' attempt at avoiding the tyranny of a central government, such as the English monarchy from which they had fled. As noted previously, the guiding principle of the U.S. democratic framework is that power vests first in the people, who grant the authority to govern to the government. The ability to speak, assemble, and practice one's own religious beliefs free from undue government involvement, coupled with the right to complain to (and seek redress from) the government, were all considered essential to ensuring that the power to govern remained fundamentally with the citizens.

DOI: 10.4324/9781003197966-3

Initially, the courts held that the First Amendment applied only to the federal government, and did not extend to state governments, relying on the fact that the plain language of the amendment makes reference to "Congress." In 1925, however, in *Gitlow v. New York*,[1] the Supreme Court was asked to consider whether a New York state statute that made it illegal to advocate for the overthrow of the government violated the First Amendment. The court ultimately found that the statute was constitutional, but in so doing, it held that the freedoms guaranteed by the First Amendment were among those that were "incorporated" to the states through the Fourteenth Amendment, adopted in 1868. The Fourteenth Amendment, among other things, prohibits the federal and state governments from depriving citizens of life, liberty, or property without due process of law.

In its opinion, the Court observed that

> freedom of speech and of the press – which are protected by the First Amendment from abridgment by Congress – are among the fundamental personal rights and "liberties" protected by the due process clause of the Fourteenth Amendment from impairment by the States.

Ever since, it has been understood that the First Amendment guarantees afforded citizens by the First Amendment apply not only to the federal government but also to state and local governments.

WHAT IS SPEECH?

Although the First Amendment refers specifically to "speech," courts have interpreted the term to include anything that serves a symbolic or expressive purpose. The Supreme Court has observed that "[s]ymbolism is a primitive but effective way of communicating ideas."[2] Accordingly, we sometimes refer to the First Amendment as protecting "expression" as opposed to merely "speech," in the traditional sense of the word.

The Supreme Court has developed a two-part test by which to determine if particular conduct rises to the level of **expressive conduct** or **symbolic speech** worthy of First Amendment protection. First, the court considers whether the conduct was undertaken with the intent to convey a particular message; and second, whether it is likely that the message would be understood by those who viewed it.[3]

In *Spence v. State of Washington*, the Court was asked to determine whether Washington state could punish a college student for displaying a U.S. flag adorned

---

1 268 U.S. 652 (1925)
2 *West Virginia State Board of Education v. Barnette*, 319 U.S. 624, 633 (1943).
3 *See Texas v. Johnson*, 491 U.S. 397, 404 (1989) (citing *Spence v. State of Washington*, 418 U.S. 405, 410–11 (1974)).

with the circular peace symbol made of black tape in violation of a state law that made it illegal to superimpose figures or symbols to the flag. In concluding that Washington's law violated the First Amendment, the court first determined that Spence's conduct was expressive in nature because it:

> was not an act of mindless nihilism. Rather, it was a pointed expression of anguish … about the then-current domestic and foreign affairs of [the] government. An intent to convey a particularized message was present, and in the surrounding circumstances the likelihood was great that the message would be understood by those who viewed it.[4]

In a subsequent case, *Texas v. Johnson*, it was concluded that burning a U.S. flag during a political protest rally constituted expressive conduct that was entitled to First Amendment protection.[5] Courts have also recognized burning a draft card as protected symbolic speech,[6] as are peaceful "sit-in"-style protests, which were commonly used during the civil rights movement of the 1950s and 1960s to draw attention to racial inequality[7] and wearing certain items of clothing or accessories intended to convey a particular political message.[8]

WHAT IS "THE PRESS?"

In 1786, Thomas Jefferson wrote that "[o]ur liberty depends on the freedom of the press, and that cannot be limited without being lost."[9]

At the time, the First Amendment was drafted, the "press" meant books, newspapers, and pamphlets, such as those printed by the likes of Thomas Jefferson in support of the American Revolution.

Times have changed in the ensuing 230-plus years since the Constitution was adopted. Today, "the press" can be best understood as what we now call "the media" – those enterprises that develop, produce, and distribute news and information about the government, current affairs, and other matters of public importance – such as radio and television stations, book, magazine, and newspaper publishers, online streaming services, podcasters, and bloggers.

The press or media, as a collective group, is sometimes referred to as **the fourth estate** because it serves as a fourth branch of government, a government "watchdog"

---

4 *Spence*, 418 U.S. at 410.
5 491 U.S. 397 (1989).
6 See *U.S. v. O'Brien*, 391 U.S. 367 (1968).
7 See *Garner v. Louisiana*, 368 U.S. 157 (1961).
8 See *Tinker v. Des Moines Independent Community School District*, 393 U.S. 503 (1969).
9 Letter from Thomas Jefferson to James Currie, January 28, 1786, available at https://founders.archives.gov/documents/Jefferson/01-09-02-0209.

by keeping the public apprised of its activities so that citizens may make informed decisions about government policies and elected officials. As Justice Black observed, the First Amendment "gave the free press the protection it must have to fulfill its essential role in our democracy. The press was to serve the governed, not the governors."[10]

Justice Black's statement raises an important concept: the idea of an **adversarial press**. Politicians and other government leaders have something of a "love-hate" relationship with the press: on the one hand, the press is a key mechanism by which political leaders communicate with their constituencies. On the other hand, serving in its watchdog function, the press often has an adversarial relationship with those that it watches. This dynamic has become known as the adversarial press.

Speaking to Chuck Todd of NBC's *Meet the Press* in 2017, the late Senator John McCain, an Arizona republican, noted that "a fundamental part of the new world order was a free press." He went on to say (half-jokingly): "I hate the press. I hate you especially. But the fact is we need you."

McCain concluded:

> We need a free press. We must have it. It's vital. If you want to preserve democracy as we know it you have to have a free – and many times adversarial – press, and without it I'm afraid we would lose so much of our individual liberties over time. That's how dictators get started.

THE RIGHT TO RECEIVE INFORMATION

Courts have also recognized that an important part of the First Amendment is not only a speaker's right to express themselves freely but also the opposite side of that coin: citizens' rights to receive the messages conveyed by those expressing themselves. As the Supreme Court has explained, "[f]reedom of speech presupposes a willing speaker. But where a speaker exists ... the protection afforded is to the communication, to its source and to its recipients both."[11]

The Supreme Court first described this idea in 1969 in *Stanley v. Georgia*,[12] which involved a statute that criminalized the possession of obscene material. In its opinion holding the law unconstitutional, the Court said that it is "well established that the Constitution protects the right to receive information and ideas ... regardless of their social worth" and that such a right is "fundamental to our free society."[13]

---

10 *New York Times Co. v. U.S.*, 403 U.S. 713, 717 (1971) (Black, J., concurring).
11 *Virginia State Board of Pharmacy v. Virginia Citizens Consumer Council, Inc.*, 425 U.S. 748 (1976).
12 394 U.S. 557 (1969).
13 *Id.* at 564.

Several years later, the court relied on this concept when it extended First Amendment protection to advertising. In *Virginia State Board of Pharmacy v. Virginia Citizens Consumer Council, Inc.*,[14] the Court considered the constitutionality of a Virginia statute that made it unlawful to advertise prescription drug prices. The Court determined that the law was unconstitutional, observing that although the speaker's motives for the speech at issue – advertising drug prices – were purely economic in nature, a consumer's interest in access to drug prices is likely just as strong, if not stronger, than their interest in debating political ideas.[15]

The Supreme Court expanded the principles in *Stanley* and *Virginia State Board of Pharmacy* in a subsequent case, *Pico v. Board of Education, Island Trees Union Free School District No. 26*,[16] which involved a school district's removal of certain books from school libraries. The Court held that the school district could not remove books simply because the school board disagreed with the substance of those books, reasoning that the right to receive information and ideas is the natural complement to the speaker's First Amendment right to express those ideas, and because receiving such information or being exposed to such ideas, is a "necessary predicate to the *recipient's* meaningful exercise of his own rights of speech, press, and political freedom."[17]

In sum, courts recognize the First Amendment as a "two-way street" – in order for our right to express ourselves freely to be of any value, the people to whom we direct that expression must also have a corresponding right to receive or have access to that expression.

COMPELLED SPEECH

We typically think of the First Amendment as protecting an individual's right to speak or express themselves free from government intervention, but courts have concluded that the First Amendment also protects against the government mandating or compelling individuals to speak or express themselves against their will.

In *Rumsfeld v. Forum for Academic and Institutional Rights*,[18] Justice Roberts observed that some of the Supreme Court's "leading First Amendment precedents have established the principle that freedom of speech prohibits the government from telling people what they must say."[19]

He went on to refer to what is perhaps the most frequently cited Supreme Court cases on the point. In *West Virginia State Board of Education v. Barnette*,[20] several students

---

14 425 U.S. 748 (1976).
15 *Id.* at 763.
16 457 U.S. 853 (1982).
17 *Id.* at 867 (emphasis in original).
18 547 U.S. 47 (2006).
19 *Id.* at 61.
20 319 U.S. 624 (1943).

had been expelled from school, and some were even threatened with commitment
to juvenile reformatories, for refusing to salute the U.S. flag and recite the Pledge of
Allegiance, as required by state law. The students challenging the statute, all Jehovah's
Witnesses, claimed that the conduct required by state law violated their religious beliefs.

The Court agreed with the students, noting that

> if there is any fixed star in our constitutional constellation, it is that no official,
> high or petty, can prescribe what shall be orthodox in politics, nationalism,
> religion, or other matters of opinion or force citizens to confess by word or act
> their faith therein.[21]

As described in a later case, "[t]he right to speak and the right to refrain from speaking are
complementary components of the broader concept of 'individual freedom of mind.'"[22]

Simply put, the government cannot force someone to speak against their will.

The Supreme Court has put limits on that principle, however. In a 2005 case, it
determined that although the government could not compel an individual person
or entity to speak, one could not prevent the government from using tax dollars to
advance its own messages, a principle known as the **government speech doctrine**.[23]

REGULATING SPEECH

As we will see throughout the rest of this book, in the years since the framers wrote
that "Congress shall make no law" restricting the various freedoms set forth in the
First Amendment, the Courts have concluded that there are, in fact, some limited circumstances in which the government may impose reasonable restrictions on the First
Amendment's central freedoms.

GOVERNMENT OR PRIVATE ACTION?

As an initial matter, it is important to understand that the restrictions outlined in the
Constitution, including the First Amendment, limit only **government action** or
what is sometimes called **state action**. Private parties are generally not bound by the
constitution unless they are engaging in functions that are traditionally performed by
the government or if they are directed by some statute, regulation, or government
policy to engage in such conduct.

Put differently, only the government, or someone acting under the authority of the
government, can violate an individual's constitutional rights.

21 *Id.* at 642.
22 *Wooley v. Maynard*, 430 U.S. 705, 714 (1977).
23 *See Johanns v. Livestock Marketing Association*, 544 U.S. 550 (2005).

For example, a shopping mall might impose a rule that prohibits people from distributing political literature on the premises. Even though distributing political literature is an expressive activity clearly protected by the First Amendment, that protection does not prevent the shopping mall from imposing its rule, because the mall is a private business, and the First Amendment does not apply. However, if that same prohibition were imposed by a government-run airport, it would probably be held unconstitutional, because the airport, as a state actor, is subject to the limitations of the First Amendment.

It is worth noting that even though the federal constitution would not prevent a shopping mall from imposing a rule against the distribution of political literature, some state laws would. In California, for instance, the state constitution has been held to guarantee political protesters the right to assemble in private shopping centers.[24] Recall from Chapter 2 that under the principles of federalism and supremacy, state governments may not interpret their constitutions in such a way, or pass laws, that conflict with federal law, but they may offer protections to their citizens that are more expansive.

Discussions about the distinction between private and state action have traditionally been reserved for constitutional scholars, lawyers, students studying political science, and the like, but over the past several years, it has begun to show up in common conversation, as the use of internet-based platforms such as Facebook and Twitter have become popular forms for political discourse. During the 2020 presidential election cycle, and the global COVID-19 pandemic, many internet platform operators began identifying or, in some extreme cases removing, user-generated content that they believed to be false or misleading.

In response, some who have had their content flagged have asserted that the platforms are abiding their First Amendment rights by not letting them speak freely. But those complaints are misguided because social media platforms are owned by private companies and the First Amendment simply does not apply to them. Moreover, those companies have their own First Amendment rights that guarantee them the right to speak (or as we saw in the last section, the right not to speak) freely.

We will discuss this dynamic, and other issues pertaining to online platforms later in this book.

TYPES OF REGULATION

Once we have determined that a particular restriction on speech is imposed by the government as opposed to a private actor, the next question to ask is whether the restriction is **content based** or **content neutral**.

---

24 *See PruneYard Shopping Center v. Robbins*, 447 U.S. 74 (1980).

CONTENT-BASED RESTRICTIONS

Content-based restrictions are, as the name suggests, government restrictions that regulate speech based on the nature of its content. Such restrictions can be further categorized into **subject matter restrictions**, which are restrictions that apply based on the particular topic of a message, and **viewpoint restrictions**, which restrict speech based on a particular perspective or ideology. A law restricting the distribution of political literature at a public park would be a subject matter restriction, while a law restricting the distribution of political literature from the Democratic Party would be a viewpoint restriction. Both are examples of content-based restrictions.

The Supreme Court has explained that even where a law may not obviously restrict speech based on its content, it may still be considered content based if the law cannot be "justified without reference to the content of the regulated speech" or where the government's motivation for enacting the law was because it disagrees with the message that the targeted speech conveys.[25]

Content-based restrictions are among the most heavily scrutinized by the courts because they are among the restrictions that are most likely to run afoul of an individual's First Amendment rights. Accordingly, the Supreme Court has established the **strict scrutiny** test to determine whether a content-based restriction comports with the Constitution. As the name implies, the strict scrutiny test is the most exacting standard that courts apply to constitutional questions. Beyond the First Amendment, courts also use the strict scrutiny test to evaluate the constitutionality of laws or government actions that discriminate based on someone's race, national origin, religion, or alienage.

For a law to survive a constitutional challenge under the strict scrutiny test, the *government* must establish that the law serves a *compelling* government interest and that the law is *narrowly tailored* to advance that interest.

Note that the burden is on the *government* to establish the constitutionality of the law. To challenge a content-based restriction on speech, all a plaintiff needs to establish is that the law restricts speech based on its content. The burden then shifts to the government to demonstrate a compelling interest and prove that the law in question is narrowly tailored to achieve it.

CONTENT-NEUTRAL RESTRICTIONS

A content-neutral restriction imposes limitations on speech but without regard to the content of the message. A law prohibiting the distribution of *any* literature (regardless

---

25 *Reed v. Town of Gilbert*, 576 U.S. 155, 163–64 (2015).

of whether it has a political message) in a public park is an example of a content-neutral restriction.

Content-neutral restrictions are less offensive to traditional First Amendment values because they do not aim to regulate speech based on its topic or message, but they are still subject to close review using a test called **intermediate scrutiny**.

Under the intermediate scrutiny test, to survive a constitutional challenge, the *government* must be able to demonstrate that a content-neutral restriction on speech serves an *important government objective* and that the law is *substantially related* to achieving that objective.

The test is similar in structure to the strict scrutiny test, but the standards are relaxed slightly. Instead of needing to show a "compelling" interest, the government need only establish an "important" objective, and that the law is "substantially related" to achieving that objective, as opposed to being "narrowly tailored." As with strict scrutiny, under intermediate scrutiny, the burden is on the government to establish the facts necessary to uphold the law. A plaintiff who challenges a content-neutral restriction need only show that a law imposes restrictions on speech.

LAWS THAT DO NOT REGULATE SPEECH

Laws that do not regulate speech are analyzed using a much less stringent test – the least stringent test for constitutional questions – known as **rational basis review**. Under a rational basis review, to invalidate a law, the *plaintiff*, not the government, must show that the government has no *legitimate interest* in the law or policy, or that there is *no rational connection* between the government's purported interest and the regulation.

Notably, unlike the strict and intermediate scrutiny standards, the burden is on the *plaintiff* to establish that the government has failed to establish a legitimate interest or a rational relationship to that interest.

A SPECTRUM OF SCRUTINY

You can think of the three tests for evaluating whether a particular restriction on speech as falling along a spectrum, as shown in Figure 3.1, with strict scrutiny on one side and rational basis on the other. Intermediate scrutiny sits in the middle.

TIME, PLACE, AND MANNER REGULATIONS

As you can see, the government must meet a high bar to regulate speech based on its content. But the courts have construed the First Amendment to permit reasonable

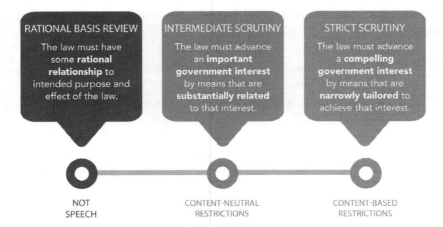

Figure 3.1 Levels of judicial scrutiny for constitutional questions.

restrictions on the basis of where, when, or how certain speech takes place. Such laws are known as **time, place, and manner restrictions**.

Because a central goal of the First Amendment is to ensure that the public has the ability to freely discuss and debate ideas, the courts have construed its protections to apply more broadly in those venues where such speech has traditionally taken place, while allowing more stringent regulations in those venues that are not generally associated with free speech activities.

Therefore, to evaluate whether a particular time, place, and manner restriction is Constitutional, we must first identify the nature of the venue in which the speech takes place. Courts consider venues for speech as falling into three categories: public forums, designated public forums, and non-public forums.

PUBLIC FORUMS

A **public forum** is public property that has traditionally been made available for or associated with speech-related activities – things like protests, marches, or the distribution of literature. Common examples of public forums include streets, sidewalks, and parks.

Generally, the government may limit speech in such venues only if the restriction:

1. Is *content neutral*;
2. Is *narrowly tailored* to achieve an *important government interest*; and
3. Leaves open *alternative channels* of communication.

In this context, "narrowly tailored" means that it burdens no more speech than necessary to achieve the government interest, though it need not be the *least restrictive* means of achieving it.

For example, in *Ward v. Rock Against Racism*, the Supreme Court concluded that an ordinance requiring those using the city's amphitheater to use the city's sound system was a reasonable time, place, and manner restriction because it was narrowly tailored to achieve the city's interest in controlling the noise level within the community.[26]

Note that if a time, place, and manner restriction fails to meet the elements of the test, it is not necessarily unconstitutional, rather, it will be analyzed under the strict scrutiny test discussed earlier in this chapter.

Sometimes, the government will require those using public forums for speech activities to get a permit before doing so. Such laws are generally permissible, so long as the conditions used to grant the permit comport with the test above, and that public officials have no discretion over whatever fee may be charged to grant the permit.

DESIGNATED PUBLIC FORUMS

Designated public forums are public spaces that are not traditionally open to speech-related activities but are made available on some limited basis for such purposes. For example, a public library, which is itself not a public forum, might make its conference rooms available to private organizations, making the conference rooms, when used for those purposes, designated public forums. Similarly, a public school is generally not a public forum, but if it were to allow a civic organization to host a political townhall or debate in the gymnasium, it would be considered a designated or limited-purpose public forum.

Restrictions on the use of designated public forums must meet the same test that applies to public forums set forth above. Accordingly, the school or library would be entitled to impose reasonable restrictions on the use of their facilities, so long as they were content neutral, narrowly tailored, and leave open alternative channels of communication. For example, the school might impose a rule that its facilities are only open for public forum activities during hours that school is not in session, or the library might impose rules restricting loud music or other sound amplification devices while using its conference rooms so as not to disturb other patrons.

Provided such rules are applied in a nondiscriminatory manner, they will likely be considered reasonable time, place, and manner restrictions.

NON-PUBLIC FORUMS

All those areas that are not traditionally open for speech-related activities, or not designated as such, are considered **non-public forums**. Military bases, schools, mass

---

26 491 U.S. 781 (1989).

transit facilities, airports, post offices, mailboxes outside an individual's home, and polling places have all been determined to be non-public forums.

A restriction on speech in a non-public forum is constitutional if it:

1. Is *viewpoint neutral*; and is
2. *Reasonably related* to a *legitimate government purpose.*

For example, the Supreme Court has held that a rule banning solicitation within an airport terminal was constitutional because it was reasonably related to the government's legitimate purpose of preventing passenger congestion and undue exploitation of travelers who are too focused on their travels to properly evaluate the solicitor's request.[27] But, in a subsequent case involving the same parties, the Court held that the government could not prevent the distribution of literature at the airport because the limitation was not reasonably related to any legitimate purpose, and distributing literature was not as intrusive as solicitation.[28]

UNPROTECTED SPEECH

There are some categories of speech that the Supreme Court has held receive no First Amendment protection.

INCITEMENT

The government generally may not restrict speech because it promotes violence or encourages breaking the law, however, the Supreme Court has said that a law may be upheld if the law seeks to restrict speech that is directed to producing or inciting imminent lawless action and is likely to produce or incite such action.[29]

FIGHTING WORDS AND TRUE THREATS

Similar to incitement, but less immediate or imminent, are "true threats," which the Supreme Court described as "where the speaker means to communicate a serious expression of intent to commit an act of unlawful violence to a particular individual or group of individuals."[30] Closely related to true threats are "fighting words," which refers to speech that, when directed at an ordinary citizen, is likely to provoke or incite an immediate physical response.[31]

27 *International Society of Krishna Consciousness v. Lee*, 505 U.S. 672 (1992).
28 *Lee v. International Society of Krishna Consciousness*, 505 U.S. 830 (1992).
29 *Brandenberg v. Ohio*, 395 U.S. 444 (1969).
30 *Virginia v. Black*, 538 U.S. 343, 360 (2003).
31 *Chaplinsky v. New Hampshire*, 315 U.S. 568 (1942).

Neither fighting words nor true threats are protected by the First Amendment, which means that the government is free to pass laws to restrict or punish such speech.

HARASSMENT AND HATE SPEECH

Some are surprised to learn that the First Amendment has not been held to prohibit hate speech – that is, vitriolic speech aimed at a particular individual or group, often based on a person's association with particular classes, such as race, gender, or national origin. That said, there is a fine line between hate speech, which is entitled to First Amendment protection, and incitement, fighting words, and true threats which, as discussed earlier, are not so protected.

In *R.A.V. v. St. Paul*, then juvenile identified only as R.A.V. burned a cross, an act widely understood to be associated with the Ku Klux Klan, on a black family's lawn. R.A.V. was convicted under a St. Paul ordinance that banned the display of symbols that "arouse ... anger, alarm or resentment in others on the basis of race, color, creed, religion or gender."[32] He subsequently challenged the constitutionality of the ordinance.

The Minnesota Supreme Court upheld R.A.V.'s conviction, holding that the ordinance was constitutional because it banned the equivalent "fighting words" as contemplated by the Supreme Court, specifically it held that burning a cross on the lawn of a black family was likely to incite a violent response. The U.S. Supreme Court, however, reversed that decision, holding that the ordinance was unconstitutional because it was an impermissible content-based restriction on speech and that St. Paul could have achieved its policy objective – preventing or mitigating violence – without limiting the law to address specific types of content, namely speech that involves race, color, creed, religion, or gender.[33]

OBSCENITY

Obscenity is another category of speech that is afforded no protection by the First Amendment, which means that the government is free to regulate it. The Court defines obscenity more narrowly than mere sexual material – it is material which, when taken as a whole, by an average person, applying contemporary community standards, appeals to the prurient interest, portrays sex in a patently offensive way, and lacks any serious literary, artistic, political, or scientific value, based on a nationwide standard.[34]

Note the distinction between the two parts of the test. Whether the material at issue "appeals to the prurient interest" and "portrays sex in a patently offensive way" is measured by a *community* standard, while the second part of the test that evaluates the

---

32 505 U.S. 377, 391 (1992).
33 *Id*. at 392–393.
34 *Roth v. United States*, 354 U.S. 476 (1957); *Miller v. California*, 413 U.S. 15 (1973).

"literary, artistic, political, or scientific value" of the material – sometimes referred to as the *Miller* test, after the Supreme Court case that established it[35] – is measured by a national standard.

It is also worth noting that the courts have drawn a distinction between possessing obscene material and distributing it. The Supreme Court explained it as follows:

> [w]hatever may be the justifications for other statutes regulating obscenity, we do not think they reach into the privacy of one's own home. If the First Amendment means anything, it means that a State has no business telling a man, sitting alone in his own house, what books he may read or what films he may watch. Our whole constitutional heritage rebels at the thought of giving the government the power to control men's minds.[36]

Thus, while the government may regulate the distribution and exhibition of obscene material, the government cannot stop somebody from merely possessing it.

Pornography featuring visual depictions of children is always considered obscene, even if the material would not be considered obscene if it featured adults.[37] But note that the Court has also held that simulated child pornography, producing featuring adults made to appear as children, or computer-generated images, is not obscene.[38]

Finally, take care to distinguish obscenity, which receives no First Amendment protection, from the less egregious versions, **indecency** and **profanity**. In contrast to obscenity, indecent or profane speech receives some First Amendment protection, but as we will see later in this book, the government is free to regulate it in certain contexts, namely when broadcast through radio or television.

DEFAMATION

Defamatory speech – speech that wrongfully harms the reputation of another – is not entitled to First Amendment protection. What constitutes defamatory speech varies based on a variety of criteria, including the nature of the statements at issue and the individual, group, or entity about which they are made. Because defamation is so important to media law, we will discuss it at length in Chapter 4.

A SPECTRUM OF PROTECTION

Taking into account the underlying purpose of the First Amendment, the free speech doctrines we discussed earlier in this chapter, and the exceptions to First Amendment

---

35 *Miller v. California*, 413 U.S. 15 (1972).
36 *Stanley v. Georgia*, 394 U.S. 557 (1969).
37 *New York v. Ferber*, 458 U.S. 747 (1982).
38 *Ashcroft v. Free Speech Coalition*, 535 U.S. 234 (2002).

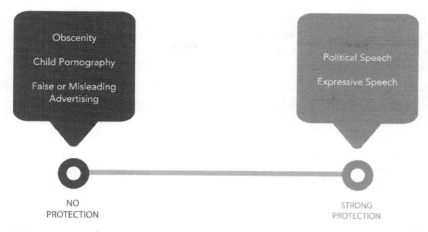

Obscenity

Child Pornography

False or Misleading Advertising

Political Speech

Expressive Speech

NO PROTECTION

STRONG PROTECTION

Figure 3.2 Degrees of First Amendment protection for certain types of speech.

protection discussed in the prior section, we start to see that the First Amendment establishes a spectrum, with varying degrees of protection based on the nature or type of speech at issue. At one end of the spectrum are categories of speech that the Supreme Court has held are entitled to no First Amendment protection, while at the other end are types of speech that the Court has held to be among the most sacrosanct to a properly functioning republic. In the middle are types of speech that enjoy limited protection and are discussed more fully later in this book.

VAGUENESS AND OVERBREADTH

Even if a law or other restriction on speech passes muster under strict or intermediate scrutiny, or the rational basis test, there are two additional reasons why a restriction on speech might be invalidated: overbreadth and vagueness. Although these concepts exist throughout constitutional law, they tend to be applied strictly in the First Amendment context because the right to free speech is so central to our form of democracy.

A restriction is **overbroad** if it restricts substantially more speech than is necessary to achieve the government's intended purpose. A restriction is **vague** if an individual cannot determine from the language of the law what is or is not permitted. Vague laws are especially problematic in the free speech context because the uncertainty may lead to a **chilling effect**, where people are afraid to engage in certain types of speech or expressive conduct for fear of being punished, even if the speech would ultimately be considered constitutionally protected.

PRIOR RESTRAINT

A central feature of the First Amendment's free speech rights is a strong presumption against the legality of prior restraints. A **prior restraint** is where the government seeks to restrict speech or expression before it happens, and they are generally disfavored because they could put too much power in the hands of the government, contrary to the framers' notion of democracy.[39] As we have seen throughout this chapter, there are circumstances where the government may regulate speech, and speakers may be held responsible for violating those regulations, but the presumption against prior restraints means that the government must generally let the speech happen and impose consequences after the fact, where justified.

The Supreme Court has recognized, however, that there are some circumstances where prior restraint may be appropriate if it is necessary to achieve a compelling government purpose. In *Near v. Minnesota*, the Court described several "exceptional cases" where prior restraints may be appropriate, including matters of national security, obscenity, and incitements to the violent overthrow of the government.[40] The Court has also held that prior restraints may be appropriate where there are compelling competing interests that justify it, such as ensuring a criminal defendant receives a fair trial.[41]

In 1971, the federal government sought to apply the national security exception described in *Near* when it sought an injunction against *The New York Times*, ordering it not to publish classified documents relating to the government's policies regarding Vietnam (the so-called "Pentagon Papers"). The documents had been unlawfully leaked to reporters by a source inside the government, and the government argued that further dissemination could harm the security interests of the country. The courts disagreed, however, and concluded that the material at issue was primarily historical and that the government had failed to establish its burden.[42] The paper published the material and the leaker, Daniel Ellsberg, was later prosecuted for disclosing classified information.

More recently, prior restraint became a familiar topic in the run-up to the 2020 presidential election. In June of 2020, the Trump administration sought to prevent former national security advisor John Bolton from publishing a memoir about his time working for President Trump, citing national security concerns. Although the district court concluded that Bolton "likely published classified materials," it declined to enjoin Bolton because it failed to show that the release of the book would cause irreparable injury, and because the books were already percolating through the supply chain or, as the court put it, "the 'horse is already out of the barn.'"[43]

Although the court did not grant the injunction, the case persisted, as the government sought to recoup Bolton's profits from the book. The government also launched a criminal investigation into whether Bolton had illegally disclosed classified

39 *See Near v. Minnesota*, 283 U.S. 697, 732–733 (1931).
40 *Id.* at 716.
41 *See Nebraska Press Association v. Stuart*, 427 U.S. 539 (1976).
42 *United States v. New York Times Co.*, 403 U.S. 713 (1971).
43 *United States v. Bolton*, 458 F. Supp. 3d 1, 6 (D.D.C. 2020).

information. In mid-2021, the Biden Administration announced it was dropping the civil lawsuit as well as the criminal investigation.[44]

Shortly after the Trump Administration sued Bolton, President Trump's brother, Robert Trump, brought a suit against their niece, Mary Trump, and her publisher, seeking to enjoin the release of her book *Too Much and Never Enough: How My Family Created the World's Most Dangerous Man*. The elder Trump argued that Mary's book violated an agreement she had signed to settle certain family disputes in which she promised not to write about the Trump family and consented to the granting of an injunction if there were ever a dispute. The trial court initially granted Robert Trump's motion for an injunction, but ultimately withdraw it, noting that constitutional law "trumps [c]ontracts."[45]

STUDENT SPEECH

Over the years, courts have recognized certain types of speech that, by virtue of the status of the speaker, or the context in which the speech takes place, justify giving the government more latitude to regulate it. One such area is student speech, or speech that takes place within an educational setting.

In a seminal case on the issue, the Supreme Court was called upon to determine whether a public school rule prohibiting black arm bands worn in protest of the military conflict in Vietnam was a violation of students' First Amendment rights.[46] The Court concluded that it did because the school district failed to demonstrate that the restriction was necessary to ensure proper order and discipline, or to avoid disruption to the learning environment. Writing for the majority, Justice Fortas wrote that students do not "shed their constitutional rights to freedom of speech or expression at the schoolhouse gate"[47] and that "state-operated schools may not be enclaves of totalitarianism."[48]

Still, the courts have concluded that there are circumstances where schools may limit or regulate student speech "in light of the special characteristics of the school environment."[49]

For example, in *Bethel School District No. 403 v. Fraser*,[50] the Supreme Court concluded that a public school did not violate a student's First Amendment rights by punishing

44 Michael S. Schmidt and Katie Benner, *Justice Dept. Ends Criminal Inquiry and Lawsuit on John Bolton's Book*, The New York Times, June 16, 2021, available at https://www.nytimes.com/2021/06/16/us/politics/john -bolton-book-justice-department.html.

45 *Trump v. Trump*, 128 N.Y.S.3d 801, 822.

46 *Tinker v. Des Moines Independent Community School District*, 393 U.S. 503 (1969).

47 *Id*. at 506.

48 *Id*. at 511.

49 *Hazelwood School District v. Kuhlmeier*, 484 U.S. 260, 266 (1988).

50 478 U.S. 675 (1986).

the student for using an "elaborate, graphic, and explicit sexual metaphor" during a speech given at a school assembly (he had been previously warned that including the explicit language would result in "severe consequences").[51]

Similarly, in 2007, the Supreme Court upheld a school district policy under which a student was punished for displaying a banner that said "BONG HiTS 4 JESUS" during a school-sanctioned and school-supervised event.[52] The Court explained that despite the general rule that students are entitled to their First Amendment rights, even while at school, "schools may take steps to safeguard those entrusted to their care from speech that can readably be regarded as encouraging illegal drug use."[53] The Court has also upheld restrictions involving student speech that bears the imprimatur of the school, such as that published in a school-sponsored student newspaper.[54]

More recently, the Supreme Court added to its jurisprudence in this area in *Mahanoy Area School District v. Levy*,[55] which represents the first time that the Court has addressed the extent to which schools may regulate the speech-related activities of its students away from campus and, in particular, on the internet. In *Levy*, a high school student who failed to make the school's varsity cheerleading squad turned to Snapchat to express her dissatisfaction with the decision by making two posts, one of which contained profane language and gestures. The school suspended her from the junior varsity cheerleading squad for the remainder of the school year, arguing that because the posts pertained to a school-sponsored extracurricular activity, they violated the school and team rules against using profanity.

The trial court found in favor of Levy and ordered the school to reinstate her role on the junior varsity squad, and the circuit court agreed. The school district then sought a writ of certiorari from the Supreme Court.

The Supreme Court agreed with the lower courts that the school's actions violated Levy's First Amendment rights. Writing for an 8-1 majority, Justice Breyer opined that there are three reasons why a school's interest in regulating off-campus speech is different than regulating on-campus speech. First, it observed that we traditionally consider schools to be acting *in loco parentis*, that is, acting in place of a child's parents while at school, "where the children's actual parents cannot protect, guide, and discipline them."[56] Since off-campus speech takes place, by definition, when the student is away from school, it is "within the zone of parental, rather than school-related, responsibility."[57]

---

51 *Id.* at 678.
52 *Morse v. Frederick*, 551 U.S. 393 (2007).
53 *Id.* at 396.
54 See *Hazelwood*, 484 U.S. at 260.
55 141 S.Ct. 2038 (2021).
56 *Id.* at 2046.
57 *Id.*

Second, the Court observed that allowing schools to regulate students' off-campus speech activities, while also allowing regulation of a student's on-campus speech, raises the specter that a student is under the school's control 24 hours a day. Accordingly, "courts must be more skeptical of a school's effort to regulate off-campus speech, for doing so may mean that the student cannot engage in that kind of speech at all."[58]

Finally, the Court explained that "America's public schools are nurseries of democracy"[59] and that democracy only works if we protect the "marketplace of ideas." Accordingly, says Justice Breyer, schools have a strong interest in ensuring that their primary constituency – students – understand "the workings in practice of the well-known aphorism, 'I disapprove of what you say, but I will defend to the death your right to say it.'"[60]

THE INTERNET AND THE FIRST AMENDMENT

Although the issues raised in *Levy* were specific to the student/school context, the fact that the speech took place on a social media service, Snapchat, makes the case a useful example of how courts are increasingly being asked to consider how the staple doctrines of the First Amendment will work in practice on the internet.

In *Reno v. American Civil Liberties Union*,[61] a landmark case involving free speech on the internet, the Supreme Court described the internet as a:

> dynamic, multifaceted category of communication [that] includes not only traditional print and news services, but also audio, video, and still images, as well as interactive, real-time dialogue. Through the use of chat rooms, any person with a phone line can become a town crier with a voice that resonates farther than it could from any soapbox. Through the use of Web pages, mail exploders, and newsgroups, the same individual can become a pamphleteer.[62]

The Court went on to quote the district court's observation that "'the content on the [i]nternet is as diverse as human thought,'"[63] ultimately concluding that content on the internet was entitled to no more or less protection than speech that occurs in traditional venues.

---

58 *Id.*

59 *Id.*

60 *Id.*

61 521 U.S. 844 (1997).

62 *Id.* at 870. The case was also one of the first in which the Supreme Court was confronted with the internet generally, as evidenced by the laborious and now somewhat quaint description of how the internet works, *id.* at 849-53, and in particular, describing the internet as "a unique medium – known to its users as 'cyberspace'" *Id.* at 851.

63 *Id.* (quoting *American Civil Liberties Union v. Reno*, 929 F. Supp. 824, 842 (E.D. Pa. 1996)).

But granting speech on the internet the same degree of protection as non-internet-based speech raises a host of new questions. For example, we learned earlier in this chapter that the government can, in some circumstances, regulate speech, and we learned that the scope of the government's authority to do so varies based on the type of regulation, but also where the speech takes place. Specifically, recall that in public forums, the government may impose reasonable time, place, and manner restrictions.

As the Supreme Court noted in *Reno*, the internet has become the *de facto* new public square, featuring the modern-day equivalent of town criers and pamphleteers, which is true even more so today than it was in 1996 when the Court made its observation. Today, owing to the rise of social media services and mobile technologies, neither of which had been widely adopted in 1996, one can engage in political conversations within just a few seconds of having a thought. One need only read the comments to virtually any news report to see that the internet has become ground zero for political discourse.

In many ways, then, it would seem as though the internet is a public forum – it has become a place where people are invited to engage in speech. But the internet is controlled primarily by private actors – companies like Google, Facebook, Twitter, Apple, and Amazon – that are not subject to the limitations of the First Amendment, and which also have their own First Amendment rights, including not only the right to free speech, but the right not to be compelled to speak.

In 2019, the U.S. Court of Appeals for the Second Circuit held that President Trump's Twitter account, which he routinely used in his official capacity as President, was a public forum, and that he engaged in impermissible viewpoint discrimination when he "blocked" certain users with whom he disagreed.[64] Because blocking a user has the effect of preventing the blocked user from expressing their viewpoint, either through replies, "likes," or retweets, the court concluded that the President's "block" violated the blocked individuals' First Amendment rights.[65]

Thus, in that instance, Twitter functioned as a public forum, but only because the person using it was a government official acting in their official capacity and was using the platform in such a way that infringed on the rights of others. The court held that it was President Trump's conduct – blocking certain users with whom he disagreed – that gave rise to the First Amendment violation. Had Twitter itself blocked those same users, it would have been protected not only by its own First Amendment rights but also under the immunities found in Section 230 that are discussed later in this book.

---

64 When one user blocks another on Twitter, the blocked user cannot see, follow, "like," or re-tweet posts from the account of the person who blocked them. Although Twitter does not affirmatively advise blocked users that they have been blocked from a particular account, if the blocked user attempts to visit the Twitter profile of someone who has blocked them, Twitter will indicate that the user has been blocked.
65 *Knight First Amendment Institute v. Trump*, 928 F.3d 226, 239–40 (2d Cir. 2019).

Indeed, in early January 2021, Twitter permanently banned President Trump from the platform in the days following the January 6, 2021 insurrection at the U.S. Capitol in Washington, DC. Twitter had previously banned him for 12 hours citing "severe violations of [its] Civic Integrity policy,"[66] and upon further review, banned him permanently for violating its Glorification of Violence policy.[67]

In July 2021, President Trump, on behalf of himself and other conservative social media users, filed suit against Twitter, along with Facebook and YouTube, which had also blocked him by that point, alleging that by blocking them, the platform violated their rights.[68] The lawsuit asserts that Twitter is essentially functioning as an arm of the government and is therefore capable of infringing on users' constitutional rights, despite the fact Twitter is clearly a private actor. In May of 2022, Trump's claims against Twitter were dismissed. The other cases remain pending.

All of this is to say, the notion of "free speech" on the internet remains murky, largely untested, and the differing approaches that the various platforms have taken to addressing misinformation about political issues have either gone too far, or have not gone far enough, depending on who you ask. The Freedom Forum Institute has developed a chart that evaluates the terms of service – the contract between the internet platforms and their users – of various social media platforms and compares their limitations with the scope of the First Amendment relating to hate speech, obscenity, misinformation, and harassment. Generally, it found that YouTube tends to be the most restrictive, while Reddit is the least restrictive.[69] That is, of course, within the rights of the services that have implemented such policies, but some have begun to question whether such unfettered control over what have become essential communication platforms is consistent with our democratic ideals.

As Justice Clarence Thomas observed, "applying old doctrines to new digital platforms is rarely straightforward." He went on to say that "[t]oday's digital platforms provide avenues for historically unprecedented amounts of speech, including speech by government actors. Also unprecedented, however, is the concentrated control of so much speech in the hands of so few parties."[70]

---

66 Ben Collins & Brandy Zadrozny, *Twitter Permanently Suspends President Donald Trump*, NBC News, January 8, 2021, available at https://www.nbcnews.com/tech/tech-news/twitter-permanently-bans-president -donald-trump-n1253588.

67 Twitter, *Permanent Suspension of @realDonaldTrump*, January 8, 2021, https://blog.twitter.com/en_us/topics /company/2020/suspension.

68 *See* Jill Colvin & Matt O'Brien, *Trump Files Suit against Facebook, Twitter, and YouTube,* Associated Press, July 7, 2021, https://apnews.com/article/lawsuits-business-government-and-politics-c7e26858dcb553f92d9 8706d12ad510c.

69 Lata Natt and Brian Peters, *Free Expression on Social Media,* Freedom Forum Institute, https://www.fre edomforuminstitute.org/first-amendment-center/primers/free-expression-on-social-media (last accessed July 31, 2021).

70 *Biden v. Knight First Amendment Institute*, 141 S.Ct. 1220, 1221 (Thomas, J., concurring).

How the First Amendment works, in practical terms, on the internet, will no doubt be an ongoing subject of discussion and debate and likely the subject of future legislative or regulatory initiatives.

KEY POINTS AND TAKEAWAYS

1. The rights granted by the First Amendment are very broad and considered sacrosanct to our form of democracy, but they are not absolute. Courts have concluded that the government may sometimes need to regulate speech, but they must meet the high burden of either strict scrutiny (for content-based regulations) or intermediate scrutiny (for content-neutral regulations). The government may also impose reasonable time, place, and manner restrictions for speech that takes place in public forums.
2. Some speech has been construed to receive no First Amendment protection, including obscenity, true threats, incitement, and defamation.
3. For First Amendment purposes, "freedom of speech" has been construed to mean not only the right to speak, but also the right to engage in expressive conduct, the right to receive information, and the right to be free from being compelled to speak.
4. Courts recognize a strong presumption against prior restraints. Our system of democracy commands that we allow as much speech as reasonably possible, though the government is free to punish those engaged in improper speech, but after the speech occurs.
5. Speech on the internet is entitled to the same degree of protection as speech in traditional venues, however, the nature of the internet raises questions, many of which remain unanswered, about how to apply traditional First Amendment values in the online environment.

QUESTIONS FOR DISCUSSION

1. The tests for determining whether restrictions on speech are permissible for public and non-public forums are based on other constitutional tests discussed in this chapter. What is the connection between these tests? How are they similar? How are they different?
2. The *Levy* case stands for the proposition that schools can generally not punish students for free speech activities that take place outside of the school environment. Do you think the school decided the case correctly? What are the implications of the court decision for cyberbullying? What if Levy's social media post had been on a school-managed or school-sanctioned platform?
3. Twitter, Facebook, and YouTube have banned former President Trump from using their platforms. Current law dictates that such bans are well within the rights of

the platforms, but should that change, given how important those platforms have become for political discourse?

4. Justice Thomas observed that the internet is largely controlled by a small handful of powerful players that now write the rules for how we engage in speech online. What implications does such consolidation have for the future of political discourse online? If you were a judge, or a Member of Congress, what changes would you look to make, if any, to improve conditions for online free speech?

4

CHAPTER 4
DEFAMATION

What obligations do media organizations have to report fairly and accurately about the subjects of their stories? What are the consequences if they don't meet those obligations? How can media organizations balance the risk of exposure with the need to produce and distribute content quickly?

Recall that in Chapter 3 we discussed several categories of speech that do not receive First Amendment protection. Among those categories is defamatory speech. In this chapter, we will discuss the nature of defamatory speech generally, the elements of a successful defamation claim, the various defenses, and the factors used to calculate damages in a defamation action.

DEFAMATION, LIBEL, AND SLANDER

In its simplest form, **defamation** is speech that damages the reputation of another. There are two types of defamatory speech: libel and slander.

Historically, **slander** was defamatory speech that was spoken, while **libel** was published in writing. Today, those concepts have evolved somewhat given advances in technology and the way speech is produced and distributed. Back before the internet became a significant distribution mechanism, if someone's reputation was harmed by a television or radio news report, it was considered slander because it was spoken, transmitted to the public live during the broadcast, and then disappeared. A newspaper or magazine that made defamatory statements would be considered libel because it was published in written form. The distinction between the two was essentially the degree of permanence or persistence of the defamatory statement: slander applied to relatively fleeting speech, while libel applied to more permanent speech.

Today, virtually all forms of mass communication are characterized by some enduring quality. Broadcast news reports today typically get posted on a website along with a written version of the same report. And, of course, there are new forms of distribution that are intended to facilitate on-demand consumption, such as podcasts or streaming services, that essentially render the content available forever.

Thus, today it is far more common to encounter claims of libel as opposed to slander, so much so that for all practical purposes, it is easier simply to talk about defamation as a single, unified concept that encompasses both libel and slander.

The distinction between the two still exists in many states, but generally applies only when it comes time to calculate damages. Although the elements to prove libel and

DOI: 10.4324/9781003197966-4

slander are the same, the way a defamed party establishes harm is distinct. Generally, it is easier to establish harm from libel because of the relative permanence of the speech – the persistence of the speech means it is more likely that the defamed party will sustain harm, whereas with slander, the relatively fleeting nature of the speech makes it less likely that the defamed person will sustain injury, and therefore the standard of proof is higher. We discuss defamation damages more fully later in this chapter.

WHO CAN BE DEFAMED?

Any living person can be defamed, though dead people cannot. The cause of action for defamation is said to "die with the person," which means that even if someone makes false statements about a deceased individual, the deceased individual's estate cannot sue or recover damages.

Companies and organizations can also be defamed, though as we will see later in this chapter, it is often more difficult for companies and organizations to satisfy the "fault" element required to succeed with a defamation claim.

Government agencies and organizations cannot be defamed.

INTRODUCTION TO THE ELEMENTS

Recall from Chapter 2 that to establish a viable claim against a defendant, a plaintiff must show proof of each element of a claim, and that to defeat a claim, a defendant simply needs to show that the plaintiff has failed to prove facts that support at least one element. Also in Chapter 2, we discussed the distinctions between federal and state laws and the various source of laws.

Defamation law is a creature of state common law and, in some cases, state statutory law. That means that, strictly speaking, the elements of defamation vary on a state-by-state basis. Fortunately, most states' laws are substantively quite similar, and there is a restatement of law that has synthesized them into a single definition of defamation.

Under the Restatement of Torts, to establish a viable claim for defamation, a plaintiff must show that the defendant made: (a) a false and defamatory statement concerning another; (b) an unprivileged publication to a third party; (c) fault amounting at least to negligence on the part of the publisher; and (d) either actionability of the statement irrespective of special harm or the existence of special harm caused by the publication.[1]

In essence, to prove a defamation case, a plaintiff must show:

1. Falsity
2. Identification
3. Defamatory
4. Publication
5. Fault
6. Harm

We will discuss each of the elements in turn in the following sections.

FALSITY

A foundational element of any defamation claim is that the allegedly defamatory statement is **false**. No matter how harmful a statement may be to an individual's reputation, unless it is false, it cannot be defamatory. Put differently, truth is an absolute defense against defamation (a statement that has become something of a mantra among journalists and lawyers that practice media law).

Media enterprises routinely receive complaints from, and in some cases are sued by, people who are upset about reports of their arrest, or the use of their mugshot, and the like. While those reports may well harm the reputation of the subject individual, provided the reports accurately convey what actually happened, they cannot be defamatory.

IDENTIFICATION

Beyond being false, the statement must identify a particular party with enough detail that the subject party's reputation could be harmed. This element is sometimes referred to as the "of and concerning" requirement because the allegedly defamatory statement must be "of and concerning" another party. The identification element is necessary because defamation law aims to give parties a mechanism for redress if their reputation or character has been unfairly maligned by a false statement. If someone hearing the statement could not easily identify the party about which the statement is made, then the subject's reputation could not be harmed.

---

1 Restatement (Second) of Torts § 558 (Am. L. Inst. 1971).

DIRECT IDENTIFICATION

The clearest and most obvious form of identification is direct, unambiguous identification. A statement such as "Chris Reed is a plagiarist" clearly and unambiguously identifies the individual about whom the statement is made. If the statement is
untrue, Chris may have a claim against the speaker for defamation.

INDIRECT IDENTIFICATION

A speaker need not identify the person by their exact name, however. The identification element may also be satisfied if the speaker includes details sufficient to identify
the individual. For example, if the speaker said that "the author of the 2022 textbook
Digital Media Law is a plagiarist," to someone who is familiar with the book, and
therefore the identity of the author is readily ascertainable, it may be defamatory if
the statement is false.

IDENTIFICATION AS A SWORD AND A SHIELD

Although we have discussed identification as an element of a defamation claim, using
accurate, detailed identification of subjects can serve as a defense, of sorts, against
defamation claims.

This is one reason why the media often identify criminal suspects not only by their
name but also by other identifying characteristics, such as age or where they live.
Doing so makes it less likely that someone with the same or a similar sounding name
will be able to claim they were defamed by the story. For example, it is not uncommon to hear or read something like "police arrested 27-year-old John Smith, of the
2300 block of Sycamore Avenue."

By providing the additional elements of identity, it is clear that the report of the arrest
is about a *specific* John Smith, and not some other person named John Smith. Absent
those additional details, some other John Smith – one who had not been arrested –
might have a plausible defamation claim against the media enterprise that broadcast the
report if people reasonably believed, as a result of the report, that he had been arrested.

Avoiding defamation claims based on misidentification is also a good reason to
include a photograph, such as a mugshot, of the arrested individual if one is available. *But beware* that you should only use the image if you are absolutely certain that
the person in the image is actually the person who was arrested. Using a photo of
the *wrong* person only creates more trouble, because the photograph is itself a form of
identification, creating potential liability to the person depicted in the photograph.

This sort of thing happens with unfortunate frequency in today's rapid, 24/7 media
environment. A harried producer searches social media for an image of someone that
recently did something newsworthy, such as getting arrested for a well-publicized

crime. The producer finds an image of someone with the same name as the individual who was arrested, publishes it alongside the story, and then subsequently discovers that the person depicted in the photo is not the same person who was just arrested, despite the fact they share the same name. Now the person depicted in the photo has a potential claim against the media enterprise for defamation, provided he or she can establish the other elements of such a claim as discussed in this chapter.

For this reason, newsroom personnel must take extra care, ideally through multiple-source reporting, to ensure that names, photographs, and the substance of reports all properly match up and refer to the appropriate person or people, especially when reporting on events that, if attributed to the wrong person, could harm their status or reputation in the community.

GROUP DEFAMATION

Defamatory statements about groups of people are not actionable by any one member of the group unless the group is so small that the statements could be reasonably understood to refer to the individual or other circumstances where it is reasonable to infer that the statement was actually intended to relate to a single person.

For example, if a speaker were to say "reporters are corrupt hacks" at a political rally, and there is only one easily identifiable reporter at the rally, then it is likely that the reporter could show that the statement was sufficient to identify the individual reporter, even though the statement referred to a broader group – reporters. If that same statement were made at a major party's political convention, where dozens of reporters are present, it would be less likely that any one reporter could establish that the statement identified him or her individually.

Note, however, that even if a particular reporter could establish that the statement sufficiently identified him or her, there are various other reasons why the statement may not be considered actionable defamation, as we will see later in this chapter.

INADVERTENT IDENTIFICATION OF REAL
PEOPLE IN FICTITIOUS WORKS

Although a defamation claim is most likely to arise in connection with reporting on real individuals, such as in news reporting or documentaries, defamation claims may also arise out of works of fiction, if the producers do not take care to ensure that their fictional characters are not so similar to real-life individuals that the audience might reasonably believe that the fictional story is "of and concerning" the real-life person.

To minimize the threat of such claims, producers of fictional works will often per-form public records searches within the geographic area where their story is set and will avoid naming characters after people that might reasonably be confused with real individuals. Of course, if the story is set in a fictional location, then the risk of someone reasonably confusing a character with a real-life person is minimized.

Another way producers often hedge against defamation risk in connection with a fictional work is to include a disclaimer in the credits that indicates the work is fictitious and that any resemblance to real-life individuals, places, or incidents, is neither intended nor inferred. Although disclaimers are not a sure-fire way to avoid a defamation claim, they certainly do not hurt.

DEFAMATORY

It may seem obvious, but the third element of an actionable defamation claim is that the statement must be defamatory. That is, it must harm the reputation of the party that is the subject of the statement or lower the status of the party within their community. Defamatory statements fall into one of two categories: **defamatory *per se*** and **defamatory *per quod***.

DEFAMATORY *PER SE*

Per se is a Latin term that means "by itself" or "intrinsically." Thus, defamation *per se* is a statement that is, on its face, likely to harm the reputation of the party about which the statement is made. There are several categories of statements the law considers *per se* defamatory, including statements that falsely state or imply that the person:

1. Is engaged in criminal conduct;
2. Has a loathsome disease;
3. Has engaged in sexual misconduct; or
4. Engaged in conduct that is contrary to the individual's business, trade, profession, or office.

The first three categories are self-evident, but it is helpful to look at some examples of the fourth category to see how courts have construed the impact of false statements on one's "business, trade, profession, or office."

For example, an Alaska court concluded that it was *per se* defamatory when a patient at a health clinic falsely accused a clinic employee of improperly accessing the patient's medical record and discussing the patient's pregnancy with another employee. The court reasoned that because the falsely alleged violation of patient confidentiality would have negative implications for the employee's fitness to work in a medical environment, the statement was properly characterized as defamation *per se*.[2]

---

2 *Greene v. Tinker*, 332 P.3d 21, 38–39 (Ala. 2014).

In contrast, when a television station falsely reported that a dentist had filed for personal bankruptcy (it was his corporation that had filed for bankruptcy), the court concluded that because filing for personal bankruptcy had nothing bearing on whether the plaintiff was fit to practice dentistry, the statement was not *per se* defamatory.[3]

DEFAMATORY *PER QUOD*

Per quod is a Latin term that, literally translated, means "whereby." In defamation law, it means that the statement at issue, taken together with some other piece of information – what lawyers call **extrinsic evidence**, that is, something other than the statement – is defamatory. In practical terms, any potentially defamatory statement that does not fall into the *per se* category is considered defamation *per quod*.

THE RELEVANCE OF THE DISTINCTION

The distinction between defamation *per se* and defamation *per quod* is relevant for establishing harm. Where the statement at issue is defamation *per se*, the plaintiff generally does not need to prove that they were harmed. Rather, the court is allowed to infer that the plaintiff was harmed because of the *per se* nature of the statement. In cases where the statement does not rise to the *per se* level, and is instead considered defamatory *per quod*, a plaintiff must typically show that suffered actual harm as a result of the statement.

THE DEFAMATION-PROOF PLAINTIFF

A **defamation-proof** plaintiff is one whose reputation is already so poor that no statement, no matter how false and defamatory it may be, could make it any worse. Notorious criminals who have been convinced of especially heinous crimes generally fall into this category. The reputation of someone convicted of a mass killing spree, for example, is unlikely to be further harmed by a false statement that they also robbed a bank on their way to the murder site.

PUBLICATION

Once it is established that there is a false and defamatory statement that sufficiently identifies the plaintiff, the plaintiff must show that it was communicated to at least one third party other than him or herself. In defamation law, we call this **publication**, even though it may not necessarily mean that the statement has been "published" in the traditional sense of the word. In this context, it simply means that the statement has been communicated to a third party, and the third party understands

---

3 *Shipp v. Malouf*, 439 S.W.3d 432, 441 (Court of Appeals, Dallas 2014).

the defamatory nature of the statement. Because the law requires not only that the statement be communicated, but also that it be understood, statements made in a language other than one understood by the audience are not enough to establish publication.

The publication requirement makes sense because without a communication to a third party it would be impossible to harm someone's reputation which is, by definition, a measure of how one is perceived by others. The population to which the communication is made need not be large, but it must be at least one person other than the person who is the subject of the defamatory statement. No matter how vile or disparaging the statement, and no matter how offensive it may be to the subject, unless it is communicated to at least one third party, it is not actionable defamation.

FAULT

A successful defamation plaintiff must next show that the party that made the statement did so with some degree of fault, that is, there must be some degree of culpability on the part of the speaker. Put differently, defamation law is not intended to hold speakers responsible for innocent mistakes or offhanded remarks. Rather, the person who claims to have been defamed must show that the speaker fell short of their responsibility under an appropriate legal standard.

STANDARDS OF FAULT

There are two such standards in defamation law – negligence and actual malice – each applicable in certain circumstances, depending on the nature of the party alleging defamation. Specifically, courts apply the heightened actual malice standard where the party alleging defamation is a public official or a public figure, and the lower standard, negligence, in cases where the allegedly defamed party is a private figure.

The higher the standard, the more difficult it is for the person claiming to have been defamed to successfully bring a lawsuit against the speaker.

ACTUAL MALICE

The highest standard of fault is **actual malice**, which was established by the Supreme Court in the famous case *New York Times v. Sullivan*.[4] For that reason, actual malice is sometimes also referred to as ***New York Times* malice**.

In *Sullivan*, the Supreme Court considered a defamation action brought by an elected city commissioner of Montgomery, Alabama, L.B. Sullivan, over a full-page paid

---

4 376 U.S. 254 (1964).

editorial advertisement that had run in *The New York Times*, paid for by civil rights leaders, protesting the treatment of Martin Luther King, Jr. by local authorities. Sullivan sued the newspaper for defamation, claiming that certain factual inaccuracies in the ad defamed him personally because he was responsible for overseeing the police department in his capacity as an elected official.

Sullivan prevailed at the state trial court, which awarded him a judgment of $500,000, even though he was unable to establish any actual damages. The state supreme court affirmed the trial court's decision, observing that the First Amendment does not protect defamation. *The New York Times* sought certiorari from the U.S. Supreme Court.

In a unanimous decision reversing the state court, the Supreme Court said that "debate on public issues should be uninhibited, robust, and wide-open, and that it may well include vehement, caustic, and sometimes unpleasantly sharp attacks on government and public officials."[5]

Accordingly, the Court held that in cases where the speech at issue was about a public official or a public figure, a plaintiff alleging defamation must establish either that the speaker either knew that statement was false at the time it was made, and made the statement anyway, or that the statement was made with a "reckless disregard for the truth." In subsequent cases, the Court explained that "reckless disregard for the truth" means that the person making the statement either knew it was false when they made it, or that they "entertained serious doubts as to the truth" of the statement.[6]

NEGLIGENCE

The concept of **negligence** appears throughout tort law and applies in various circumstances beyond defamation. Broadly speaking, it stands for the idea that when we, as individual members of society, undertake certain activities, there is a social contract to do so with reasonable care. To measure "reasonable care," the law looks to what a hypothetical "ordinary reasonable person" would do when presented with similar circumstances. Tort law refers to this as the **duty of care**. When someone acts in a way that falls short of the duty of care, that person is legally negligent.

In some jurisdictions, media organizations are held to a higher standard of care based on the theory that they have specific knowledge, expertise, and experience in investigating, reporting, and fact checking, and are therefore held to a higher standard of care. This approach, called the "professional malpractice" model, is consistent with the way standards of care work in other professional contexts. Under the professional malpractice model, the speaker's conduct is compared with that of other similarly situated journalists or media professionals, instead of an ordinary reasonable person,

5 *Sullivan*, 376 U.S. at 270.
6 *St. Amant v. Thompson*, 390 U.S. 727, 731 (1968).

just as a doctor's conduct in a medical malpractice case would be compared with how other reasonable doctors would act when confronted with similar circumstances.

PUBLIC AND PRIVATE FIGURES

As noted above, courts apply the actual malice standard where the subject of the speech is a public figure and a negligence standard where the subject is a private figure. Thus, to determine the appropriate standard of fault to use, we must first identify the nature of the subject of the speech at issue.

GENERAL-PURPOSE PUBLIC FIGURES

A **general-purpose public figure** is an individual that holds "persuasive power and influence" such as celebrities, business and civic leaders, commentators, news personalities, social media personalities, and public officials. In defamation law, a **public official** includes anyone who is elected to a government office, at any level – federal, state, and local – and every position ranging all the way from the President to a city attorney in the nation's smallest town. Not every government employee is necessarily a government official, however. The Supreme Court has observed that only those who have "substantial responsibility for or control over the conduct of government affairs."[7]

We apply the heightened actual malice standard to public officials because, as the Court noted in *Sullivan*, cultivating and maintaining an environment conducive to robust debate about issues of public importance "may well include … sometimes unpleasantly sharp attacks on government and public officials."[8] Put differently, public officials must be held accountable to the public that elected them, and therefore speech about those officials must be afforded wide latitude, which the law provides by requiring them to establish actual malice to succeed on a defamation claim.

Regarding public figures more generally, the Court has explained that the media "are entitled to act on the assumption that public officials and public figures have voluntarily exposed themselves to increased risk of injury"[9] from defamation by virtue of taking on roles or positions that are reasonably, and often by definition, very public in nature. In addition, the Court has held that the heightened standard of fault is appropriate because public figures generally have more "effective opportunities for rebuttal,"[10] or put another way, a defamed public figure, by virtue of his or her "persuasive power and influence," has the ability to "correct the record," as it were, in a way that a private figure may not.

For example, a defamed political figure may simply call a press conference and there is a strong likelihood that it will receive media attention. Similarly, a social media

---

7 *Rosenblatt v. Baer*, 383 U.S. 75 (1966).
8 *Sullivan*, 376 U.S. at 270.
9 *Gertz v. Robert Welch, Inc.*, 418 U.S. 323, 345 (1974).
10 *Id.* at 344.

personality can simply publish a new post or video and respond directly to his or her followers (which, in some cases, might garner media attention depending on the significance of the controversy). A person without the same degree of persuasive power and influence – a private figure, discussed more fully below – is unlikely to be able to command public attention such that they can effectively respond to a defamatory statement made about them.

LIMITED-PURPOSE PUBLIC FIGURES

A **limited-purpose public figure** is a private figure who, by virtue of certain circumstances, has become a public figure for a particular purpose, or in the context of a particular issue or debate. As the Supreme Court describes it, they have "thrust themselves to the forefront of particular public controversies in order to influence the resolution of the issues involved," and in so doing, "invite attention and comment."[11]

Courts have struggled over the years to establish a precise definition of a limited-purpose public figure. The Eleventh Circuit, for example, has established a relatively simple two-part test that evaluates whether: (1) the subject of the statement played a central role in the controversy; and (2) the alleged defamation was germane to the subject's role.[12]

The Sixth Circuit has articulated a more involved, five-factor test that examines whether: (1) the subject had access to channels of effective communication; (2) the subject voluntarily assumed a role of social prominence in the controversy; (3) the subject sought to influence the issue or controversy; (4) the controversy existed prior to the publication of the allegedly defamatory statements; and (5) the subject retained public-figure status at the time of the alleged defamation.[13]

Limited-purpose public figures are treated like public figures if the alleged defamatory statement relates to the controversy or issues for which the subject has been determined to be a public figure. Accordingly, in those circumstances, the plaintiff must show actual malice, just like general-purpose public figures. If, however, an allegedly defamatory statement is made against the same person, but outside the context in which the individual is a limited-purpose public figure, they are treated as a private figure, as discussed below.

INVOLUNTARY LIMITED-PURPOSE PUBLIC FIGURES

Some courts have recognized another category of public figures known as the **involuntary limited-purpose public figure**, under which a private figure could be considered a public figure if they became enmeshed in a matter of public concern, regardless of whether the person intentionally sought publicity or notoriety in relation to their involvement. The Supreme Court appears to have recognized such a

11 *Id.* at 345.
12 *Berisha v. Lawson*, 973 F.3d 1304, 1310 (11th Cir. 2020).
13 *Carr v. Forbes*, 259 F.3d 273, 280 (4th Cir. 2001).

concept when it wrote that "the instances of truly involuntary public figures must be exceedingly rare,"[14] however, subsequent opinions have reaffirmed the notion that the public-figure designation typically requires some degree of voluntariness. That is, the subject must have intentionally done something to justify treating them as a public figure. Still, some state laws still recognize involuntary limited-purpose public figures in narrow circumstances.

PRIVATE FIGURES

A **private figure** is anyone who does not fall into the public figure or public official categories. Private figures need only show that the speaker was negligent to establish fault for defamation. Private figures have, by definition, not "thrust themselves" into a particular issue or controversy, and do not have wide "persuasive power or influence." Private figures, therefore, did not willfully subject themselves to the limelight, nor do they typically have the ability to command public attention to respond in kind to an allegedly defamatory statement. Accordingly, the law provides an easier path for such individuals to bring a defamation claim by requiring only a showing of negligence.

HARM

The sixth and final element of a successful defamation claim is harm or damages – that is, some compensable loss attributable to the alleged defamatory statement. Without some showing of harm, a plaintiff may not recover for defamation. However, sometimes the law will presume harm based on the nature of the statement or the context in which it was made.

There are three principal types of harm, or damages, that are relevant in defamation law – general damages, special damages, and presumed damages. Like most of defamation law, the precise definitions vary by jurisdiction, but generally, they can be described as follows.

GENERAL DAMAGES

The term **general** damages, sometimes also referred to as **actual damages**, refers to damages that are provable through some form of admissible evidence. Although evidence is required, the figures need not be established with precision. A plaintiff might, for example, introduce a declaration from a psychiatrist that says the plaintiff suffered severe mental anguish as a result of a defamatory statement made against them. Based on that evidence, and the circumstances surrounding the statement, it is up to the judge or jury to determine the appropriate dollar amount attributable to the harm suffered.

---

14 *Gertz*, 481 U.S. at 345.

SPECIAL DAMAGES

Special damages are what you might have been thinking of when you saw the term "actual damages." Special harm is a subcategory of actual harm that refers to damages that are provable with a specific dollar figure. For example, if a plaintiff lost an employment opportunity as a result of a defamatory statement (and can establish a causal link between the statement and the lost job), the value of the salary and benefits that the plaintiff would have received had they been offered the job would be considered special harm. In many jurisdictions, to recover damages for *per quod* defamation, a plaintiff must show special damages (that is, a showing of general damages is not sufficient).

PRESUMED DAMAGES

Finally, **presumed damages** are exactly what it sounds like. In some cases, the law will allow a judge or jury to award a plaintiff damages without any proof at all. Rather, the court may infer injury based on the nature of the statement made and the circumstances surrounding it. In many jurisdictions, a plaintiff – regardless of whether they are a public or private figure – must show that the defendant acted with actual malice to recover presumed damages.

OTHER DAMAGES CONCEPTS

PUNITIVE DAMAGES

Punitive damages are, as the name suggests, intended to punish a defendant for misconduct, and serve as a deterrent for future misdeeds, either by the same defendant or others, since court judgments are accessible by the public and, in significant cases, are widely reported. Because punitive damages are not based on harm to the plaintiff, the determination of the appropriate amount is entirely in the hands of the judge or jury, based on the perceived severity of the defendant's statement and the circumstances that gave rise to it.

Not all states allow for the recovery of punitive damages in defamation cases, and in those states that do, there are often limits on the type of cases in which they apply, and some jurisdictions require a showing of actual malice.

NOMINAL DAMAGES

Nominal damages are, in some ways, the opposite of punitive damages. A judge or jury might award nominal damages where there is no showing (or a very scant showing) of actual harm but nevertheless wants to signal to the defendant that their conduct was improper or simply that the statement they made was, indeed, defamatory. Sometimes, courts will grant nominal damages of $1 because the plaintiff was unable to show actual harm but grant significant punitive damages to send a message to the defendant.

DEFENSES AND PRIVILEGES

A plaintiff who can establish each of the six elements of defamation is said to have made a *prima facie* case, meaning that on its face, it appears as though the plaintiff was defamed by the defendant. The burden then shifts to the defendant to show that they have a defense to one or more of the elements of defamation or qualify for a privilege. Defenses are aimed at poking holes in one or more of the elements of defamation, whereas privileges are circumstances where the law will not hold a defendant liable for defamation even if the plaintiff has established each element.

ABSOLUTE PRIVILEGE

Some statements, no matter how false or defamatory they may be, are simply not actionable because of the nature of the speaker or the context in which the statements are made. These are called **absolute privileges** because they serve as a complete defense to defamation and cannot be abridged or waived in most cases. Examples include statements made in judicial or legislative proceedings that are reasonably related to the proceeding or statements made by government officials in the course of their official duties.

A Member of Congress can, for example, say whatever he or she wants about a person or company during a committee hearing or on the floor of the House or Senate no matter how defamatory it may be without fear of legal retribution. The litigation privileged nature of judicial proceedings is one reason why well-represented parties will typically decline to comment on litigation outside of the official proceedings. Defamatory allegations or statements that are made in the course of the proceedings are privileged, while those same statements made outside of the proceedings may not be.[15]

CONSENT

Consent is a straightforward defense that means exactly what it sounds like: the defendant has permission or consent from the plaintiff to make the defamatory statement. Obviously, no reasonable person would ever directly consent to someone making a defamatory statement, but in the media industry, it is very common for participants – for example, game show contestants, reality show competitors, and the like – to sign broad releases that absolve the producer of liability for a variety of potential legal claims, including defamation.

---

15 The other reason litigants generally decline to comment publicly about proceedings is that statements made by a party outside of court are generally admissible against that party in court. To avoid making statements that could later come back to haunt them, most parties simply decline to say anything.

TRUTH

Because falsity is an essential element of defamation, as discussed in the last section, truth is an absolute defense against defamation. A true statement simply cannot be defamatory because it is not, by definition, false, and falsity is an essential element of a defamation claim.

SUBSTANTIAL TRUTH AND INCREMENTAL HARM

The substantial truth doctrine provides that a statement need not be entirely correct to benefit from the truth defense. Put differently, the law will not hold a speaker liable for defamation if the "gist" or "sting" of the statement is generally the same as it would have been had the minor inaccuracies not been present.

For example, if a news report states that an individual was arrested for robbing a liquor store on their way home from work, but they were in fact heading home from a baseball game, the statement will not be considered "false" for defamation purposes even though the statement is inaccurate. The gist or sting of the statement – that the individual robbed a liquor store – is the same regardless of whether the individual was coming from work or a baseball game.

Closely related to the concept of substantial truth is the doctrine of **incremental harm**, which stands for the proposition that if a statement is mostly true, additional false elements that do not materially change the statement do not make the statement actionable.

OPINION

Statements of opinion are not defamatory. That doesn't mean that you can take a false, declarative statement and simply add "in my opinion" and it suddenly becomes protected speech. The precise contours of what constitutes an "opinion" are somewhat elusive, with standards changing over time and in different courts and jurisdictions. One commonly cited test for determining whether a particular statement qualifies as opinion comes from *Ollman v. Evans*,[16] in which the court asked:

1. Whether the common usage or meaning of the allegedly defamatory words are likely to give rise to clear factual implications;
2. Whether the statement is objectively capable of being proved or disproved;
3. The extent to which the statement can be read to imply facts based on the context in which it appears;
4. The broader social context of the statement and how that might affect how the statement is interpreted. As the *Ollman* court explained: "It is one thing to be

---

16 750 F.2d 970 (D.C. Cir. 1984).

assailed as a corrupt public official by a soapbox orator and quite another to be labelled corrupt in a research monograph detailing the causes and cures of corruption in public service."[17]

Under the *Ollman* test, a statement such as "the media law professor is untrustworthy" made in an offhanded way between two students would likely be construed as opinion because "untrustworthy" is not necessarily capable of being proved or disproved, and the context does not suggest that there are underlying facts or suggest that people will believe.

But suppose a similar statement was published in a school newspaper article discussing the rise of petty theft on campus. Under those circumstances, it is reasonable to think that a reader might imply there are facts to suggest the media law professor is involved in the increase in crime on campus. Accordingly, the speaker would have a more difficult time asserting that the statement was protected opinion.

RHETORICAL HYPERBOLE

Closely related to opinion is the defense of **rhetorical hyperbole**, which has been described as "'loose, figurative, or hyperbolic language'"[18] that no reasonable person would believe was intended to be construed as factual.

In a particularly colorful example of the doctrine in practice, the Supreme Court of Virginia concluded that a Virginia Tech administrator could not sue the school newspaper for describing her as the "Director of Butt Licking." The court agreed with the trial court's assertion that the phrase is "'void of any literal meaning,' and that it would be unreasonable to interpret the phrase as conveying any factual information" about the administrator,[19] and concluded that although "[t]he phrase is disgusting offensive, and in extremely bad taste," it was "no more than 'rhetorical hyperbole.'"[20]

FAIR COMMENT AND CRITICISM

The fair comment and criticism privilege applies where statements are made about parties that put themselves or their work into the public sphere. Essentially, this privilege is defamation law's version of a broader principle in tort law known as "assumption of the risk." If one willingly publishes or releases their work to the world – for example, an artist releases an album, an actor appears in a new blockbuster, a scientist authors a book about a controversial topic – they are essentially opening themselves up to fair comment and criticism of their work and, in some cases, themselves as individuals.

17 *Id.* at 983.
18 *Milkovich v. Lorain Journal Co.*, 497 U.S. 1, 21 (1990).
19 *Yeagle v. Collegiate Times*, 497 S.E.2d 136, 137 (Va. 1988).
20 *Id.* at 138.

You can think of fair comment and criticism as a specialized application of two other defenses we have already discussed: consent and opinion.

FAIR REPORT PRIVILEGE

The **fair report privilege** applies specifically to the media. It immunizes media from defamation claims arising from fair, accurate reports about statements made in judicial or legislative proceedings, court papers, police reports, and the like. The precise scope of the privilege – that is, the type of documents or proceedings about which can be reported – varies by state, but generally, it covers media coverage of official documents and proceedings.

The privilege generally does not cover statements made by officials outside of official circumstances, such as interviews or press conferences, and it is possible to lose the privilege's protection if a story is unreasonably embellished or it otherwise departs from a fair and accurate report of the covered proceeding.

The fair report privilege serves as an exception to the usual rule that those who republish or retransmit defamatory material are themselves liable for defamation, even though they were not the original speaker. Without the fair report privilege, the media may be discouraged from covering important official proceedings.

NEUTRAL REPORTAGE PRIVILEGE

The **neutral reportage privilege** is similar to the fair report privilege in that it aims to protect the media so that it may fairly and accurately report on important matters of public concern. Unlike the fair report privilege, however, it is typically not limited to reporting on official proceedings, rather, it aims to protect reporting of accusations made by prominent people, groups, or organizations against other prominent people, groups, or organizations on a matter of public importance, even if the media enterprise may not believe that the statement is true.

In other words, neutral reportage aims to protect reporting about statements or allegations where the fact that a statement or allegation was made is, itself, the newsworthy event. So long as the media cover it fairly and accurately, it is protected from defamation claims arising out of the republication or retransmission of those statements, even if they turn out to be false.

NOTICE AND RETRACTION STATUTES

Many states have enacted retraction statutes that require a plaintiff to request a retraction, or at least provide notice of an allegedly defamatory report, before filing a lawsuit. The purpose of such statutes is to give the media a reasonable opportunity to investigate and retract or correct the story, as appropriate. In some states, a plaintiff's failure to request a retraction or provide notice will prevent them from filing a lawsuit, while in others it merely limits the damages award to which they may be entitled.

FOOD DISPARAGEMENT

Although defamation claims most often come up in the context of a media organization making statements about an individual or an entity, some states have laws that specifically prohibit the disparagement of food or agricultural products. Such laws have become known as **food disparagement laws** or **veggie libel laws**.

Perhaps the most well-known example of a food disparagement law in action is *Texas Beef Group v. Winfrey*.[21] In that case, the Texas beef industry sued television personality Oprah Winfrey, and a guest who appeared on an episode of her daily talk show, alleging violations of Texas's veggie libel statute, the Texas False Disparagement of Perishable Food Products Act, by suggesting that the U.S. beef supply was unsafe following the "Mad Cow Disease" scare in the mid-1990s, leading to a decline in the value of cattle. Specifically, after one of her guests raised the specter that something similar to the Mad Cow Disease outbreak could happen in the United States, Winfrey said she was "stopped cold from eating another burger."[22]

Following a trial that lasted nearly six weeks, Winfrey prevailed, a jury concluding that she had not disparaged the cattle industry in violation of the state statute. Asked for comment following her win, Winfrey said "that free speech not only live, it rocks!"[23]

Several years later, Beef Products, Inc. (BPI) sued ABC News alleging that it had violated South Dakota's food libel law in connection with a series of reports that suggested BPI's meat filler product was, in fact, not entirely beef, but rather an ammonia-laden "pink slime." ABC News moved to dismiss on grounds its speech was constitutionally protected, but the trial court disagreed and allowed the case to continue.[24] The parties ultimately settled before the case went to trial, a common occurrence in litigation of all types, but especially in defamation litigation, because the time and expense involved to bring a case to verdict are so significant.

---

21 201 F.3d 680 (5th Cir. 2000).

22 *Id.* at 688.

23 Sue Anne Pressley, *Oprah Winfrey Wins Case Filed by Cattlemen*, The Washington Post, February 27, 1998, https://www.washingtonpost.com/archive/politics/1998/02/27/oprah-winfrey-wins-case-filed-by-cattlemen/dd4612f5-ccbf-4e3d-a1c1-f84d1f4fd23c.

24 *Beef Products, Inc. v. American Broadcasting Companies*, 2014 WL 1245307 (S.D. Cir. Mar. 27, 2014).

ANTI-SLAPP STATUTES

Knowing that the cost of defending a lawsuit is so high, sometimes well-resourced plaintiffs will attempt to use litigation, or the threat of litigation, to stifle speech with which they disagree.

For instance, imagine an investigative blogger working on a story about a local meat packing plant that is thought to be dumping toxic chemicals into a nearby river leading to environmental damage and public health concerns. The meat packing company catches wind of the upcoming report and threatens to sue the blogger and the website for which she works for defamation and violations of her state's food disparagement law. Fearing that the high cost of litigation could lead to severe financial woes, the website refuses to publish the story and the blogger ultimately abandons it, despite the fact that the story brought an issue of significant public importance to light.

Such suits, when brought for the purposes of stifling discourse about important matters of public concern, are referred to as **strategic lawsuits against public participation** or **SLAPP suits**. Such lawsuits are contrary to our core First Amendment principles aimed at encouraging a free, open, and robust dialogue about important public issues.

To help combat the threat of SLAPP litigation, a number of states have adopted anti-SLAPP or SLAPP-back laws. Although the specific provisions vary widely by state, generally such laws apply where a defendant's First Amendment rights are implicated and give the defendant a fast-track mechanism to get out of frivolous litigation relatively early in the process, thereby reducing the cost of defending the suit. Anti-SLAPP laws are also intended to serve as a deterrent to those who seek to use the judicial process for nefarious or improper purposes. To that end, some states' anti-SLAPP measures contain fee-shifting provisions that hold the plaintiff responsible for the defendant's legal fees if the court dismisses the case in response to an anti-SLAPP motion.

According to the Reporters Committee for Freedom of the Press, a free press advocacy organization, 31 states currently have some form of anti-SLAPP measure in place.[25] There is no federal anti-SLAPP law, however, and it remains unclear whether federal courts may apply state anti-SLAPP measures in those states that have them. Some federal appellate courts have upheld the use of such laws, while others have found the opposite.

---

25 Arizona, Arkansas, California, Colorado, Connecticut, Delaware, Florida, Georgia, Hawaii, Illinois, Indiana, Kansas, Louisiana, Maine, Maryland, Massachusetts, Missouri, Nebraska, Nevada, New Mexico, New York, Oklahoma, Oregon, Pennsylvania, Rhode Island, Tennessee, Texas, Utah, Vermont, Virginia, and Washington. Reporters Committee for Freedom of the Press, *Overview of Anti-SLAPP Laws*, https://www.rcfp.org/introduction-anti-slapp-guide (last visited August 15, 2021).

LITIGATION AND PROCEDURAL CONSIDERATIONS

This section examines some additional concepts that have an impact on whether a defamation plaintiff will find it prudent to bring a defamation action against a media enterprise or other defendant.

THE "STREISAND EFFECT"

The administrator in the Virginia Tech matter described earlier in this chapter – the one referred to by the school paper as the "Director of Butt Licking" – might have wished that she had not brought the case when it started receiving media attention, bringing her name, and the associated "butt licking" title, into greater public view.

This dynamic – the notion that complaining about or attempting to prevent the distribution of defamatory (or just generally unsavory) material has the collateral effect of making that material more widely known – has become known as the "Streisand Effect," after a case brought by music icon Barbara Streisand. In 2003, Streisand sued a photographer and environmental activist alleging that he had invaded her privacy by taking an aerial photograph that included her Malibu estate.

The photo was posted to a publicly accessible website alongside approximately 12,000 similar images taken to document erosion and building code violations along the California coast.[26] According to one report, the image had been downloaded six times prior to the lawsuit (twice of which were by Streisand's lawyers). After the suit was filed, that figure jumped to 420,000.[27] Streisand's lawsuit was ultimately dismissed and the judge ordered Streisand to pay the photographer $177,000 to cover his legal fees.[28]

The case serves as a cautionary tale for those seeking redress for allegedly defamatory statements.

STATUTE OF LIMITATIONS

For most types of claims, the law provides a limited time during which an aggrieved party may bring a lawsuit. The period is known as the **statute of limitations**, the length of which varies by type of claim. A party that believes they have been defamed

---

26 Paul Rogers, *Streisand's Home Becomes Hit on the Web*, The Mercury News, June 24, 2003, archived version available at https://www.californiacoastline.org/news/sjmerc5.html (last accessed August 16, 2021).

27 Naveed Saleh, *Understanding the Streisand Effect*, Psychology Today, December 20, 2019, https://www.psychologytoday.com/us/blog/the-red-light-district/201912/understanding-the-streisand-effect.

28 Kenneth R. Weiss, *Judge Orders Streisand to Pay $177,000 for Photographer's Legal Fees*, Los Angeles Times, May 28, 2004, https://www.latimes.com/archives/la-xpm-2004-may-28-me-barbra28-story.html.

by someone must sue before the end of the statute of limitations, otherwise their claim will be dismissed, even if the defendant would otherwise have been found liable. The statute of limitations for defamation actions ranges from one to three years, depending on the state.

Most states apply something called the **discovery rule** to legal claims, including defamation claims, that provides that the statute of limitations "clock" does not start ticking until the defamed party becomes aware (discovers) the defamatory statement.

For example, suppose a blogger writes a defamatory story about an individual on August 18, 2022, but the individual does not become aware of the story until August 18, 2023, the statute of limitations would not begin to run until August 18, 2023.

REPUBLICATION RULE

The **republication rule** says that one who repeats or otherwise further distributes defamatory speech is just as responsible as the original speaker, which is why it is so important for media enterprises to fact check stories, vet sources, and generally exercise due care in their newsgathering and reporting activities since the media enterprise could be held responsible for statements made by those on which it reports.

For example, a local sports podcaster might conduct an interview with a high school football coach who, in the course of the discussion, makes defamatory statements about the superintendent of the school district. Under the republication rule, the superintendent could sue the coach who made the statements, but also the podcaster for publishing them.

Note that the coach and podcaster might have a strong defense to the superintendent's defamation claim because it is likely that the superintendent would be considered a public figure, at least to the extent that the statements made on the podcast were related to her role as a school administrator. Assuming that is the case, the superintendent would have the high burden of showing actual malice – that is, that the podcaster and his guest made the allegedly defamatory statements either knowing they were false or with a reckless disregard for whether they were true or not.

As we saw earlier in this chapter, the law does provide some respite for media reporting on certain types of activities, such as judicial or legislative proceedings and police activities, but generally, publishers, broadcasters, and other distributors of speech are responsible for the speech they distribute.

There is one major exception to the republication rule that applies only to internet platforms such as social media sites. Such services enjoy nearly complete immunity from liability from the actions and speech of their users thanks to a law called Section 230, which we discuss in much more detail in Chapter 10.

To illustrate, suppose the podcast episode discussed above that contains the defamatory speech was hosted (stored) on a popular podcasting service, and links to it were posted to the podcaster's Facebook and Twitter accounts. Under Section 230, neither the podcast hosting service, Facebook, nor Twitter would have any liability for the defamatory statement, even though they all played a role in distributing the offending speech.

SINGLE PUBLICATION RULE

In a situation where defamatory statements are made and then republished, the **single publication rule** says that the aggrieved party can only recover once for the alleged defamation. So, imagine that a blogger publishes an article about the podcast episode discussed above. In the story, the reporter includes a quote from the podcast that includes the defamatory statement. Under the republication rule, the newspaper would be liable for republishing the defamatory statement from the podcast (which was, itself, a republication of a statement made by a guest on that podcast). Because of the single publication rule, the superintendent would only be able to sue once or, put differently, she could not recover damages for *both* the podcast and the newspaper report.

> The superintendent would be well advised to not sue the newspaper and instead go after the coach and podcaster. Why? The newspaper may be able to assert a strong neutral reportage defense, provided that its report fairly and accurately described what the coach said on the podcast, the superintendent's response (if any), and the exchange can be reasonably characterized as a newsworthy event.

LIBEL TOURISM

Libel tourism is a defamation-specific form of **forum shopping**, which refers to when a plaintiff finds creative ways of bringing certain types of cases in certain jurisdictions where the law or relevant judicial practices are especially favorable to their cause, or there is an unusually high bar to defend such cases. In defamation cases, plaintiffs often try to bring cases in England or Wales because the law of those jurisdictions makes it easier for public figures to pursue defamation claims, whereas in the United States they are confronted with the high bar of the actual malice standard of fault. Prevailing plaintiffs then take their judgments to other countries where they hope to enforce them.

In an attempt to prevent this practice, in 2010, Congress passed the Securing the Protection of our Enduring and Established Constitutional Heritage (SPEECH) Act, which renders foreign defamation judgments unenforceable in the United States if they do not comport with basic First Amendment principles and certain other procedural requirements.[29]

RELATED CAUSES OF ACTION

When suing for defamation, many plaintiffs will include additional causes of action that arise out of the same allegedly defamatory statement. Among the most common are negligent infliction of emotional distress and intentional infliction of emotional distress, both types of personal injury claims.

Negligent infliction of emotional distress or **NIED** occurs when a defendant engages in some sort of negligent conduct that leads to undue emotional distress of the defendant. Recall from our discussion earlier in this chapter about fault, a defendant is negligent when a plaintiff can show that (1): the defendant's actions gave rise to a duty; (2) the defendant breached that duty by failing to act as an "ordinary reasonable person" would do in similar circumstances; (3) the plaintiff suffered some cognizable injury; and (4) the defendant's conduct was the cause.

Some states require that the plaintiff suffer some physical injury to recover for NEID, but others will allow the plaintiff to recover based solely on mental anguish.

Intentional infliction of emotional distress or **IIED** is similar to NIED but, as the name implies, there is an additional element of intention or purpose. Unlike in negligent infliction of emotional distress, where the defendant allegedly caused harm but did not set out to do so, to be found liable for IIED, the plaintiff must show that the defendant intended to do harm. Specifically, a plaintiff must show: (1) that the defendant engaged in extreme and outrageous conduct; (2) that the defendant knew at the time they engaged in the conduct should have known that the plaintiff had some kind of emotional weakness or sore spot; and (3) the extreme or outrageous conduct caused the plaintiff to experience severe emotional distress. Unlike NEID, in most states, the plaintiff need not show any physical manifestation of the distress. A plaintiff will generally be allowed to recover upon a showing of mental anguish alone.

IN THE NEWS: *SANDMANN V. THE MEDIA*

Although dealing with defamation claims (most of them without merit) is fairly routine for most significant media enterprises, occasionally, such claims become stories unto themselves. That's what happened to CNN, *The Washington Post*, and several other media organizations throughout 2019 and 2020 when they were sued

---

29 Pub. L. 222–334 (2010).

for defamation by Kentucky high school student Nicholas Sandmann over a series of photos, videos, and articles that "went viral" following a confrontation at a political demonstration on the National Mall.

The photos and videos at issue show Sandmann, wearing a red hat featuring President Trump's election slogan "Make America Great Again," in an apparent staredown with a Native American protester, Nathan Phillips, who was on the mall for a separate Indigenous Peoples Rally. Sandmann alleged that news reports and articles written about the video clips and photos created the impression that he had been the aggressor when, in fact, says Sandmann, Phillips and his group approached the Covington students as they waited for their busses to take them back to Kentucky. Indeed, shortly after the initial posts, longer videos emerged that revealed a more comprehensive view of what happened, supporting Sandmann's assertions.

In his lawsuits, Sandmann cites dozens of examples of how he believes CNN and *The Washington Post* defamed him. Among them, he says CNN characterized the group as "[a] crowd of teenagers [that] surrounded a Native American elder and other activities and mocked them" and characterized Phillips as a "Native American man confronted by teens."[30] Similarly, Sandmann alleged that *The Washington Post* defamed him by making statements describing the interaction using words such as "ugly," "aggressive," and "taunting," among several others.[31]

Both CNN and *The Washington Post* moved to dismiss Sandmann's claims. The court granted *The Washington Post*'s motion, finding that the statements about which Sandmann complained either were not "of or concerning" Sandmann, not defamatory, or statements of opinion or rhetorical hyperbole. In other words, the court concluded that even if every one of the statements had been made, and the circumstances surrounding them were exactly as Sandmann alleged, *The Washington Post* still would not have been liable for defamation.

> Note that on a motion to dismiss, the court is to consider only whether the plaintiff has stated sufficient facts to give rise to a plausible legal claim. The court is not concerned at this juncture with whether the facts stated are true or not, only that they establish a legal cause of action if they are, in fact, true. This is because a motion to dismiss is filed before either party has taken discovery, so the facts are still very much "in the eye of the beholder."

Despite the dismissal, following some procedural machinations, the judge reinstated Sandmann's case against *The Washington Post* and similarly allowed the lawsuit

30 Complaint at 27, *Nicholas Sandmann v. Cable News Network, Inc.*, No. 19-00031 (E.D. Ky. Mar. 12, 2019).
31 *Nicholas Sandmann v. WP Company LLC*, 401 F. Supp. 3d 781, 792 (E.D. Ky. 2019).

against CNN to continue. Shortly thereafter, CNN settled with Sandmann for an undisclosed sum, and *The Washington Post* followed soon after. As of this writing, Sandmann's litigation against other media outlets, including ABC, CBS, *Rolling Stone*, and *The New York Times*, remains pending.

> Settlements in defamation cases are not unusual, especially where a defendant is unsuccessful at getting the case dismissed relatively early in the process – for example, at the motion to dismiss stage. That's because often, the cost of litigating the case to resolution often far exceeds what the plaintiff would accept to drop the case, and business imperatives command a swift, economic resolution. Still, sometimes a media enterprise will believe so strongly in the underlying principles at stake in the litigation to fight on despite the cost. The decision of whether to settle or litigate is a complex question that generally requires extensive discussion and coordination between a company's business and legal executives.

KEY POINTS AND TAKEAWAYS

1. Defamation is a legal cause of action that allows living individuals, companies, and other organizations to seek redress for harm done to their reputation as a result of false statements.
2. A successful defamation claim requires that a plaintiff show the statement at issue was false, defamatory, properly identified the plaintiff, was communicated to at least one other person, caused harm to the plaintiff, and was the result of at least negligence on the part of the defendant.
3. There are myriad defenses to defamation, including truth (an "absolute" defense), opinion, rhetorical hyperbole, fair report and comment, neutral reportage, and various other privileges that apply in certain circumstances.
4. Reporters and others making statements about what could be construed as defamatory should carefully fact check each statement and, ideally, corroborate the information from multiple sources.
5. Take care to identify subjects of reports accurately and with as much detail as possible by including middle names or initials, ages, and general location information, to the extent possible. For example, referring to a subject "24-year-old John Q. Public of Evanston" is less likely to lead to misidentification than merely saying "John Public."
6. Use precise language when describing allegations or legal charges. For example, it is preferable to say someone was "arrested on suspicion" of a particular crime rather than saying they were "arrested for" that crime.
7. Similarly, avoid characterizations such as "alleged murderer" or "accused rapist," in favor of "alleged to have committed murder" or "charged with first-degree sexual assault."

8. Where possible, rely as much as possible on official documents, proceedings, or statements from public officials. In some cases, it may be beneficial to show portions of the relevant documents to your audience so they can see the context.

QUESTIONS FOR DISCUSSION

1. The local police department releases a mugshot of someone who was recently arrested on suspicion of murder. The local media, relying on the police department's representation, publish the photograph. It turns out, however, that the person depicted in the photograph was actually arrested on suspicion of drunk driving and the charges were ultimately dropped. The person in the photograph sues the police and the media for defamation. Will he prevail? What defenses, if any, do the police have? The media?

2. Before the mugshot had been withdrawn and replaced with the correct image, a locally famous chef and restaurateur retweeted one of the media reports about the murder and the arrest, adding "We have to get these lowlife degenerates off the street." The person in the photograph responds by holding a well-attended press conference during which he calls the culinary magnate an "opportunistic, capitalist bovine, unfit to run a soup kitchen, let alone a five-star restaurant" and encourages the public not to patronize any of the restaurateur's establishments. The local media pick up the story, and the restaurateur sues the man in the photograph, for defamation. Will he prevail? What defenses, if any, does the man in the photograph have? The media?

3. What steps could members of the local media have taken to minimize whatever exposure they may have from the circumstances described above?

4. Recall that among the categories of *per se* defamation are statements relating to an individual's trade or profession. Recall also that many states have specific laws dealing with agricultural product disparagement. Why do you think defamation law puts so much emphasis on a person's trade or profession and agricultural industries?

5

CHAPTER 5
PRIVACY AND PUBLICITY

Defamation law addresses the extent to which media organizations must report truthfully, but what are the limits of a media enterprise's ability to report true facts about individuals or use an individual's name or likeness without their permission?

In this chapter, we will consider the four main privacy torts, including false light invasion of privacy, misappropriation of the right of publicity, disclosure of private facts, and various statutory protections for private information and personal data.

INTRODUCTION TO PRIVACY

Unlike free speech, which finds its roots clearly articulated in the Constitution, privacy is not expressly guaranteed by the federal constitution, although some state constitutions have expressly recognized it. Rather, the right to privacy has been developed over the years by the Supreme Court's interpretation of various constitutional principles and rights guaranteed by the Bill of Rights.

In a famous Supreme Court case involving access to birth control, Justice William O. Douglas described the right to privacy as emanating from a "penumbra" cast by several amendments to the Bill of Rights, namely the First, Third (quartering of troops during peacetime), Fourth (search and seizure), Fifth (self incrimination and due process), and Ninth (affirming the existence of "unenumerated" rights).[1]

Over the years, courts have fashioned the broad privacy principles that exist in the constitutional penumbra into four distinct privacy torts: false light invasion of privacy, public disclosure of private facts, appropriation, and intrusion upon seclusion. Although constitutional principles undergird all four of these doctrines, they are primarily creatures of state law, which means the elements and defenses of each will vary depending on the jurisdiction, but we can still make some broadly applicable generalizations.

Beyond the four torts, Congress and various state legislatures have also recently begun legislating in the privacy arena, enacting laws that aim to protect data and other information about individuals in specific contexts, such as the Health Insurance Portability and Accountability Act, which aims to protect individuals' medical records, and the Family Educational Rights and Privacy Act, which protects educational information and records.

---

1 *Griswold v. Connecticut*, 381 U.S. 479, 484 (1965).

DOI: 10.4324/9781003197966-5

FALSE LIGHT INVASION OF PRIVACY

Of all the privacy torts, **false light invasion of privacy** or simply **false light** is the most like defamation. In fact, some states have determined that it's so similar that false light isn't recognized as a separate cause of action.

False light is similar to defamation in that it creates a cause of action for individuals who believe their reputation or character has been impugned. However, unlike defamation, which requires that the statements at issue are defamatory, in a false light case, the statements at issue are simply presented in a way that gives the public a false impression about the plaintiff and constitutes a major misrepresentation of the plaintiff's character, history, activities, or beliefs.[2] Or, put more succinctly, the statements must cast the plaintiff in a false light, as the name of the tort suggests.

For a defendant to be responsible for placing an individual in a false light, a plaintiff must show that:

1. The false light in which they were placed would be highly offensive to a reasonable person; and
2. The defendant either knew they were placing the plaintiff in a false light or acted with a reckless disregard as to the falsity of the publicized matter and the false light in which the plaintiff is placed.[3]

PUBLIC DISCLOSURE

For a plaintiff to have a viable claim for false light, the information that casts them in a false light must have been disclosed publicly. This is fairly obvious since, without a disclosure to the public, there can be no harm. Unlike "publication" in the defamation context, which requires communication to only one person, the public disclosure in a false light case must be broad. A California court, for instance, held that the communication must be to the public at large or to a group broad enough that it is "substantially certain" to become public knowledge.[4]

FALSITY

Although a statement need not be defamatory to give rise to a false light claim, it generally must still be false, although some courts have determined that so long as the statement "at least [has] the capacity to give rise to a false public impression as to the plaintiff,"[5] it is actionable. That said, the statements at issue must still be capable of creating a false impression that is reasonably believable.

---

2 *Romine v. Kallinger*, 573 A.2d 284, 295 (N.J. 1988) (citations omitted).
3 Restatement (Second) of Torts § 652E.
4 *New Show Studios, LLC v. Needle*, 2016 U.S. District. LEXIS 129077, *15 (C.D. Cal. 2016).
5 *Romine*, 573 A.2d at 294.

A Utah court, for example, dismissed a false light claim where the plaintiff's husband, and a number of his coworkers, were interviewed for a video thinking that they were answering questions about household chores that they disliked. When the video was played back at a company party, however, it had been edited to appear as though the question they were answering was "What's sex like with your partner?" In dismissing the action, the Court concluded that the video could not be reasonably construed as anything more than a "joke or spoof" and was therefore not actionable.[6]

IDENTIFICATION

As in a defamation matter, the statements that give rise to a false light claim must be "of and concerning" the plaintiff, even if not identified by name. For instance, a California court determined that plaintiffs had satisfied the identification element when a producer used a photograph of the Little League team for which they played, in connection with a documentary about adult coaches who sexually abused their players (the team's coach had pleaded guilty to such charges). The court concluded that despite the fact that the plaintiffs had not been identified by name, the use of their photograph in connection with the story could create the false impression that the individuals in the image had been sexually abused.[7]

HIGHLY OFFENSIVE TO A REASONABLE PERSON

To be actionable, the false light in which the defendant placed the plaintiff must be highly offensive to a reasonable person of ordinary sensibilities. That is, if an ordinary, reasonable person would have reason to be offended, the statement is considered "highly offensive" for the purposes of bringing a false light claim.

For example, courts have held that being falsely accused of a crime[8] or labeled as an alcoholic[9] are highly offensive, but dramatic portrayals of a person that are generally positive but feature certain negative characteristics or tragic flaws have been held to not be highly offensive.[10]

Some courts have also recognized that where the facts that comprise a particular portrayal may include some minor inaccuracies or omissions but is mostly true, and the "gist" or "sting" is the same as it would have been had the statements been entirely correct, the portrayal cannot be considered highly offensive,[11] essentially borrowing the concept of "substantial truth" from defamation law.

---

6 *Stein v. Marriott Ownership Resorts, Inc.*, 944 P.2d 374 (Utah Ct. App. 1997).
7 *M.G. v. Time Warner, Inc.*, 89 Cal.App.4th 623 (2001).
8 *Fanelle v. LoJack Corp.*, 79 F. Supp. 2d 588, 563 (E.D. Pa. 2000).
9 *Dean v. Guard Pub. Co.*, 744 P.2d 1296 (Or. App. 1987).
10 See *Sarver v. Hurt Locker, LLC*, 2011 WL 11574477, *10 (C.D. Cal. 2011), *aff'd*, *Sarver v. Chartier*, 813 F.3d 891, 907 (9th Cir. 2016); *Polsby v. Spruill*, 25 Media L. Rep. 2259, 2266 (D.D.C. 1997), *aff'd*, 1998 U.S. App. LEXIS 7908 (D.C. Cir. Mar 11, 1998).
11 See, e.g., *Arpaio v. Zucker*, U.S. Dist. LEXIS 189291, *10 (D.D.C. 1998).

KNOWN FALSITY OR RECKLESS DISREGARD

Also borrowed from defamation law is the requirement that a false light plaintiff shows that the defendant acted knowing that the statements they were making were false or made with a reckless disregard for the truth – that is, "actual malice."

However, unlike in defamation law, where the actual malice standard is applied only to public figures (while private figures must show only negligence), most courts have held that in a false light case, both public and private plaintiffs must show actual malice for the claim to be actionable.

DEFENSES

Because of the close relationship between the two causes of action, the defenses applicable in a defamation case are generally also available to defendants in a false light case. Courts have rejected plaintiffs' false light claims based on opinion or rhetorical hyperbole defenses, for example, as well as the various privileges that defeat a defamation claim, and, of course, the various procedural defenses such as that the statute of limitations has run.

PUBLIC DISCLOSURE OF PRIVATE FACTS

Described by the Restatement of Torts as "publicity given to private life," but more commonly known as **disclosure of private facts** or more simply, **disclosure**, occurs when a party discloses private facts about another person, without any legitimate basis for doing so. The tort of disclosure gives people a mechanism to seek redress for harm associated with the unreasonable disclosure of their private information.

In contrast to defamation, where the statement at issue had to be false, disclosure deals with facts that are true but should nevertheless have not been publicized because there is no legitimate reason to do so. Some states, such as New York, do not even recognize it, but under the Restatement, unlawful disclosure occurs when one:

> Gives publicity to a matter concerning the private life of another is subject to liability to the other for the invasion of his privacy, if the matter publicized is of a kind that:
>
> (a) would be highly offensive to a reasonable person and
> (b) is not of legitimate concern to the public.

PUBLICITY

Recall that in defamation law, a statement had to be "published" to be actionable, which simply means that it is communicated to, and understood by, at least one other person. Here, the standard is a bit higher. The plaintiff must show that the statement was "publicized," which means that the statement was made broadly and communicated to a wide enough range of people such that it is reasonable to assume that it will become public knowledge. Some courts have held that publication to smaller groups is sufficient, but only if there is some sort of special relationship between the group and the person about whom the statements were made, such as members of a close-knit trade or profession, parents of students at the same school, and the like.

"PRIVATE" FACTS

To be considered a "private" fact, the fact must truly be private – that is, not generally known *nor knowable* to the general public and something that an average person would reasonably expect to be private. Thus, information obtained from public records, no matter how much effort it takes to find them, to that an average person would likely have difficulty finding them, would not be considered "private" for purposes of a disclosure claim. As a result, information found on birth certificates, marriage and divorce certificates, corporate filings, state licensing databases, criminal records, court documents, government employee salary data, and the like are all fair game because they are publicly accessible. Courts have even concluded that disclosing nonpublic information that pertains to a matter of public concern, provided it was lawfully obtained, does not give rise to an invasion of privacy claim.[12]

Private information that an individual discloses themselves is no longer considered "private," so somebody who simply repeats a private fact about a subject, which they learned from that subject directly, could not be held responsible for improper disclosure. But merely disclosing to a close circle of family and friends is not sufficient to render a private fact public. For example, a person may wish to confide in a family member or close confidant about the fact that they have been diagnosed with cancer or that they have been engaged in an intimate relationship with a particular person. Those private disclosures do not render otherwise "private" facts public for the purposes of disclosure liability.

Also note that there is no equivalent to defamation's "republication rule" in a disclosure case because the first disclosure of the information, by definition, makes it publicly known, and the disclosure of information that is already in the public sphere is not actionable.

IDENTIFICATION

Although not expressly described in the Restatement's rule, and often glossed over by courts, embedded in the principle of "private facts" is the notion that the person about whom the facts pertain has to be reasonably identifiable. If private,

---

12 *See Times-Mirror Co. v. Superior Court*, 198 Cal.App.3d 1420 (1988).

embarrassing facts are disclosed, but it is not known to whom they pertain, then nobody can claim to have been injured by such disclosure.

The identification requirement does not require great detail or precision, however. For example, a California court concluded that a plaintiff had been sufficiently identified in a broadcast segment that featured "her first name … her voice, her general appearance and the recounted circumstances of the accident" in which the plaintiff had been involved, which had also been covered extensively by other media that had published her full name and city of residence.[13]

HIGHLY OFFENSIVE TO A REASONABLE PERSON

Beyond simply being a "private" fact, the disclosure of that fact must be highly offensive to a reasonable person of ordinary sensibilities. The Restatement provides that "minor and moderate" annoyances are not actionable; rather, to be highly offensive, the disclosure must be so serious "that a reasonable person would feel justified in feeling seriously aggrieved by it."[14] The analysis is therefore highly context specific, depending on the nature of the private facts disclosed and the person to whom those facts pertain and how they were disclosed.

For instance, suppose a college newspaper discloses the confidential grades of several students that were obtained through improper means in an article intended to shame low-performing students. Most courts would likely conclude that such conduct is highly offensive. However, when confronted with similar facts, a Maryland court concluded that the disclosure was not highly offensive because the students whose grades had been leaked were athletes who had "sought and basked in the limelight" and because the basketball player's grades determined whether they were eligible to play.[15] Accordingly, the court determined that the disclosure of their grades "was not unreasonable and did not trample upon community mores."[16]

NOT OF LEGITIMATE PUBLIC CONCERN

One of the reasons that the Maryland court determined that the disclosure of the student's grades was not highly offensive was because there was a legitimate public interest in the performance of the university's basketball team.[17] The court reasoned that if the students had been removed from the team due to poor academic performance, "the public would be entitled to ask and speculate as to the reasons for such action."[18]

13 *Shulman v. Group W Productions, Inc.*, 955 P.2d 469, 489 (Cal. 1998).
14 Restatement (Second) of Torts § 652D.
15 *Bilney v. Evening Star Newspaper Co.*, 405 A.2d 652, 660 (Md. App. 1979).
16 *Id.*
17 *Id.*
18 *Id.*

The Supreme Court has held that one cannot be held liable for disclosing private facts, no matter how offensive the disclosure may be, if they pertain to a matter of legitimate public concern, thus every state that recognizes the tort of disclosure will also have such an exception.[19]

Determining whether something is properly characterized as a matter of legitimate public concern typically centers around how "newsworthy" it is. Generally, the disclosure of what would ordinarily be private facts is excusable if the public's interest in those facts derives from a newsworthy event and is not "morbid and sensational prying into private lives for its own sake."[20] Note that although the courts use the term "newsworthy," it actually extends well beyond pure news. Courts have recognized that the principle applies to entertainment content as well.

There are various tests used to determine whether a particular disclosure is sufficiently newsworthy. In California, for example, courts consider:

1. The social value of the facts published;
2. The depth of the publication's intrusion into ostensibly private affairs; and
3. The extent to which the party voluntarily acceded to a position of public notoriety.[21]

If the third item gives you a sense of déjà vu, you aren't imagining things. The general principles that underlie the test for newsworthiness in the disclosure setting are more or less the same as the principles that undergird the distinction between public and private figures that we saw in our discussion of defamation in Chapter 4.

Courts have determined that public figures – those that voluntarily put themselves into the public spotlight, either by virtue of their roles or positions (e.g., celebrities, politicians) or by their actions – have a higher bar to clear when trying to show that their private facts have been disclosed. Or, put differently, there is a greater likelihood that private facts pertaining to public figures will be considered of legitimate public concern compared with private figures.

Where things get tricky is in the context of involuntary public figures – those that have become public figures by virtue of being involved in some event of public concern but did not voluntarily put themselves in that position. For example, an accident victim might be the subject of unwanted news coverage simply by being involved in the accident. In those cases, courts have held that the disclosure of private facts about the victim is not an invasion of privacy so long as the facts disclosed are reasonably

---

19 *See Cox Broadcasting Corp. v. Cohen*, 420 U.S. 469, 492 (1975).
20 Restatement (Second) of Torts § 6252D, Comment (h).
21 *Briscoe v. Reader's Digest Association, Inc.*, 483 P.2d 34, 43 (Cal. 1971).

related to the newsworthy subject, and disclosure is not disproportionate to the newsworthiness of the matter reported.

Under this standard, it would likely be appropriate for the media to disclose information about the victim's health and welfare as it pertains to the accident, but not the fact that the victim has a chronic disease if the disease has nothing to do with the accident.

DEFENSES

The most common and viable defenses to a disclosure claim are that the information is derived from public sources or that it is a matter of legitimate public concern. As with all torts, a defendant can assert various other procedural defenses, including consent, or that the statute of limitations has run.

APPROPRIATION AND RIGHT OF PUBLICITY

Appropriation is a privacy tort that involves the improper use of the likeness of an individual. By **likeness**, we mean anything that serves to identify an individual, such as their name, voice, signature, image, or other identifying characteristics. Appropriation is really two separate but closely related causes of action: **appropriation** and **right of publicity**. The two are largely the same except for the nature of the plaintiff involved.

Appropriation deals with circumstances where a *private individual's* likeness is used without permission in a manner that causes injury to the plaintiff's emotional well-being. Right of publicity involves the same conduct, using one's likeness without permission, but where the plaintiff is a *public figure* such as a celebrity. In contrast to the other privacy protections we discuss in this chapter, the right of publicity is often considered to be a property right that can be licensed and otherwise commercialized. As one court observed:

> Television and other media create marketable celebrity identity value. Considerable energy and ingenuity are expended by those who have achieved celebrity value to exploit for profit. The law protects the celebrity's sole right to exploit this value whether the celebrity has achieved her fame out or rare ability, dumb luck, or a combination thereof.[22]

For example, when Post Malone and Cedric the Entertainer appeared in a Bud Light commercial during the 2021 Super Bowl, for example, they were exploiting their rights of publicity.

---

22 *White v. Samsung Electronics America, Inc.*, 971 F.2d 1395, 1399 (9th Cir. 1992).

Because misappropriation and right of publicity are substantively the same, except as to the nature of the plaintiff, we discuss the two here as though they are interchangeable, although there may be some distinctions at the margins in some states, depending on the nuances of each states' laws. Note that many states have codified their appropriation and rights of publicity laws, whereas in others, they have developed through case law.

An individual's likeness is misappropriated, or their right of publicity violated, where a defendant:

1. Uses the plaintiff's identity;
2. To the defendant's advantage;
3. Without consent;
4. Resulting in the plaintiff's injury.

PLAINTIFF'S IDENTITY

To be actionable, the defendant must have identified the plaintiff in some way. There are the obvious ways, of course, through the use of their name or image, but as noted above, likeness can be virtually anything so long as it serves to identify the plaintiff.

In *Midler v. Ford Motor Co.*,[23] the Ninth Circuit held that Ford's use of a "sound-alike singer," intended to closely mimic the sound and style of performer Bette Midler, improperly exploited Midler's likeness. In that case, Ford's advertising agency had tried to license Midler's original performance for use in a commercial, but Midler's representatives denied the request. The agency then hired a singer to re-record the song that was ultimately used in the commercial. In finding that Ford had violated Midler's right of publicity, the court explained that "[t]he human voice is one of the most palpable ways identity is manifested. ... To impersonate her voice is to pirate her identity."[24]

Note that there are at least two rights at issue: one is the copyright in the musical composition and the other is Midler's right of publicity. Each is owned by separate parties. Typically, the rights in a musical composition are owned by a music publisher, while a person's right of publicity is owned by the individual. Here, Ford's advertising agency had sought and received a license from the copyright owner to use the song,[25] leaving only the right of publicity at issue. We discuss copyright law more fully in Chapter 11.

23 849 F.2d 460 (9th Cir. 1988).
24 *Id.* at 463.
25 *Id.* at 462.

In a subsequent case, the Ninth Circuit extended the concept of identity to essentially anything that evokes the personality of the plaintiff. In *White v. Samsung Electronics America, Inc.*,[26] Samsung had produced a television commercial featuring a robot dressed to look like television personality Vanna White. As described by the court, "[t]he robot was posed next to a game board which is instantly recognizable as the Wheel of Fortune game show set, in a stance for which White is famous."[27] White had not given her permission and was not paid for the robotic rendition and sued for, among other things, a violation of her right of publicity.

The district court rejected White's claim, but the appellate court reversed, observing that the various features of the advertisement – the female-shaped robot wearing a gown, wig, and jewelry, the *Wheel of Fortune*-style set setting, turning letters on a game board – taken individually, are not especially unique to White, but taken together, evoke the unmistakable image of White and was therefore a violation of her publicity rights.[28]

DEFENDANT'S ADVANTAGE

It is not enough for an appropriation or right of publicity claim that the defendant simply uses the plaintiff's identity. The defendant must use the identity to its benefit or advantage. Some jurisdictions and courts require that the advantage be *commercial* in nature, that is, something that proposes a commercial transaction (an advertisement).

Use of a plaintiff's identity in an advertising campaign, such as in the Vanna White and Bette Midler cases, is a clear commercial use, but others are closer calls, or the result will depend on the nuance of the local law. For example, in *Pott v. Lazarin*,[29] a California appellate court determined that using an individual's name and image in social media posts and at a press conference aimed at raising money for suicide prevention was not a commercial use because they were not advertising or selling products or services.[30] If that case had been brought in Tennessee, however, the court likely would have held such use to be commercial, since the misappropriation statute there expressly includes fundraising.[31]

Note that merely generating revenue as a result of a particular use is not usually sufficient to render the use "commercial." Using someone's likeness in a movie or television show, for instance, is generally not considered commercial even if the

---

26 971 F.2d at 1395.
27 *Id.* at 1396.
28 *Id.* at 1399.
29 47 Cal.App.5th 141 (Cal. App., Sixth Dist., Mar. 30, 2020).
30 47 Cal.App.5th at 150–51.
31 Tenn. Code Ann. § 47-25-1105.

producer makes money by licensing the content to movie theaters, television broad-casters, and streaming services. We discuss this concept more fully in the defenses section below.

WITHOUT CONSENT OF THE PLAINTIFF

As with the other privacy torts, consent is generally a defense to an appropriation claim, though many states view it as an affirmative element of the claim – that is, a plaintiff has to specifically allege a lack of consent when they file a lawsuit.

As a practical matter, consent in the right of publicity arena occurs by virtue of a formal agreement between the parties. When a celebrity agrees to participate in an advertising campaign, for instance, there is typically a comprehensive written agree-ment that outlines the ways in which the party exploiting the individual's publicity rights is allowed to do so.

For instance, suppose a sports celebrity signs a deal with an athletic wear manufac-turer that contemplates the manufacturer using the celebrity's likeness in connection with a series of television commercials. Unbeknownst to the celebrity, after the com-mercials have been recorded, the athletic wear company begins using the celebrity's image *on* a line of products (not just in commercials for the products). Each use – the commercials and the use on the products – represents an exploitation of the celebrity's publicity rights. But, because the agreement only contemplated use in commercials, the use on products would exceed the scope of the celebrity's consent and the athletic wear manufacturer could be responsible.

Consent can also be implied by conduct. Although it is common for producers of reality television programs to secure consent from those who appear in their shows, at least one court has concluded that it was not necessary to get express written consent where a party conducts themselves in such a way that implied consent.[32]

> One of the factors the court looked to when determining whether the plaintiff in *Greenstein* had consented to the use of his likeness was the presence of promi-nent signage at the filming location that explicitly said that a reality show was being recorded in the area and that one's presence in the area "shall be deemed consent to photograph you, to record your voice, and to exploit such image, photographs and sound recordings in this program and other programs in all media worldwide, in perpetuity."

---

32 *Greenstein v. Greif Co.*, 2009 WL 117368, *10 (Cal. App. 2d Dist. Jan. 20, 2009).

Posting such signs is common practice in the media production industry, especially when filming takes place in public areas where people may unwittingly wander through a scene or otherwise find themselves recorded. Generally, so long as the signs are sufficiently prominent, courts have found them to be a sufficient basis upon which to imply consent.

INJURY TO THE PLAINTIFF

In most jurisdictions, it is sufficient for a plaintiff to show that there is either economic or emotional harm, but there must be a demonstrable link between the harm and the violation of the privacy right. As a practical matter, average people alleging misappropriation would seek redress for emotional harm, while celebrities and other public figures alleging violations of their right of publicity would seek damages for economic harm since they are generally in the business of monetizing such rights.

THE EXPRESSIVE WORK DEFENSE

The most common defense to an appropriation or right of publicity case is that the use of the plaintiff's likeness is protected by the First Amendment as an *expressive use*, as opposed to a commercial use. That means that it is not a misappropriation of one's likeness to cover newsworthy events involving that person, write truthful articles or books about a person, or produce truthful films and television shows about them. Thus, the determination of whether someone's likeness has been improperly appropriated often rises and falls on the determination of whether a particular use was expressive or commercial.

As you might imagine, the line between what constitutes an expressive work versus a commercial work is sometimes not entirely clear.

In 1977, the Supreme Court explained that although news reporting generally would not give rise to a misappropriation claim, it was a violation of a performer's right of publicity when a television station broadcast the entirety of his act.[33] Hugo Zacchini had developed a "human cannonball" act in which he was shot from a special cannon into a net approximately 200 feet away. Zacchini had asked the station not to record the act, but it did so anyway, broadcasting the entirety of it during a news program. The Supreme Court observed that "[t]he broadcast of a film of [the] entire act poses a substantial threat to the economic value of that performance"[34] and that the station's

---

33 *Zacchini v. Scripps-Howard Broadcasting*, 433 U.S. 562 (1977).
34 *Id.* at 575.

use of the entire performance was akin to preventing Zacchini from charging an admission fee.

In 2010, army sergeant Jeffrey Sarver brought a suit against the producers of *The Hurt Locker*, claiming that it violated his privacy rights because it was based, in part, on interviews that the screenwriter, Mark Boal, had done with him while on assignment for *Playboy* magazine, embedded with the military in Iraq.[35] Sarver relied on the Supreme Court's decision in *Zacchini* to support his claim, but the Ninth Circuit saw it differently. The court observed that unlike Zacchini, who had spent time and effort to develop a character and performance of interest to the public, Sarver was a private person who had "expressly disavowed the notion that he sought to attract public attention to himself."[36] The court continued to note that the movie did not steal Sarver's "entire act" as it were, and did not exploit "any performance or persona that he had worked to develop," and explained that the First Amendment "safeguards the storytellers and artists who take the raw materials of life – including the stories of real individuals, ordinary or extraordinary – and transform them into art, be it articles, books, movies, or plays."[37]

In contrast, in 2014, the Seventh Circuit held that a supermarket's attempt at congratulating Michael Jordan for his induction into the Basketball Hall of Fame was an unauthorized exploitation of Jordan's publicity rights.[38] In that case, supermarket chain Jewel-Osco had placed a full-page advertisement in a special commemorative issue of *Sports Illustrated*. The relatively minimalist ad featured two shoes, each bearing Jordan's number, 23, some congratulatory text with the headline "A Shoe In!" along with the Jewel-Osco logo and slogan "good things are just around the corner."[39]

Jewel-Osco argued that the advertisement did not constitute commercial speech because it did not propose a commercial transaction, but rather, merely congratulated Jordan for his success. The court disagreed, however, finding that when viewed in context, the congratulatory message was aimed at enhancing the Jewel-Osco brand. "The commercial message is implicit but easily inferred," said the Seventh Circuit, "and it is the dominant one."[40]

Jewel-Osco and Jordan ultimately settled for an undisclosed amount, but a similar ad run by another grocery chain resulted in an $8.9 million jury award against it.[41]

----

35 *Sarver*, 813 F.3d at 896.
36 *Id*. at 905.
37 *Id*.
38 *Jordan v. Jewel Food Stores, Inc.*, 743 F.3d 509 (7th Cir. 2014).
39 *Id*. at 512.
40 *Id*. at 518.
41 Associated Press, *Michael Jordan, Jewel-Osco Reach Settlement Over Use of Name*, November 23, 2015, https://apnews.com/article/6f2c975acf3644199882d28f17e1c7f3.

POSTMORTEM RIGHT OF PUBLICITY

In most cases, the right to privacy is considered personal, which means it extends only so long as an individual is alive. Put differently, the right to privacy dies with the person. Right of publicity is sometimes an exception to that general rule.

As cases like *Zacchini* and *Jewel-Osco* make clear, the purpose of the right of publicity is to allow celebrities and other public figures to reap the benefits of their efforts to develop and maintain their public personas. As a result, the law tends to treat the right of publicity as a property right, akin to other forms of intellectual property (discussed more fully in Chapters 11 and 12), and some jurisdictions allow the right to subsist beyond an individual's death, though usually only for a limited time. For example, California allows the right to continue for 70 years,[42] while New York recognizes it for 40 years.[43]

There is a robust market for licensing postmortem rights of publicity in those states where such rights exist, and licensing representatives tend to be fairly aggressive and, as one might expect, take rather expansive views of what constitutes commercial speech and therefore a licensable exploitation of the rights of their clients.

For example, in 2017, Muhammad Ali Enterprises sued the Fox television network for alleged violations of Muhammad Ali's postmortem right of publicity arising from a three-minute tribute video that the network broadcast before Super Bowl LI, just eight months after his death.[44] Echoing the *Jewel-Osco* case (likely because the lawsuit was filed by the same lawyer), Muhammad Ali's representatives said in court papers that the spot was not a tribute, but rather a promotional video for Fox and specifically the Super Bowl telecast. They sought $30 million in damages, but the matter was ultimately settled before the court rendered a decision.[45]

Whether it's shilling for an athletic brand or triumphantly announcing that they're going to Disney World after winning the Super Bowl, sports figures are no strangers to leveraging their right of publicity for various commercial purposes. There is one group, however, for whom such opportunities have traditionally not been available: college athletes. That's because until recently the National Collegiate Athletic Association had a rule that prohibited them from profiting off of their name, image, or likeness, and limited the ways NCAA member schools could provide financial support to their athletes.

42 Cal. Civ. Code § 3344.1.

43 N.Y. Civ. Rights Law § 50-f.

44 *Muhammad Ali Enterprises LLC v. Fox Broadcasting Co.*, No. 17-cv-7273, *complaint filed*, 2017 WL 4516708 (N.D. Ill. Oct. 10, 2017).

45 Jon Parton, *Fox Settles $30 Million Muhammad Ali Lawsuit*, Courthouse News Service, July 17, 2018, https://www.courthousenews.com/fox-settles-30-million-muhammad-ali-lawsuit.

In 2021, the Supreme Court decided *NCAA v. Alston*,[46] which held that the NCAA's limits on student aid, including its restrictions on student commercializations of name, image, and likeness, violated federal antitrust laws. Around the same time, a number of states enacted laws that specifically allowed college athletes to profit from their rights of publicity, setting up a potential conflict with the NCAA's rules. Just before those laws were set to take effect, the NCAA relaxed its position, allowing athletes to monetize their likenesses so long as they continued to comply with applicable state laws and school or conference rules, many of which continue to impose certain restrictions on athletes.

INTRUSION UPON SECLUSION

Intrusion upon seclusion (or sometimes referred to simply as **intrusion**) is, in some ways, the most straightforward privacy tort, and the one that most people think of when they think about an invasion of privacy. Unlike the other privacy torts, which require communication of the offending speech to external parties, intrusion is focused on the conduct of the defendant in the course of gathering information.

In most jurisdictions, to establish intrusion upon seclusion, a plaintiff must show that the defendant:

1. Intentionally intruded upon the solitude or seclusion of another, or his or her private affairs; and
2. The intrusion would be highly offensive to a reasonable person.

INTENTIONAL INTRUSION UPON THE SOLITUDE OR SECLUSION OF ANOTHER

Determining whether a defendant has unreasonably intruded on the seclusion of a plaintiff often centers on the legal doctrine of **reasonable expectation of privacy**, which arose out of criminal law cases that developed the principles of the Fourth Amendment, which protects citizens from unreasonable searches and seizures. Broadly speaking, courts have held that there is no reasonable expectation of privacy in public places, the curb (including one's trash placed at the curb for collection), unfenced areas around a home, or things that are viewable from overhead by aircraft. Beyond those categories that have been specifically addressed by courts, determining whether someone has a reasonable expectation of privacy is essentially an exercise in applying social norms and standards to determine whether a person would reasonably expect, given the circumstances, that their conduct, conversations, and affairs would be private in a particular situation.

---

46 141 S.Ct. 2141 (2021).

One might reasonably expect that their e-mail is private, for example, but at least one court has held that there is no reasonable expectation of privacy when the e-mail flows through a corporate e-mail system that warns users that their e-mail may be monitored. Essentially, the court said that the warning that their corporate e-mail may be monitored defeats the expectation that the communications are private.

Although one generally does not have a reasonable expectation of privacy in a public location, even public locations have areas where a person may have a reasonable expectation of privacy. Restrooms, locker rooms, fitting rooms, hotel rooms, and the like are all areas of public accommodations where, despite the generally public nature of the venue, a person may still have a reasonable expectation of privacy.

HIGHLY OFFENSIVE TO A REASONABLE PERSON

In California, for instance, courts consider the following factors when determining whether a particular intrusion is "highly offensive":

1. Degree of intrusion;
2. The context;
3. The conduct and circumstances surrounding the intrusion;
4. The intruder's motives;
5. The setting in which the intrusion occurs; and
6. The expectation of those whose privacy is invaded.[47]

Take, for example, someone taking a selfie in the mirror of a public gym locker room. They snap the picture at exactly the wrong time and happen to inadvertently catch another person in the background of the photo. That would probably constitute an intrusion on the other person's privacy because, in the locker room, there is a reasonable expectation of privacy. However, given the context, the conduct and circumstances surrounding the intrusion, and the intruder's motives, it would probably not be considered highly offensive.

Now suppose the person taking the picture was a celebrity gossip reporter who had gained access to the locker room solely for the purpose of surreptitiously taking pictures of celebrities known to frequent the gym. Under those facts, it is more likely that a court would conclude the intrusion is highly offensive because of the intruder's motives and the context of the intrusion.

DEFENSES

Unlike other privacy torts, First Amendment principles are generally not useful defenses to intrusion claims because the essence of the claim does not involve speech.

---

47 *Miller v. National Broadcasting Co.* 187 Cal. App. 3d 1463, 1483–84 (1986).

Rather, it is focused on the nature of the conduct involved in gathering information. Still, some courts have recognized that gathering newsworthy information may be privileged by the First Amendment if it involves "routing reporting techniques,"[48] which has been interpreted to mean things like knocking on doors, photographing people or attempting to interview them from public spaces, or attempting to extract confidential information from sources.

However, the mere pursuit of a newsworthy objective is generally not sufficient to justify an intrusion. For instance, gaining access to physical locations, or convincing people to agree to interviews, through the use of misrepresentations or other false pretenses, even if for the purpose of news reporting, is unlikely to overcome an intrusion claim.

Those engaged in field reporting or investigations should be aware that often the conduct that can give rise to a civil claim for intrusion against seclusion may also create liability for trespassing. In most jurisdictions, trespassing is defined as when one enters a physical space owned or controlled by another (or instructs a third party to do so) without consent, and it is actionable as a civil tort, just like the privacy torts we have discussed in this chapter, but also as a criminal infraction, raising the possibility of fines and jail time. Such cases are rarely prosecuted (meaning that the charges are ultimately dropped), but it is unfortunately not unheard of for journalists to be detained or arrested by police, especially in circumstances where they are covering large, rapidly changing events, such as protests or marches.

Many media enterprises have policies against naming individuals involved in certain sensitive situations, most notably victims of sexual assault, because of the stigma associated with it. Despite the widespread nature of the practice, it is not rooted in the law. In fact, courts have struck government attempts at preventing the media from disclosing victims' names as contrary to the First Amendment.[49] That said, courts have also held that the government may be justified in restricting access to such information by, for example, allowing state agencies to withhold victims' names from disclosure under open records laws (discussed more fully in Chapter 6).[50]

48 *Nicholson v. McClatchy Newspapers*, 177 Cal. App. 3d 509, 518 (1986).
49 *See, e.g.*, Reporters Committee for Freedom of the Press, *Ban on Identifying Sex Crime Victims Is Unconstitutional*, December 13, 1994, https://www.rcfp.org/ban-identifying-sex-crime-victims -unconstitutional.
50 *See, e.g.*, Reporters Committee for Freedom of the Press, *Identities of Sex Crime Victims Not Public*, November 6, 2003, https://www.rcfp.org/identities-sex-crime-victims-not-public.

Although not naming victims of sexual assault has long been a common practice, some have begun to question whether broadening the policies to allow for more comprehensive reporting of sexual assault would help advance our understanding of the crime as a public health issue. Media ethics expert Kelly McBride suggests the following:

[r]ather than starting with a policy that tells us what to avoid, what if our policies encouraged us to tell the story of sexual assault more completely, so that the public might understand how it happens and how to prevent it?

She cautions that journalists should not identify victims without their consent, but rather, media enterprises "should rewrite [their] policies to encourage journalists to tell more complete stories about sexual assault."[51]

STATUTORY PRIVACY PROTECTIONS

Beyond the common law privacy torts, Congress and state legislatures have enacted a number of statutory privacy laws aimed at protecting privacy in certain specific categories. Some of the most commonly cited laws include:

- The **Fair Credit Reporting Act (FCRA)** regulates the consumer credit industry, namely the credit bureaus that track, maintain, and distribute information about consumer finances that are used to evaluate creditworthiness and the financial institutions that rely on that information in making credit determinations.
- The **Gramm-Leach-Bliley Act (GLBA)** requires financial institutions to protect the sensitive financial information of consumers and to routinely disclose their privacy practices to their customers and clients.
- The **Health Insurance Portability and Accountability Act (HIPAA)** regulates what healthcare providers and other players in the healthcare industry, such as insurance companies, can do with certain protected health information.
- The **Family Educational Rights and Privacy Act (FERPA)** protects student privacy and prohibits schools and other educational institutions from disclosing educational records without permission.
- The **Children's Online Privacy Protection Act (COPPA)** governs the collection of information about individuals under 13 years of age.

---

51 Kelly McBride, *To Tell the Stories of Sexual Assault Victims, it's Time for a New Look at Anonymity Policies*, Poynter, January 29, 2018, https://www.poynter.org/newsletters/2018/to-tell-the-stories-of-sexual-assault -victims-its-time-for-a-new-look-at-anonymity-policies.

As vaccines for COVID-19 became available following the global COVID crisis, and some schools, businesses, and other venues began requiring proof of vaccination (or evidence of a medical justification for not being vaccinated) as a condition of entry, social media became riddled with misunderstandings about the scope of HIPAA. Some who were opposed to vaccine mandates argued that requiring disclosure of an individual's vaccination status constituted a violation of their HIPAA rights. But it doesn't.

HIPAA applies only to "covered entities," which are specifically defined in the statute, and essentially comprise healthcare providers and insurance companies, as well as certain enterprises that support them. There is nothing in HIPAA that prevents private parties from requiring people to disclose certain health information as a condition of entry and nothing about HIPAA that prohibits the media from asking individuals to disclose information about their health or medical treatment. Of course, those individuals are free to decline providing such information, but it certainly isn't against the law to ask.

Although none of these privacy laws impose obligations or restrictions on the media directly, they have an impact on the media's ability to gather information, since many sources are bound by such laws.

For example, ambulance operators, hospitals, doctors, nurses, and related professionals are barred by HIPAA from disclosing detailed information about the medical condition of their patients. HIPAA does, however, permit the disclosure of the "general condition" of a patient, if asked for by name, unless the patient specifically asked that the information not be released.[52] That's why, for instance, statements by hospitals following casualty events will only say that a particular individual was brought to the hospital and is in "serious condition" or was "treated and released," or something similar.[53] Anything more than that would require the patient's permission.

FERPA offers another example of where journalists often run into challenges with gathering information. FERPA applies only to the disclosure of personally identifiable information about students that derives from records maintained by educational institutions. It does not prohibit school officials from discussing information based on their personal knowledge or observations of a particular student, nor does it prevent the disclosure of aggregated statistical information about students so long as the information is not identifiable to any particular student.

---

52 45 C.F.R. § 164.510(a).

53 *Id.* at 164.510(a)(1)(i). The law goes so far as to enumerate the standard categories that healthcare providers may use to describe a patient's condition: undetermined, good, fair, serious, critical, treated and released, or treated and transferred to another facility.

In a recent Pennsylvania case, a reporter at the *Philadelphia Inquirer* sought aggregated attendance records from the School District of Philadelphia under the state's Right to Know Law, a law that allows reporters and other members of the public to obtain certain information from government agencies (we discuss such laws more fully in Chapter 6). Even though the reporter sought data that was in aggregated form, impossible to associate with any one student, the district took the position that it was exempt from disclosure under FERPA.

The reporter appealed the decision to a state board charged with overseeing the Right to Know law which agreed with her position, but the school district appealed. In a brief filed in support of the reporter, a consortium of media organizations wrote that "[i]f schools are permitted to use FERPA to cloak de-identified data in secrecy, such data might never see the light of day, leaving the public in the dark about problems that could otherwise be addressed."[54]

In early 2022, the appellate court sided with the reporter and ordered the school district to comply with the trial court's original order.

IN THE NEWS: *DE HAVILLAND V. FX NETWORKS, LLC*

In 2017, actress Olivia de Havilland sued Pacific 2.1 Entertainment Group and FX Networks for their portrayal of her in the television miniseries *Feud: Bette and Joan*.[55] The series, a dramatization of the relationship between Bette Davis and Joan Crawford, featured Susan Sarandon as Davis, Jessica Lange as Crawford, and Catherine Zeta-Jones as de Havilland, who was a close friend of Davis. Upset with the portrayal, de Havilland sued, alleging that the producers misappropriated her likeness, and the use of her likeness in advertising the series was a violation of her rights of publicity. She also alleged that certain scenes portrayed her in a false light.

The defendants sought to dismiss de Havilland's claims under California's anti-SLAPP statute, but the trial court denied the motion. The defendants appealed and the appellate court reversed the trial court, effectively dismissing the case (the Supreme Court declined de Havilland's request to hear the case).[56]

MISAPPROPRIATION AND RIGHT OF PUBLICITY

In dismissing the misappropriation claim, the California Court of Appeal quoted liberally from *The Hurt Locker* case to conclude that *Feud* constitutes speech that is "fully

---

54 Br. Of Amici Curiae at 17, *School District of Philadelphia v. Calefati, et al.*, 1285 CD 2020).
55 *De Havilland v. FX Networks, LLC*, 230 Cal. Rptr. 3d 625 (Cal. Ct. App. 2018).
56 *De Havilland v. FX Networks, LLC*, 139 S.Ct. 800 (2019).

protected" by the First Amendment because the series "'marketability and economic value' does not derive primarily from de Havilland's fame but rather comes principally from ... the creativity, skill, and reputation of *Feud's* creators and actors."[57]

Regarding the fact that neither Pacific nor FX sought permission from de Havilland, the court observed that such permission, although often sought and obtained, is not necessarily legally required for expressive works:

> Producers of films and television programs may enter into agreements with individuals portrayed in those works for a variety of reasons, including access to the person's recollections or "story" the producers would not otherwise have, or a desire to avoid litigation for a reasonable fee. But the First Amendment simply does not require such acquisition agreements.[58]

The court also determined that using de Havilland's name and likeness in promotional announcements for the series did not violate her rights of publicity. Even though the announcements were commercial in nature in that they solicited the public to watch the show, the First Amendment protections that extend to the miniseries also extend to advertising and other promotional activities that are "merely ... adjunct" to the protected expressive content.[59]

> In the entertainment industry, it is not uncommon for production companies to secure agreements for an individual's "life rights," but as the court in *de Havilland* explains, such agreements are generally not required for expressive works. Still, it has become an industry practice to obtain such agreements, largely for the reasons that the court describes: they provide an "insurance policy" of sorts against potential litigation from the subjects of a particular expressive work, and they are often coupled with a consulting arrangement through which the producers are afforded direct access to the subject, which helps the creatives craft their vision more effectively than they might be able to do relying on public sources alone.

FALSE LIGHT

De Havilland based her false light claim on four separate scenes which, says de Havilland, make her look like she used crude and vulgar language about other people and is a gossipy hypocrite. The court considered the scenes in question, which accounted for a tiny fraction of the eight-hour miniseries, and concluded that no reasonable viewer would view the accounts as intended to be entirely factual. Even

---

57 *De Havilland*, 230 Cal. Rptr. 3d at 640.
58 *Id*. at 631.
59 *Id*. at 639.

if they did, said the court, the statements cannot be said to be defamatory or highly offensive to a reasonable person, as is required for a successful defamation claim.

The court noted that "[v]iewers are generally familiar with dramatized, fact-based movies and miniseries in which scenes, conversations, and even characters are fictionalized and imagined."[60] It went on to note that when considered in the context of the entire series, the portrayal of de Havilland is "overwhelmingly positive" and "the most favorable of any character in the docudrama."[61]

IN SUM

As the court noted in its succinct summary of its order:

> Books, films, plays, and television shows often portray real people. Some are famous and some are just ordinary folks. Whether a person portrayed in one of these expressive works is a world-renowned film star – "a living legend" – or a person no one knows, she or he does not own history. Nor does she or he have the legal right to control, dictate, approve, disapprove, or veto the creator's portrayal of actual people.[62]

De Havilland died in 2020 at the age of 104.

KEY POINTS AND TAKEAWAYS

1. In contrast to free speech principles, which are explicitly described in the First Amendment to the Constitution, privacy principles are said to exist in the "penumbras" of several amendments that, taken together, have led courts to develop a right of privacy.
2. Unlike defamation, where statements must be at least false to give rise to liability, even true statements can be actionable under the various privacy torts. The focus of privacy law is on the way the information was gathered, and the way that information is used. In most cases, the standard is whether the use is "highly offensive" to a reasonable person.
3. When dealing with the likenesses of real individuals, media producers should take care to understand the nature of their work and the rights required. For example, purely *expressive* works are protected by the First Amendment, while *commercial* works may implicate an individual's right of publicity and may require licensing.
4. Although it is common practice in the entertainment industry to secure "life rights" agreements for works that are based on real-life individuals, such agreements are generally not required but could be advisable as a hedge against

---

60 *Id.* at 643.
61 *Id.* at 644.
62 *Id.* at 630.

potential litigation or to secure access to individuals and information that may not be generally accessible to the public.

5. Where media producers develop expressive works based on real-life individuals, it is advisable to include a disclaimer to protect against potential claims. Following the *Feud* case, FX Networks used the following language: "This series is inspired by true events and investigative reports. Some events are combined or imagined for dramatic and interpretive purposes. Dialogue is imagined to be consistent with these events."

6. Data privacy is an emerging and rapidly growing area of law that will have profound effects on the way internet-based distributors of content interact with their consumers. As more traditional media enterprises look to electronic distribution mechanisms (e.g., streaming services), they will need to become more conversant on data privacy issues.

QUESTIONS FOR DISCUSSION

1. The standard in most privacy torts is that the conduct at issue must be "highly offensive." Is that the right standard?

2. Why do you suppose some states have declined to recognize false light invasion of privacy as a distinct tort? Can you think of circumstances where a claim may be actionable as false light invasion of privacy but not as defamation?

3. The personal data that are used to make data-driven production decisions, drive recommendation engines, and for targeted advertising discussed in this chapter are often justified as being favorable to consumers. Do you agree? Is giving up a certain degree of privacy, or control of your personal data, worth it for improved media or entertainment options?

6

CHAPTER 6
NEWSGATHERING

How far can a media enterprise go to "get the story?" Do the media enjoy any special protections or expanded limits? Should they? What protections exist for "confidential" sources?

This chapter examines the various legal limits on a journalist's ability to report on a story and protect the identity of their sources of information.

THE LIMITS OF NEWSGATHERING

Recall from Chapter 3 that in addition to the right to speak freely, the First Amendment also protects the public's right to receive information which, the Supreme Court has said is "fundamental to our free society."[1] Notwithstanding the importance of access to information in our democracy, and the role that journalists and the media play in getting that information distributed, it is widely understood that merely being engaged in a journalistic enterprise does not immunize reporters and other members of the press from laws of general application. Put differently, it is no defense to an allegation of, say, trespassing, that the perpetrator was engaged in some journalistic enterprise.

There are a number of related laws that have an impact on the way journalists gather information.

TRESPASSING

Generally speaking, the media has a right to report on, photograph, or record anything that is readily accessible from a public location. The media may not, however, enter private land without the permission of the landowner. Conversely, owners are free to deny access to their property, even to journalists. Indeed, many commercial properties do just that. Most office buildings, shopping centers, and the like prohibit the media from accessing their property without permission (or sometimes more specifically, prohibit the use of audio or video recording). Accessing such property without permission is considered trespassing.

The media may, however, report freely from public locations surrounding private space, such as sidewalks, and are even free to aim their cameras toward private property, so long as all they capture or report on is viewable from that public vantage

---

1 *Stanley v. Georgia*, 394 U.S. 557, 564 (1969).

DOI: 10.4324/9781003197966-6

point. For instance, it would be permissible (and is quite common) for reporters and photographers to stand on the sidewalk outside of an office building, shopping mall, or some other location that will not allow cameras on its own property.

The media is also generally free to report from public accommodations such as airports and train stations, subject to certain limitations. For instance, entertainment news reporters regularly approach celebrities at Los Angeles International Airport (LAX), which they are permitted to do because LAX's media guidelines, like those of most major commercial airports, provide that journalists are welcome to report from

Los Angeles World Airports Media Guide
UPDATED JANUARY 2022

Contacting LAX PR

The LAX Public Relations staff is available to assist reporters 365 days a year, with resources available for emergencies or breaking news 24 hours a day.

Business Hours
(Monday - Friday 9 a.m. to 5 p.m.) Please contact the main Public Relations number at *424-646-5260*

After Hours / Emergencies
Please contact the on-duty public information officer by calling *424-646-5430.**

*Please note that this line is reserved for breaking news or emergencies. Please do not distribute this number to members of the public. If the PIO is not available to answer your call, leave a detailed message and it will be returned in the order it was received. Routine media requests should be directed to the main office during normal business hours.

Recorded Media Line
LAX Public Relations maintains a recorded media line, available by calling 424-646-5227. This line is updated during irregular operations or significant incidents with the latest information for media use.

Follow LAX

LAX provides frequently updated information about airport operations and projects on its website, FlyLAX.com.

LAX is very active on social media. During a breaking news situation, **Twitter** (@FlyLAXairport) is the airport's default platform for official, updated information as it becomes available.

Real-time parking and traffic information at LAX is available by following @FlyLAXstats on Twitter.

Updated information about the airport's modernization program, including fact sheets, videos and construction photos, is available at FlyLAX.com/ConnectingLAX

Rules & Regulations

Journalists are welcome to conduct reporting, filming or photography within public areas of the airport as long as they do not disrupt passenger flow or otherwise impede airport operations, tenants or passengers.

- Vehicle and pedestrian traffic may not be altered.

- Intermittent traffic control is not allowed.

- Lights, reflectors or other equipment must be handheld or on a tripod that does not impede the normal flow of pedestrians or other airport operations.

- Power cables may not be placed along the ground.

- Tripods cannot be placed within a roadway or block doors, escalators or other conveyances.

- Canopies or other tent covers are not allowed

Any access to the sterile area or other non-public areas of the airport must be requested through the LAX Public Relations office by calling 424-646-5260 during business hours

Advance notice of at least 24 hours is required for most special requests to be considered. Special requests are considered on a case-by-case basis based on overall impact to the airport and staff resources.

All journalists must follow the instructions of Los Angeles Airport Police, Los Angeles Fire Department or LAX Operations at all times.

Filming within the gate areas, concessions or other leased spaces is not allowed without the permission of the leaseholders. TSA Public Affairs must approve any filming of the TSA checkpoints in advance. U.S. Customs and Border Protection must approve any filming within customs areas in advance.

Parking At LAX

LAX is in a period of significant construction, which has reduced curbside access. While the airport recognizes the need for additional designated media parking, designated press parking is currently limited by ongoing construction to protect the safety of reporters and maintain airport operations, and is subject to change.

All media vehicles parking at designated press parking locations are required to display a current LAX parking permit. These permits are available by application to LAX Public Relations by contacting us during regular business hours.

The following locations are currently reserved for media permit parking:

1. **Upper/Departures Level curbside between Terminal 3 and Tom Bradley International Terminal***

2. **Upper/Departures Level curbside east of Terminal 7/8**

3. **LAX-it pick-up lot, north side on raised concrete area*** (Enter the LAX-it lot on the west side using Sky Way. Use the bus entrance to enter the lot and pull onto the raised concrete area on the right side before you enter the row of buses).

    * Vehicles may be left unattended. Drivers MUST call Airport Police Watch Commander at (424) 646-6100 AND MUST leave cell phone numbers in plain view next to the permits.

4. **All media vehicles may park in Central Terminal Area Parking Structures 1 and 7 for free up to eight (8) hours with validation** from the security desk in the lobby of the Los Angeles World Airports Administration Building at: **One World Way** (Monday - Friday 6 a.m. to 9 p.m.)

Validation is currently unavailable in parking structures 2a, 2b, 3, 4, 5 and 6 because of recent automation related to construction activities. If your parking ticket is not validated, you must pay for parking.

Please note that law enforcement or fire officials may ask media at any time to yield a designated media parking area temporarily for emergency response use. Media vehicles may not park in curbside zones or parking slots designated by signage for public ground transportation services, for vehicles displaying Americans With Disabilities Act (i.e., wheelchair) placards and license plates, nor adjacent to fire hydrants or in front of any terminal entrance/exit doors.

LAWA
LOS ANGELES WORLD AIRPORTS
LAWA.org | FlyLAX.com

Figure 6.1 Los Angeles World Airports' Media Guide.

the airport so long as they do not get in the way of passengers or airport operations. Reporting from public locations, but failing to follow the rules, may also be considered trespassing in certain circumstances.

We briefly discussed trespassing in Chapter 5 because of its nexus to intrusion upon seclusion. Under most states' laws, trespassing is the unlawful intrusion or invasion of a property, with intent to be there, with some injury to the property owner. In some states, the injury is the mere fact that an unwanted individual is on the owner's property; in others, the harm may flow from the resulting report from the unauthorized location (as is the case in the following *Food Lion v. ABC* discussion). Trespass is typically actionable as a tort but may also be treated as a criminal violation.

WIRETAPPING

Wiretapping refers to the use of devices to intercept or monitor private communications without the knowledge or consent of at least one party to the communication. Although most commonly applied to phone calls, laws against wiretapping also apply to the unauthorized interception of e-mail. At the federal level, wiretapping is governed primarily by the Electronic Communications Privacy Act,[2] which updated the previous wiretapping statute, passed in 1968, to include various forms of electronic communication.

In addition to the federal prohibitions on wiretapping, most states have their own wiretapping laws that may be more restrictive than the federal rules. Indeed, several states have adopted what is called an **all-party consent** or **multi-party consent** approach to wiretapping, which requires that the person intercepting or recording the communication must have the consent of not just one party, as the federal law requires, but *all* parties to the communication.

This distinction is important to journalists primarily in the context of recording conversations or interactions with sources or other interview subjects. In states that follow the federal rule, so-called **single-party consent** states, it is generally permissible for one party to a conversation to be recording it even if the others are not aware, while in multi-party consent states, it is illegal to make such recordings if the participants had a reasonable expectation that the conversation was private.

The state laws on this topic are varied, and even in single-party consent states, there are often myriad exceptions and provisions often detailing the circumstances under which the recordings are made and how they may be used. You should check with a lawyer experienced in media law issues before engaging in any kind of surreptitious recording to ensure compliance with the relevant state laws.

---

2 Pub. L. 99–508 (1986).

Using hidden camera footage is a popular newsgathering technique, especially among investigative journalists looking to catch people engaged in questionable or improper conduct. In states with multi-party consent laws, however, making or using such recordings will generally be illegal if the recordings are made where the parties have a reasonable expectation of privacy. Even in single-party consent states, there may still be nuances or exceptions to the wiretapping laws that impact a journalist's ability to use hidden cameras. Such laws often apply the "reasonable expectation of privacy" standard that we discussed in Chapter 5 in determining whether a particular use of hidden cameras is lawful.

REFUSAL TO FOLLOW LAWFUL ORDERS AND DISORDERLY CONDUCT

Refusal to comply with lawful orders and **disorderly conduct** are "catch-all" charges often used by police as a mechanism of crowd control at large gatherings and events and are also sometimes used to prevent people from gathering around crime scenes, accident scenes, mass casualty events, and the like. Although law enforcement agencies often give journalists more latitude than members of the general public when attempting to disperse a crowd, that's not always the case.

In May 2021, for instance, two reporters were arrested while covering a 50-person protest for an unarmed black man that had been killed by police. The reporters were arrested while live streaming the arrest of another protester on Twitter. Asked why

Figure 6.2 Interfering with police or failing to follow their instructions during protests, marches, or other mass gatherings can sometimes lead to arrest.

they were being arrested, police responded it was for "standing in the middle of the street in the roadway."[3] Both were released later the same evening.

HARASSMENT AND STALKING

Generally, approaching someone in a public place, calling them directly, or sending them an e-mail and asking for an interview or to obtain information for a report is entirely lawful, even if the person isn't especially happy to be hearing from the media. But go too far, and journalists could find themselves accused of harassment or stalking.

Harassment and stalking are primarily enforced at the state level, and each jurisdiction has its own definitions, though generally **harassment** involves an ongoing pattern of conduct intended to annoy, alarm, or terrorize another person, such that the person suffers emotional distress. **Stalking** is more serious, involving a pattern of conduct that would cause a reasonable person to fear for their safety generally, or that they are in reasonably imminent danger of death or bodily harm. Stalking often includes following or engaging in surveillance against that person for the purpose of scaring them.

As you can see, harassment and stalking each require a pattern of conduct, so merely asking for an interview, or following a subject for the purpose of a report or journalistic exercise, is unlikely to rise to the level of either cause of action. But repeatedly hounding someone for an interview, or attempting to scare or cajole them into participating, could lead to such charges.

Perhaps you have heard of Borat Sagdyev, a fictional Kazakhstani journalist played by comedian Sacha Baron Cohen. In 2009, he released a mockumentary entitled *Borat! Cultural Learnings of America for Make Benefit Glorious Nation of Kazakhstan*, and in 2020, released the sequel *Borat Subsequent Moviefilm*. In the films, Cohen's schtick is to interview people believing that he is a legitimate journalist, often mischaracterizing the nature of the interview, asking embarrassing questions, or otherwise putting the interview subject in a position of looking foolish or otherwise vulnerable.

Given what we know about fraud and false light invasion of privacy? How is Cohen able to get away with it?

Cohen has been sued in the past by some of his interview subjects, but he has yet to lose. The reason? Cohen and his production team use strong appearance releases that grant them the right to use the footage notwithstanding whatever

---

3 Elinor Aspegren, *Two USA Today Network Reporters Arrested, Release After Covering Andrew Brown Jr. Protest*, USA Today, May 20, 2021, available at https://www.msn.com/en-us/news/crime/two-usa-today-network-reporters-arrested-released-after-covering-andrew-brown-jr-protest/ar-AAKb3dU.

sleight of hand may have been used to secure the interview and immunizes them from litigation for the various privacy torts we discussed in Chapter 5.

Portions of one of the releases made an appearance in an Alabama Supreme Court decision, and it provides that: "[t]he participant agrees to be filmed and audiotaped for a documentary-style film … It is understood that the Producer hopes to reach a young adult audience by using entertaining content and formats."[4] The release also grants the producer the exclusive right to "use … any recorded material that includes the Participant without restriction in any media throughout the universe in perpetuity and without liability to the Participant, and the Participant hereby grants any consents required for those purposes."

FRAUD

Fraud occurs when a defendant makes a representation of a material fact, knowing it is false, with the intent to induce the person to whom the representation is made into taking some action that they then undertake, relying on the representation to their detriment, resulting in an injury. Fraud is actionable as a tort, and if certain thresholds for harm are met, it can result in criminal charges as well.

For media enterprises, fraud allegations could arise if journalists, producers, or other employees make misrepresentations to induce someone to participate in an interview that they might not otherwise have agreed to if they knew the intended purpose or to gain access to a location that would not otherwise have been made available to the public or journalists specifically.

Unfortunately, it is more common for reporters to be the victims of harassment or stalking than the perpetrators, due to the public nature of the work. For example, in 2021, a former seminary professor was charged with stalking a local television investigative reporter who had been working on an investigation into allegations of clerical sexual abuse. The professor allegedly made 11 phone calls to the reporter, including a death threat and accusations that his reporting had caused the seminary to be shut down.[5] The former professor entered into a plea agreement with the prosecution and was sentenced to a year in prison.[6]

4 *Ex parte Cohen*, 988 So.2d 508, 510 (Ala. 2008).
5 *See* Pete Madden, *Teacher at Buffalo Seminary Charged with Threatening Reporter Who Investigated Church*, ABC News, February 12, 2020, https://abcnews.go.com/US/teacher-buffalo-seminary-charged-threatening -reporter-investigated-church/story?id=68943736.
6 Jeff Tims, *Hamburg Man Going to Prison for Stalking a Local News Reporter*, Shore News Network, November 9, 2021, https://www.shorenewsnetwork.com/2021/11/09/hamburg-man-going-to-prison-for-stalking-a -local-news-reporter.

A CAUTIONARY TALE: *FOOD LION V. ABC*

Fraud was among the various claims brought against ABC News in one of the most widely cited cases about the limits of newsgathering. In 1992, ABC News sent two of its reporters to a Food Lion supermarket in North Carolina to investigate allegations that the store was repackaging and selling out-of-date found beef.[7] Rather than appear as reporters, however, the ABC employees applied for jobs with Food Lion, using false names, addresses, and references, and without reference to the fact that they also worked for a television network. Food Lion hired the pair, one as a meat wrapper, the other as a deli clerk. In addition to performing their ordinary duties they also secretly:

> used tiny cameras ("lipstick" cameras, for example) and microphones concealed on their bodies to secretly record Food Lion employees treating, wrapping and labeling meat, cleaning machinery, and discussing the practices of the meat department. They gathered footage from the meat cutting room, the deli counter, the employee break room, and a manager's office.[8]

During the brief course of their employment (one reporter stayed for two weeks; the other for just one), the duo recorded approximately 45 hours of footage, much of which was from areas of the store that would not have been accessible to the reporters but for their misrepresentation. Some of that footage was subsequently used in a report on ABC's *Primetime Live* news magazine program. The broadcast footage:

> appeared to show Food Lion employees repackaging and redating fish that had passed the expiration date, grinding expired beef with fresh beef, and applying barbecue sauce to chicken past its expiration date in order to mask the smell and sell it as fresh in the gourmet food section. The program included statements by former Food Lion employees alleging even more serious mishandling of met at Food Lion stores across several states.[9]

After the segment aired, Food Lion sued ABC, but not for defamation. Instead, it alleged fraud, breach of the duty of loyalty, trespass, and unfair trade practices. Following a trial, the jury found ABC liable for fraud, and the two individual producers liable for breach of the duty of loyalty and trespass. Interestingly, however, the jury awarded Food Lion only $1,400 in compensatory damages for its fraud claim, and only $1.00 each for its duty of loyalty and trespass claims, but more than $5.5 million in punitive damages.[10] That suggests the jury's goal was to punish ABC for its unscrupulous practices, but not necessarily reward Food Lion, whose own deceptive

---

7 *Food Lion, Inc. v. Capital Cities/ABC, Inc.*, 194 F.3d 505, 510 (4th Cir. 1999).
8 *Id.* at 510–11.
9 *Id.*
10 *Id.* at 512.

practices raised serious questions about food safety, which likely would not have been known but for ABC's conduct.

> The duty of loyalty is a common-law legal doctrine that requires employees to act in the best interest of their employers. Allegations of breach of the duty of loyalty most commonly arise when an employee either operates a side business or is assisting another business that competes with their primary employer.

> In most states, employers are required to indemnify and defend their employees for lawsuits arising out of their employment. Although the indemnity obligations usually do not apply to unlawful conduct, such as trespassing, here, because the reporters engaged in the unlawful conduct at the behest of their employer, it is very likely that ABC covered the cost of the reporters' legal defense as well as the damages award, even though the two were named as individual defendants, along with ABC.

Notwithstanding the jury's determination, the court found the punitive damages award excessive and reduced it to $315,000 through a process called **remittitur**. Both parties appealed and the appeals court ultimately reversed the fraud claim and the punitive damages because Food Lion had failed to establish it had been harmed by ABC's fraudulent conduct; it allowed the breach of loyalty and trespass claims to stand.

The *Food Lion v. ABC* case is a cautionary tale for investigative journalists. Even though newsgathering and reporting have been recognized as essential to our form of democracy, reporters are not immunized from laws of general applicability just because they are engaged in a journalistic enterprise. As a practical matter, running afoul of the law can be enormously expensive. Although the court ultimately dismissed the significant punitive damages award against ABC, the case very likely cost the network millions of dollars in legal fees to get to that point and required ABC's employees to commit considerable time dealing with the case – time and money that would have no doubt been better spent on new journalism endeavors.

USING INFORMATION OBTAINED UNLAWFULLY

Although the law is clear that having a journalistic purpose is no defense to unlawful conduct, the Supreme Court has held that there is a First Amendment right to publish information gained through illicit means, provided that the publisher was not involved in the unlawful conduct.

In *Bartnicki v. Vopper*,[11] talk radio host Frederick Vopper broadcast portions of an illegally intercepted telephone call between two teachers' union officials who were involved in contentious negotiations with a local school board. Vopper obtained the recording from the head of a local taxpayers' organization opposed to the union, Jack Yocum, who found the tape in his mailbox and was apparently unaware of who left it there.

Gloria Bartnicki, the union's lead negotiator was one of the people whose voice was recorded on the call. She sued Vopper and Yocum claiming that they "knew or had reason to know" that the recording of the phone call had been made illegally and that Yocum should never have given a copy to Vopper, and Vopper never should have put it on the air.

Whoever made the recording almost certainly violated the Electronic Communications Privacy Act. The open question for the Court was whether it was unlawful for Yocum and Vopper, who themselves had obtained the recording lawfully, to use it knowing that it had been made unlawfully. Quoting one of its earlier decisions, the Court observed that "'state action to punish the publication of truthful information can seldom satisfy constitutional standards'"[12] and recited its holding that "'if a newspaper lawfully obtains truthful information about a matter of public significance, then state officials may not constitutionally punish publication of the information, absent a need … of the highest order.'"[13]

The court then applied that precedent to the facts of the Bartnicki matter and determined that the state interest in punishing the surreptitious recording of phone calls did not outweigh the public interest in disseminating truthful information about the school district's negotiations with the teachers' union and concluded that the ECPA could not be used to punish Yocum and Vopper.[14]

The upshot for journalists is that they are generally free to publish information obtained legally, even if the information was originally obtained through illegal means, provided the journalist was not involved and provided its disclosure advances some public interest.

Journalists should take great care, however, to not become ensnared in, aware of, or familiar with the criminal enterprises of their sources. If a journalist can be said to have participated in any way in the unlawful conduct of his or her sources, then they could face liability for aiding and abetting the crime or serving as an accessory to it.

---

11 532 U.S. 514 (2001)
12 *Id.* at 527 (quoting *Smith v. Daily Mail Publishing Co.*, 443 U.S. 97, 102 (1979)).
13 *Id.* at 528 (quoting *Smith*, 443 U.S. at 103).
14 *Id.* at 535.

NEWSGATHERING WITH DRONES

Media organizations, particularly television stations, have long used helicopters in the course of news gathering. Indeed, hardly a day goes by in the Los Angeles area without a televised police pursuit. But helicopters have significant operating limits due to their size, noise, and cost. In recent years, advances in unmanned aircraft systems – drones – have made the technology a cheaper and more efficient way of gathering news, or simply capturing images from the air.

Drones have also become commonplace in other industries such as agriculture, real estate, and infrastructure inspection and maintenance. Many people also fly drones as a hobby. As a result, drones have become somewhat ubiquitous in modern society, leading to more regulation of when, where, and how drones can be used, including how journalists use them for newsgathering.

FEDERAL LICENSING CONSIDERATIONS

The Federal Aviation Administration (FAA), part of the Department of Transportation, is the agency that has oversight over all civil aviation in the United States. The FAA's regulations require that anyone operating a drone for commercial purposes, which is defined broadly as essentially anything other than recreational use, has a "remote pilot license." That means that journalists using drones in the course of their news gathering must be licensed by the FAA.

There are four basic requirements to become a licensed remote pilot:

1. Be at least 16 years old;
2. Be able to read, write, speak, and understand the English language;
3. Be in acceptable physical and mental condition to safely fly a drone;
4. Pass a two-hour FAA knowledge test comprising 60 multiple-choice questions; and
5. Pass a background investigation conducted by the Transportation Security Administration.

The knowledge test is administered by authorized FAA test centers around the country and covers airspace classifications, operating requirements, flight restrictions, weather considerations, emergency procedures, and aeronautical decision making and judgment. There are numerous books and online courses that can help prepare you for the exam.

Beyond the pilot's licensure, drones used for commercial purposes must be registered with the FAA, just like all other commercial aircraft. Registration costs a nominal fee and is easily accomplished through the FAA's website. The drone owner must affix the registration number to the drone, which helps identify it in the event it ever gets lost (and presumably also helps the FAA identify who is responsible if a drone shows up where it shouldn't be).

STATE CONSIDERATIONS

The Supreme Court has held that individuals do not have a reasonable expectation of privacy in the publicly accessible, navigable airspace above their property.[15] The court noted that although there may be circumstances where flying over someone's private property can give rise to a privacy violation, generally, people are aware that planes, helicopters, and other aircraft routinely pass above and that their property is viewable from that vantage point, negating any reasonable expectation of privacy.[16]

Still, a number of states have begun attempting to regulate the use of drones, especially over private property. Texas, for example, has one of the more restrictive drone laws in the country, which renders it unlawful to "capture an image of an individual or privately owned real property … with the intent to conduct surveillance on the individual or property captured in the image."[17]

The law goes on to provide several enumerated exceptions, many of which are extremely specific. For example, images captured by satellite for the purpose of mapping[18] or by the owner or operator of oil, gas, water, or other pipelines for inspection or maintenance[19] are excluded from the law's broad prohibition. None of the exclusions can be fairly characterized as applying to journalists or for the purposes of newsgathering.

Violations are subject to misdemeanor criminal penalties as well as potential civil liability to the owner of the property (or a tenant) over which a drone is flown illegally.

Another part of the law, the so-called "no fly" provisions, impose misdemeanor criminal sanctions for flying drones over correctional facilities, critical infrastructure facilities,[20] and sports venues,[21] although the prohibition excludes drone flights performed for a commercial purpose provided they otherwise comply with applicable FAA regulations.

In 2019, photographer Joseph Pappalardo, backed by the Texas Press Association and the National Press Photographers Association, sued the State of Texas to invalidate the drone law, alleging that the surveillance provisions are impermissible content- and speaker-based restrictions on speech because the exemptions are based on the purpose

15 *Florida v. Riley*, 488 U.S. 445, 450 (1989).
16 *Id.* at 451.
17 Texas Government Code § 423.003.
18 *Id.* at § 423.002(4).
19 *Id.* at § 423.002(16).
20 *Id.* at § 423.0045.
21 *Id.* at § 423.0046.

for which an image is captured or used, and because the surveillance provision is vague and overbroad because the term "surveillance" is not defined.[22] The plaintiffs also alleged that the no fly provisions are vague and overbroad because the term "commercial purpose" is not defined and is often construed to exclude newsgathering.[23]

In March of 2022, the court ruled in favor of the plaintiffs, finding that the law was a content-based restriction on speech and were not narrowly tailored to achieve the government's stated purpose. The court also agreed that parts of the statute were unconstitutionally vague.[24]

PROFESSIONAL CONSIDERATIONS

In addition to the legal issues, drone journalists should be aware of the Drone Journalism Code of Ethics that was developed collaboratively by the National Press Photographers Association, the Society of Professional Journalists, and the Radio and Television Digital News Association. You can find a full copy at https://nppa.org/sites /default/files/Done%20Code%20of%20Ethics.pdf, but its key provisions are:

1. Safety is the first concern. Do not endanger people, animals, or property;
2. Newsrooms should not encourage others to fly illegally;
3. Ask "Would you 'do that' if you were capturing the image while on the ground?";
4. Respect privacy;
5. Respect the integrity of the photographic moment;
6. Do not improperly enhance the resulting image or video;
7. Newsrooms should recognize that the pilot in command makes the decision about whether a flight can be accomplished safely;
8. Drone-journalism pilots in command should not be expected to report or perform other duties while commanding an aircraft;
9. Drone journalists have an obligation to hone their flight skills and "stay sharp";
10. Coach others to be responsible and follow the rules. As the Code says "[t]he public's perception of drone flights depends on how professionally pilots operate in these early days of this emerging technology."

PROTECTING JOURNALISTS' SOURCES

The relationship between journalists and their sources is among the most sacrosanct in the entire profession, and it is widely understood that for journalism to work effectively, journalists must commit to keeping the identity of their sources confidential unless the source is willing to be identified publicly.

---

22 *National Press Photographers Association v. McCraw*, 504 F.Supp.3d 568, 574 (W.D. Tx. 2020).
23 *Id.* at 575.
24 *National Press Photographers Association v. McCraw*, 2022 WL 939517 (W.D. Tex. 2022).

The theory behind this longstanding journalistic practice is that sources would be less likely to disclose to journalists sensitive or confidential information about matters of public importance if they might face retribution or retaliation. And if sources are unwilling to speak with journalists, it becomes more difficult for the media to serve their role as the "fourth estate" or "government watchdog."

Put more succinctly, assuring sources' confidentiality is an essential part of a journalist's or media enterprise's role to report on matters of public importance.

Journalists who breach a confidential source's trust are said to have "burned" their source, and journalists known for such conduct are often ostracized from the industry.

COMPELLED DISCLOSURE

In the U.S. legal system, parties may be compelled to testify or provide documents in court by way of a **subpoena**, which is essentially a court order issued by the clerk of the court upon the request of one of the parties to a dispute. A party who receives a subpoena must appear in court or produce the requested material within a period of time specified by the court, or else they will be considered in **contempt of court**, which can be handled either civilly or criminally.

Criminal contempt is punishable by a fine or imprisonment, while **civil contempt** is not itself a crime, but it allows a judge to detain a subpoenaed individual indefinitely until they comply with the subpoena. Thus, "civil contempt" is somewhat oddly named since it can result in a journalist being incarcerated despite the lack of a criminal conviction or pending prosecution.

Perhaps one of the most widely publicized instances of a reporter being jailed for contempt was in 2005 when *The New York Times* reporter Judy Miller served nearly 90 days in jail for refusing to testify before a federal grand jury in connection with the outing of CIA spy Valerie Plame. She eventually relented after getting permission from her source, who turned out to be Lewis "Scooter" Libby. He was never charged for the leak but was convicted of lying to investigators. His sentence was commuted by President Bush and he was later pardoned by President Trump.

There are various ways to cancel or **quash** a subpoena that renders it unenforceable. One such way is to invoke a **legal privilege** that protects the contents of the documents or testimony sought by the subpoena. A privilege in this context is legal protection against being compelled to disclose certain information in court.

Among the more common privileges is the attorney–client privilege, which protects confidential communications between an attorney and her client. Because of the privilege, the attorney may not be compelled to testify about the subject matter of conversations that she has with her client, provided the conversations were confidential. Without such a rule, clients may not be willing to have honest, forthcoming conversations with their lawyers. Similarly, in most states, communications between doctors and their patients are privileged, as are communications between spouses.

REPORTER'S PRIVILEGE

Despite the longstanding professional practice of maintaining source confidentiality, the law recognizes it only to a limited degree, putting journalists at some risk when they make such commitments. The germ of a **reporter's privilege** dates back to the 1972 Supreme Court case *Branzburg v. Hays*,[25] in which the court held that the First Amendment does not immunize journalists from being hailed before grand juries to disclose the identities of their confidential sources.[26]

But in a concurring opinion, Justice Powell observed that although the facts of the case compelled such a result, that might not always be the case and that the court should not permit journalists to be forced to testify on matters "bearing only a remote and tenuous relationship to the subject of an investigation"[27] or where the disclosure of confidential information lacks a "legitimate need of law enforcement."[28]

In a dissenting opinion, Justice Stewart, joined by Justices Brennan and Marshall, argued that the government should have to establish three elements before forcing a journalist to testify: (1) show probable cause that the journalist has information that is "clearly relevant to a *precisely* defined subject of governmental inquiry";[29] (2) that it is reasonable to think that the journalist has that information; and (3) that there is no means of obtaining the information that is "less destructive of First Amendment liberties."[30]

Although the statements in the concurring and dissenting opinions are not binding, the concepts described in them have become guideposts for journalists and their lawyers arguing against compelled disclosure of confidential source information.

SHIELD LAWS

Although there is no broad constitutional protection for journalists and their sources, most states have enacted some form of a **shield law** that specifically provides statutory reporter's privilege. The degree of protection varies by state and journalists should take some time to understand the parameters of the law in the state(s) where they work. The Reporters Committee for Freedom of the Press has compiled a Reporter's Privilege Compendium, available at www.rcfp.org/reporters-privilege/

----

25 408 U.S. 665 (1972).
26 *Id.* at 690.
27 *Id.* at 710.
28 *Id.*
29 *Id.* at 740.
30 *Id.*

that summarizes the material portions of each state's law and is a good place to start to find the law in your jurisdiction.

California's shield law is known for being among the most protective in the country, in part because it has been incorporated into the state's constitution.[31] The California statute provides that:

(a) A publisher, editor, reporter, or other person connected with or employed upon a newspaper, magazine, or other periodical publication, or by a press association or wire service, or any person who has been so connected or employed, cannot be adjudged in contempt by a judicial, legislative, administrative body, or any other body having the power to issue subpoenas, for refusing to disclose, in any proceeding … the source of any information procured while so connected or employed for publication in a newspaper, magazine or other periodical publication, or for refusing to disclose any unpublished information obtained or prepared in gathering, receiving or processing of information for communication to the public.

(b) Nor can a radio or television news reporter or other person connected with or employed by a radio or television station, or any person who has been so connected or employed, be so adjudged in contempt for refusing to disclose the source of any information procured while so connected or employed for news or news commentary purposes on radio or television, or for refusing to disclose any unpublished information obtained or prepared in gathering, receiving or processing of information for communication to the public.

(c) As used in this section, "unpublished information" includes information not disseminated to the public by the person from whom disclosure is sought, whether or not related information has been disseminated and includes, but is not limited to, all notes, outtakes, photographs, tapes or other data of whatever sort not itself disseminated to the public through a medium of communication, whether or not published information based upon or related to such material has been disseminated.[32]

APPLYING SHIELD LAWS TO NEW FORMS OF MEDIA

Notice that paragraphs (a) and (b) of the California law restrict the law to those working for traditional or "legacy" media organizations – that is, newspapers, magazines, press associations, wire services, radio and television stations, or press associations. This language illustrates a growing concern among some journalists about the scope

31 *See* Cal. Const., Art. I, § 2(b).
32 Cal. Evidence Code § 1070.

of current reporter's privilege protections. Laws that expressly include certain types of media raise questions about the extent to which new forms of journalism, such as blogging or podcasting, are covered by existing laws.

In Nevada, for instance, a state trial court denied a blogger protection of the state shield law because he was not a member of a press association and because his blog was not printed in physical form and therefore did not constitute a newspaper, as required by the statute.[33] The Nevada Supreme Court reversed, concluding that even though the Nevada legislature could not have contemplated a newspaper existing in digital form when it enacted the shield law, the court determined that it could consider advances in technology when construing a statute, and held that "a blog should not be disqualified from the news shield statute … merely on the basis that the blog is digital, rather than appearing in an ink-printed, physical form."[34] The court declined broader guidance on whether blogs should be considered "newspapers."

Although the court ultimately held that the blogger was entitled to the protection of the shield law in this instance, the fact that the trial court initially thought differently underscores the challenges that journalists may face when reporting for more modern distribution platforms that were not in existence when most shield laws were created.

Merely adding online journalists to existing laws may seem like an easy fix, but some are concerned that expanding the scope of such protections to anyone who posts anything online could cause political blowback resulting in a narrowing of shield laws for everybody.[35]

FEDERAL REPORTER'S PRIVILEGE

There is no federal shield law, which means even in states where there is a robust reporter's privilege under state law, a journalist may still be compelled to testify in federal proceedings.

There have been attempts at establishing a federal shield law over the years, the most recent of which is the Protect Reporters from Exploitative State Spying Act (the "PRESS Act") that was introduced by Maryland Representative Jamie Raskin in 2021.[36] An earlier version of the bill had been introduced previously as the Free Flow of Information Act.[37]

33 *Toll v. Wilson*, 453 P.3d 1215 (Nev. 2019).

34 *Id.* at 1219.

35 *See, e.g.*, Reporters Committee for Freedom of the Press, *Two Recent Cases Highlight Tension in Applying Shield Law to New Media*, available at https://www.rcfp.org/journals/news-media-and-law-summer-2011/two-recent-cases-highlight/.

36 H.R. 4330, 117th Cong., 1st Sess. (2021).

37 H.R. 4382, 115th Cong., 1st Sess. (2017).

The bill aims to protect journalists from being compelled to disclose the identity of their sources or newsgathering materials unless the government can show that the disclosure of information is necessary to prevent an act of terrorism (or to identify a terrorist) or a threat of imminent violence, bodily harm, or death.[38] The bill also restricts government access to journalists' phone and internet records unless a court determines that there is a reasonable threat of imminent violence.[39]

The 2017 version of the bill was more restrictive, requiring that the government first exhaust "all reasonable alternative sources" before seeking to compel a journalist to disclose information.[40] The 2017 version also contained a balancing test, requiring that in addition to the standards described previously, the government show that the public interest in compelling the disclosure by the journalist outweighs the public interest in gathering or disseminating news or information.[41]

Both versions of the bill would extend their protections only to professional journalists, defined as those who regularly gather or report news or information concerning local, national, or international events or other matters of public interest for dissemination to the public for a substantial portion of the person's livelihood or substantial financial gain.

As of this writing, there has been little movement on Rep. Raskin's bill since it was introduced in July 2021.

You have probably heard journalists talk about interviewing people "off the record" or "on background." Those terms have little legal significance but have become standards among journalists and their sources. A source speaking to a reporter **off the record**, for instance, means that the reporter is not allowed to use the information disclosed by the source, whereas a conversation **on background** means that the journalist is free to use the information so long as she does not identify the source. A conversation that is **not for attribution** is one where the journalist may quote the information, but not identify the source by name, only by more generic identifying characteristics such as a general title or description of the source's relationship to the story (e.g., "a source close to the investigation" or "a senior government official"). An **on the record** conversation is the most open discussion a journalist may have with a source. Such conversations are free to be quoted and used without restriction.

Both journalists and their sources need to understand the ground rules before engaging in an interview or exchanging documents.

---

38 H.R. 4330 at § 3.
39 *Id.* at § 4.
40 H.R. 4382 at § 2(a)(1).
41 H.R. 4382 at § 2(a)(4).

THIRD-PARTY SUBPOENAS

One of the key features of the PRESS Act is a limitation on the government's ability to seek information from phone companies and internet service providers about journalists' activities as a way to identify individuals who leak confidential government information to reporters. The practice has been long criticized, and in 2013, Attorney General Eric Holder imposed new rules that established a higher standard for government investigators.

Under the higher standard, those seeking to subpoena records pertaining to journalists were required to show that they had exhausted all other ways of accessing the information before asking a reporter to identify a source and to notify journalists in advance that they would be issuing a subpoena for their records or data.

Those rules were largely abandoned during the Trump Administration. Although it did not come to light until 2021 after President Trump had left office, in 2017, shortly after President Trump took office, the Justice Department obtained a court order to seize journalist's phone records and e-mail logs of several prominent *New York Times* reporters, a CNN pentagon correspondent, and the phone records of several *The Washington Post* reporters. The reporters involved had covered various stories that marred President Trump's early days in office, including the firing of FBI director James Comey and the FBI's investigation into Russian interference in the 2016 election.

Later in 2021, Attorney General Merrick Garland issued a policy statement indicating that the Department of Justice will no longer use subpoenas for the purpose of obtaining information about journalists, unless the reporter is him or herself a target of an investigation unrelated to their work, if they are suspected of working with a foreign power or terrorist group, or if there is an imminent threat of bodily harm or death.

Such policy statements are just that – statements of the administration's policy – and do not have the force of law. Indeed, it is common for new administrations to expressly revoke the policies of a prior administration and replace them with their own policies.

IN THE NEWS: *SEATTLE METROPOLITAN POLICE V. SEATTLE TIMES, ET AL.*

In the weeks following the May 25, 2020 murder of George Floyd outside of a Minneapolis convenience store, civil rights and community leaders staged peaceful marches throughout the country to highlight ongoing challenges with what they viewed as discriminatory police practices. Unfortunately, in many cities, the peaceful

Figure 6.3 Protests in downtown Seattle following the murder of George Floyd. Source: Cameron Thomsen, Shutterstock.

marches turned violent, as criminal actors overtook the lawful demonstrators and converted the events into violent riots.

That's what happened in Seattle on May 30, 2020. According to *The Seattle Times*, 27 people were arrested for various crimes, such as assault, arson, and looting.[42] Police cars were "burned, spray-painted and smashed" and firearms, including two assault rifles, were stolen from police vehicles (the rifles were ultimately recovered).[43] At one point, Interstate 5, the principal north–south thoroughfare through town was shut down because it had been overtaken by protesters, and all inbound ferry services were suspended.[44]

In the weeks following the melee, the Seattle Metropolitan Police Department issued a subpoena to *The Seattle Times* and the four major network-affiliated television stations seeking "[a]ny and all video footage or photographs, including but not limited to all unedited and/or raw video footage" from a 90-minute period on the afternoon of May 30, 2020, in the vicinity of the most serious rioting (defined in the subpoena by specific street boundaries).[45]

42 "Seattle Protest Updates: The city Reacts to the Death of George Floyd", *The Seattle Times*, May 30, 2020, available at https://www.seattletimes.com/seattle-news/protest-updates-as-the-country-reacts-to-the -death-of-george-floyd-follow-the-latest-developments-in-seattle-and-elsewhere/.

43 Dedee Sun, *Cars Burned, Stores Looted after Seattle Protests Saturday Turn Destructive; Dozens Arrested*, KIRO 7, May 31, 2020, available at https://www.kiro7.com/news/local/cars-burned-stores-looted-after-seattle -protests-turn-destructive-dozens-arrested/UGLTZPH2RZCOTDSX35Q2LNHAXI/.

44 *Id.*

45 *In re Subpoena Duces Tecum to Seattle News Media*, Order Enforcing Subpoena and Denying News Media's Objections, No. 20-0-616926, July 31, 2020.

The police said they needed the footage and photographs to help identify the individuals who lit the police cars on fire, and stole the firearms, two of which remained unrecovered and posed a threat to the community.

The media moved to **quash** – render unenforceable – the subpoena, arguing that they were protected by Washington's shield law, which provides that members of the news media may not be compelled to disclose the identity of their sources, or their newsgathering materials, including raw footage unless the government can show that there are reasonable grounds to believe that a crime has occurred,[46] and:

1. The news or information is highly material and relevant;
2. The news or information is critical or necessary to the maintenance of a party's claim, defense, or proof of an issue;
3. The party seeking such news or information has exhausted all reasonable and available means to obtain it from alternative sources; and
4. There is a compelling public interest in the disclosure.[47]

Specifically, the media argued that the police department's request was merely speculative – that is, they hoped there was something relevant in the materials they sought, but didn't know for sure, which did not rise to the level of being "highly material and relevant" or "critical or necessary" as required by the statute.

The media also argued that the police had not shown that they had exhausted all alternative sources, such as public social media posts or surveillance video from area businesses. Finally, they asserted that the public interest would be best served by not enforcing the subpoena because to do otherwise would create the impression that the media operate as instrumentalities of the police, subjecting journalists to serious risk of physical harm.

Following a hearing on the matter, the trial court judge sided with the police department and entered an order requiring the media organizations to turn over their professionally captured video and footage, but not images or videos from reporters' cell phones. The court limited the police department's use of the images to investigate and prosecute the arson and firearms charges only; they were barred from using the images to pursue lesser crimes such as looting and vandalism.

Days later, the media appealed the decision to the Washington Supreme Court which **stayed** – temporarily suspended – the enforcement of the trial court's order pending further review. Shortly thereafter, the police department advised that it was dropping the subpoena.

In a *Seattle Times* article summarizing the state of play, Seattle City Attorney Pete Holmes said that the subpoena "was about trying to recover dangerous weapons.

---

46 There are also provisions that pertain to civil actions.
47 R.C.W. § 5.68.010(2)(b).

The urgency of getting this evidence collided with the more ponderous process of our judicial system, and the process won out." Eric Stahl, a partner at Davis Wright Tremaine, and the lawyer who represented the media companies responded that what Holmes calls "a 'process' is actually an important protection for journalism, free speech and the public's right to know. And fortunately, in this case, the process worked."[48]

KEY POINTS AND TAKEAWAYS

1. The law recognizes that a free press is essential to a well-functioning democracy, but reporters do not get special privileges just for engaging in a journalistic enterprise. They must still follow laws that generally apply to everyone else. Journalists cannot lie, misrepresent themselves, or trespass to get access to a story, and they must follow state laws when recording conversations or using hidden cameras.
2. Although journalists cannot break the law when reporting stories, it is generally not against the law for journalists to report on materials that were obtained unlawfully – for example, surreptitious recordings or leaked documents – so long as the journalist did not participate in the unlawful conduct that led to the disclosure of the information.
3. The right to record the police in the course of their official duties is among those protected by the First Amendment. Restrictions on the right to record must meet the constitutional test for reasonable time, place, and manner restrictions.
4. All 50 states and the Federal government have open records and meetings laws that afford the public, including journalists, access to certain government information and proceedings. The degree of access and scope of materials available varies by jurisdiction, but in its simplest form, a simple written request to a government agency is sufficient to yield a response. For more complex inquiries, there are free and low-cost services available to help journalists navigate the various legal issues that may arise.
5. Many states have shield laws that protect journalists from being compelled to disclose the identity of their sources or unpublished newsgathering materials. There is no federal shield law.

QUESTIONS FOR DISCUSSION

1. Although not every state has a reporters' shield law, those that do typically limit its applicability to "traditional" journalists – those who work for newspapers, magazines, and radio or television outfits. Should shield laws be expanded to include

---

48 Lewis Kamb, *Seattle Police End Effort to Get Unpublished Media Photos and Videos from Protests*, Seattle Times, September 21, 2020, available at https://www.seattletimes.com/seattle-news/seattle-police-end-effort-to -get-unpublished-media-photos-and-videos-from-protests.

digital journalists? If so, how? Should anyone with a website or who posts a comment on a social media site have the protections of the shield law?

2. We saw in this chapter that it is generally not unlawful for a reporter to make use of information that was obtained unlawfully, so long as the reporter did not directly participate in the illegal conduct. Is that the right rule?

3. One of the media's concerns about not having an effective reporter's privilege is that they might become seen as an extension of law enforcement, which could make it more difficult to find sources willing to speak or provide information, and in some cases, could subject journalists to abuse and harassment. How should policymakers and courts balance those issues against the needs of law enforcement and the administration of justice that might sometimes require information from journalists? How would you have ruled if you were the judge in the Seattle matter?

7

CHAPTER 7
REPORTING ON THE GOVERNMENT

Reporting on and obtaining information from the government can raise unique concerns. On the one hand, the government, as an instrumentality of the people, funded by and working for the citizens, must be open and transparent, and it is the media's role to keep a watchful eye on the government and keep the public informed. On the other hand, the government must be afforded a degree of discretion in conducting its affairs. For instance, there are strong public policy reasons why law enforcement files should not be made publicly available until an investigation concludes.

This chapter examines some of the issues surrounding reporting on the government, including the police and the courts.

REPORTING ON THE POLICE

As we saw in the last chapter, reporting on or recording the police in action raises unique challenges because of two principles of our constitutional democracy that can sometimes conflict. On the one hand, the police have the authority to use force, where appropriate, to maintain the peace and to ensure law and order. On the other hand, the media's role is, in part, is to serve as a check on government power – a watchdog, or the "fourth estate" – a role that would be difficult to fulfill without the ability to closely monitor the police engaged in their government-sanctioned duties.

The tension between these two democratic imperatives has existed for as long as there has been a constitution, the police, and the media, but the issue has been brought to the fore in recent years owing to the ubiquity of cell phone cameras. In the past, outside of pre-planned events such as protests or marches, it was relatively rare for the media to capture police incidents on camera because it required them to be at the right place at the right time. Today, of course, everyone has the capacity to be a "journalist" in some manner by being able to record the police on their cell phones, either preserving the video for later distribution or live streaming it on various social media platforms.

Courts have recognized the importance of applying the same standards of newsgathering conduct to both "citizen journalists" and professional news media. In 2011, the First Circuit observed:

> The proliferation of electronic devices with video-recording capability means that many of our images of current events come from bystanders with a ready

DOI: 10.4324/9781003197966-7

cell phone or digital camera rather than a traditional film crew, and news stories are now just as likely to be broken by a blogger at her computer as a reporter at a major newspaper. Such developments make clear why the news-gathering protections of the First Amendment cannot turn on professional credentials or status.[1]

Although the Supreme Court has not directly opined on whether the public and the press have a right to record the police, it has observed that "the First Amendment goes beyond protection of the press and the self-expression of individuals to prohibit government from limiting the stock of information from which members of the public may draw."[2]

Several appellate courts have applied that broad principle to the specific act of recording the police. In 2017, for example, the Court of Appeals for the Third Circuit held that the First Amendment "protects the act of photographing, filming, or otherwise recording police officers conducting their official duties in public."[3] The court explained that such recordings advance the key First Amendment principle of encouraging discourse about matters of public importance, such as the role and effectiveness of the police.[4] The court also recognized that videos taken by the public – bystander videos – "fill … the gaps created when police choose not to record video or withhold their footage from the public"[5] and have led to important advances in addressing police misconduct and protecting civil rights.

The right to record the police has limits, however. The government is still free to regulate the recording of police activity so long as it meets the test for a reasonable time, place, and manner restriction.[6] Recall from earlier that to comply with the Constitution, a time, place, and manner restriction must be content neutral, narrowly tailored to serve a significant governmental interest, and must leave open ample alternative channels for communication. In the context of recording police, the time, place, and manner test has primarily looked at the extent to which the attempt at restricting recording police activity protects the police from unreasonable interference by the person engaged in the recording.

In *Fields v. City of Philadelphia*, for instance, the court suggested that it would be difficult to justify restrictions on making a recording across the street from where the police activity was taking place, but that it might be appropriate to restrict recording a conversation with a confidential informant that might impact an investigation or put the informant's safety at risk.[7]

---

1 *Glik v. Cunniffe*, 655 F.3d 78, 84 (1st Cir. 2011).
2 *First National Bank of Boston v. Bellotti*, 435 U.S. 765, 783 (1978).
3 *Fields v. City of Philadelphia*, 862 F.3d 353, 356 (3d Cir. 2017).
4 *See id*. at 359.
5 *Id*. at 360.
6 *Id*.
7 *Id*.

Notwithstanding the constitutionally protected right to record the police, the reality is that in a situation where a journalist or member of the public is threatened with arrest for making such recordings, the police hold all the cards. The police have the power to detain and arrest virtually anyone they want, and even if a person is ultimately not charged with a crime, or the arrest is found to be improper, the person has still had to ensure the inconvenience and trauma of the arrest and the prospect of criminal prosecution.

To minimize the risk to journalists covering police-related news, many media enterprises, and the organizations that represent them, work to foster relationships with the law enforcement community. State and local press organizations often have strong working relationships with local law enforcement officials and larger law enforcement agencies frequently have dedicated public information staff whose job is to serve as a liaison to members of the media. When such relationships are in place, it is often easier to resolve a journalist's unreasonable arrest or detention.

Journalism credentialing programs often help in this regard as well. Press passes are often thought of as providing access to certain nonpublic spaces or events and while they are sometimes used for that purpose, they are often used simply to identify members of the press in public spaces so the police know to afford them a reasonable degree of latitude as they work to fulfill their constitutionally supported mission.

In 2021, California enacted legislation aimed specifically at protecting journalists at protests. It prohibits the police from intentionally assaulting, interfering with, or obstructing journalists, and requires the police to give a detained journalist immediate access to a supervisory officer for purposes of challenging the detention.[8]

THE FREEDOM OF INFORMATION ACT

It is clear that the "First Amendment protects the public's right of access to information about their officials' public activities."[9] One of the primary ways that the public can obtain information about what the government is up to is the Freedom of Information Act (FOIA).[10] Enacted in 1966, the Supreme Court has said that the essence of FOIA "is to ensure an informed citizenry, vital to the functioning of a

---

8 Cal. Penal Code § 409.7 (2021).
9 *Fields*, 862 F.3d at 360.
10 *See U.S. Department of Justice v. Reporters Committee for Freedom of the Press*, 489 U.S. 749 (1989).

democratic society, needed to check against corruption and to hold the governors accountable to the governed."[11]

FOIA, which applies only to Executive Branch agencies, establishes a presumption that government records should be made available to the public unless they fall into one of several enumerated exemptions. Notably, FOIA does not require that agencies create new records or answer questions, it simply requires that agencies provide copies of records in their possession that are not subject to any of the FOIA exemptions.

PROACTIVE DISCLOSURES

Although FOIA tends to be best known as a mechanism by which one can request records from the government, FOIA also requires that agencies make certain information publicly available without ever being asked. Among those documents are final opinions, orders, and other adjudicatory documents, policy statements or interpretations, administrative manuals, records that have been the subject of a FOIA request three or more times in the past, and any other documents that the agency reasonably believes may be requested frequently.

Traditionally, agencies were obligated only to make such information available for "public inspection and copying," which they achieved by operating "reading rooms," often at each agency's Washington, DC headquarters. That, of course, made it difficult for those outside of the area to access information without making a formal FOIA request and incurring the costs associated with such requests.

In 2016, Congress passed the FOIA Improvement Act of 2016,[12] which, among other things, requires that agencies make information available in an electronic form. As a practical matter, many agencies had frequently requested information available on their websites long before 2016, but many now have a designated "electronic reading room" or "FOIA library" that contains electronic copies of the documents required to be disclosed proactively.

MAKING A FOIA REQUEST

For records that are not disclosed proactively, any member of the public may request a copy by following the agency's procedures for doing so which are generally published on the agency's website. Many agencies now prefer that requests be submitted electronically. The federal government also operates a central website for all things FOIA at www.foia.gov.

The law requires that the requestor "reasonably describe" the records sought, and courts have explained that "FOIA was not intended to reduce government agencies to

11 *National Labor Relations Board v. Robbins Tire & Rubber Co.*, 437 U.S. 214, 242 (1978).
12 Pub. L. No. 114-185 (2016).

full-time investigators on behalf of requesters."[13] Simply put, FOIA was not intended to promote "fishing expeditions" into agency files. Instead, the requestor must have a reasonable sense of what they are looking for.[14]

TURNAROUND TIME

Assuming the request is complete, the agency is supposed to respond within 20 days, though in reality, they rarely do. Often, the agency will send a letter acknowledging receipt but will not fulfill the request until later. The government's FOIA portal notes that "[t]he time it takes to respond to a request will vary depending on the complexity of the request and any backlog of requests already pending at the agency." The site also notes that "[a]gencies typically process requests in the order of receipt."

It is possible to expedite a FOIA request in limited circumstances, one of which is if the request is made "by a person primarily engaged in disseminating information" involving "urgency to inform the public concerning actual or alleged Federal Government activity."[15] Journalists working on time-sensitive reports are generally well positioned to assert the need for expedited services.

FEES

Although there is no fee to file a FOIA request, the law does allow agencies to charge for the time it takes their employees to search for the requested documents and the cost of copying and mailing them. Most agencies do not charge for the first two hours of search time or the first 100 pages, and agencies are not permitted to request payment in advance unless they believe the fee will exceed $250 or the requester has failed to pay fees in the past.

For requests made by members of the news media, there may be a charge for duplication (but not search time), and the law allows agencies to waive the fees entirely where the information sought will be used to contribute significantly to public understanding of the operations or activities of the government.[16]

For all requesters, FOIA requires that agencies "make reasonable efforts to search for the records in electronic form or format"[17] and provide the responsive records "in any form or format requested."[18] Cost-conscious requestors that do not qualify for treatment as a member of the news media, or for a fee waiver, would be well advised to request documents in an electronic format, so as to reduce the duplication costs.

---

13 *Assassination Archives & Research Center v. CIA*, 720 F. Supp 217, 219 (D.D.C. 1989).
14 *See* U.S. Department of Justice, Department of Justice Guide to the Freedom of Information Act 25–26 (2020).
15 5 U.S.C. § 552(a)(6)(E)(v)(II).
16 *Id.* at § 552(a)(4)(A)(iii).
17 *Id.* at § 552(a)(3)(C).
18 *Id.* at § 552(a)(3)(B).

Below is a sample FOIA request that you can use as a model:

To Whom it May Concern:

Pursuant to the Freedom of Information Act ("FOIA"), codified at 5 U.S.C. § 552, et seq., I respectfully request that the following records be provided to me: [Describe the records sought] (the "Requested Records"). To the extent possible, I would like the records to be provided to me in electronic form via electronic mail to: [Your e-mail address].

I am a representative of the news media as contemplated by 5 U.S.C. § 552(a)(4)(A)(ii)(III). I respectfully request that you waive the fees associated with my request because my intended use of the Requested Records will contribute significantly to the public understanding of the operations or activities of the government. Specifically, I will [describe how you will use the records]. My intended use of the Requested Records is not intended to primarily advance my own private commercial interests. 5 U.S.C. § 552(a)(4)(A)(iii).

Should you decline to grant my request for a fee waiver, I understand that because I am a representative of the news media, and because the Requested Records are not sought for commercial use, you will charge me only for reasonable standard charges for document duplication. 5 U.S.C. § 552(a)(4)(A)(ii)(II).

Please note that notwithstanding the foregoing, if a fee is assessed, I am willing to pay no more than [maximum amount you are willing to spend]. If you reasonably believe that the cost will exceed that amount, please contact me prior to fulfillment.

EXEMPTIONS

As noted previously, FOIA creates a strong presumption in favor of openness and disclosure. That means that unless there is a particular reason for an agency to withhold information, it must generally disclose it when asked to. FOIA describes nine categories of records that are generally exempt from disclosure:[19]

1. **Information that has been classified to protect national security**. It should be fairly obvious and noncontroversial that classified national security materials are not discoverable under FOIA.
2. **Information related solely to the internal personnel rules and practices of an agency**. Records that pertain to routine, trivial internal matters of agency

---

19 *Id*. at § 552(b).

administration that are unlikely to generate much public interest are generally exempt from FOIA.

3. **Information that is prohibited from disclosure by another federal law**. Beyond the exemptions set forth in the FOIA statute itself, various other federal laws contain specific provisions excepting certain materials from disclosure. For example, the Antitrust Civil Process Act excludes commercially sensitive materials from antitrust investigations from disclosure.[20] Similarly, the Homeland Security Act of 2002 authorizes agencies to withhold "critical infrastructure information."[21]

4. **Trade secrets or commercial financial information that is confidential or privileged**. This exemption is intended to ensure that confidential or otherwise commercially sensitive information that companies must provide to the government to comply with certain regulatory requirements – for example, sensitive information about clinical trials for a new drug that must be provided to the Food and Drug Administration – does not become public and get into the hands of competitors.

5. **Privileged communications within or between agencies**. Privileged communication includes discussions between agency staff and their lawyers that are protected under the **attorney-client privilege**, documents prepared in anticipation of litigation under the **attorney work product privilege**, and internal or interagency recommendations and analysis of emerging policies or regulations under the **deliberative process privilege** (sometimes also called **executive privilege**).

6. **Information that would violate another person's privacy if disclosed**. Generally, records that contain personally identifiable information about an individual in which the individual has a significant privacy interest are not disclosable. For instance, an individual's Medicare record would not be disclosable under FOIA because it contains sensitive, private medical information. An FBI file about a deceased individual, however, would likely be disclosable because the subject no longer has a privacy interest in the information. A living individual can obtain whatever records an agency may have about themselves including with the request a notarized statement or a statement signed under penalty of perjury certifying that the person making the request is the subject of the records sought.

7. **Information compiled for law enforcement purposes**, so as not to reveal information that might interfere with law enforcement, adversely affect an individual's right to a fair and impartial trial, jeopardize ongoing investigations or prosecutions, disclose the identity of a confidential informant, disclose techniques or procedures employed by law enforcement, or endanger the life or physical safety of any individual.

8. **Information concerning the regulation or supervision of financial institutions** to ensure the security of financial institutes by preventing unnecessary "runs" on banks that might occur if the public were to be able to access (and potentially misconstrue) regulators' assessments of a bank's financial health.

20 15 U.S.C. § 1314(g).
21 6 U.S.C. § 133(a)(1)(A).

9. **Geological and geophysical information and data, including maps, concerning wells**, originally intended to protect the oil and gas exploration industry from unreasonable competition, but courts have also recognized that the exemption applies to water wells in addition to oil and gas wells.[22]

In cases where an exemption applies, agencies must still generally disclose as much of the record as possible, redacting the material subject to an exemption, and identifying the specific basis for the nondisclosure.

REFUSALS AND APPEALS

If an agency refuses a request, either for documents or for reduced fees, or withholds more information than the requestor believes was appropriate, the requestor can file an **administrative appeal**, which is essentially just a letter to the agency asking them to reconsider. Such appeals are reviewed by people within the agency that were not involved in denying the original request. The agency may respond by either disclosing more information (or granting the request for a fee reduction) or may stand by its original decision.

Dissatisfied requestors may also file a lawsuit against the agency in federal district court. Because litigation requires that participants follow strict timing protocols – for example, a party must respond to a lawsuit within 20 days – filing a lawsuit is sometimes the most effective way to cajole a response out of an otherwise nonresponsive agency. Successful FOIA litigation can result in a court order, mandating that the agency disclose the requested records.

The downside to FOIA litigation is that it can be costly. Unlike the initial FOIA request, which can be easily made without the aid of an attorney, bringing a FOIA lawsuit usually requires a lawyer and such actions can also be time consuming because of the procedural requirements of federal litigation.

You have probably heard the phrase "I can neither confirm nor deny" in connection with requests for information that is classified or confidential.

The phrase has become known as the "Glomar response," which derives its name from *Phillipi v. CIA*,[23] a case in which the CIA sought to avoid disclosing documents pertaining to its Glomar Explorer, a drill ship used to recover a sunken Soviet submarine in 1974. A security breach at a military contractor led to the release of a document describing the project that was subsequently covered by several media outlets. The CIA sought to prevent other news organizations

22 15 U.S.C. § 552(b).
23 655 F.2d 1325 (D.C. Cir. 1981).

from writing about the project, which led a reporter from *Rolling Stone* magazine to file a FOIA request seeking documents pertaining to the CIA's attempt at suppressing the story.

In response to the journalist's request, the CIA responded that they could "neither confirm nor deny" the existence of any responsive documents. The government took the position that the mere act of acknowledging the existence or nonexistence of documents would effectively reveal enough information to deduce whether such a classified program existed (a fact which is, itself, classified). Had the CIA responded that such documents were being withheld pursuant to a FOIA exemption, it would have confirmed that such documents exist, suggesting that the classified program exists; had the CIA responded that no such documents existed, it would have confirmed the nonexistence of such a program. Accordingly, the government would neither confirm nor deny the existence of such documents. The response has become a common refrain for government agencies seeking to protect certain national security or privacy interests.

You can learn more about the Glomar response, and the then-classified military project that gave rise to it, on the podcast Radiolab from WNYC Studios. The episode "Neither Confirm Nor Deny" is available at www.wnycstudios.org/podcasts/radiolab/articles/confirm-nor-deny.

OPEN MEETINGS

Beyond FOIA's requirement that executive branch agencies make documents available to the public, the government must also ensure that the public has meaningful access to official meetings and proceedings of executive branch agencies. The Government in the Sunshine Act of 1976,[24] usually just referred to as the "Sunshine Act," requires that "every portion of every meeting of an agency shall be open to public observation"[25] and, by extension, the press is free to observe and report on such proceedings. The law also requires that agencies provide sufficient public notice of upcoming meetings and publish agendas in advance.[26]

The Sunshine Act recognizes that in some cases, open meetings would not advance the public interest, such as those that might include discussions of national security or defense information, trade secrets or other competitively sensitive information, and other information specifically exempted by other laws.[27]

24 Pub. L. 94–409 (1976).
25 5 U.S.C. § 552b(c).
26 *Id.* at § 552b(f)(2).
27 *Id.* at § 552b(c).

STATE OPEN GOVERNMENT LAWS

FOIA and the Sunshine Act apply only to federal agencies, but most states have passed some version of their own open records and open meetings laws intended to achieve the same objectives. Each state names and structures its open government laws slightly differently. For example, in Colorado, the open records act is aptly called the Colorado Open Records Act,[28] and the open meetings law is called the Colorado Sunshine Act.[29] In New Hampshire, the two are combined into a single statute called the Right to Know Law.[30] The National Freedom of Information Coalition has assembled a state-by-state guide to open government laws, available at www.nfoic .org. The Reporters Committee for Freedom of the Press has a similar offering available at www.rcfp.org/open-government-guide.

While most state statutes allow "any person" to make a request for public records, a number of states limit access to such records to state citizens, allowing agencies in those states to deny requests from out-of-state requestors solely on that basis. In 2013, two people who had been denied access to records under Virginia's Freedom of Information Act because they lived in other states sued the Commonwealth of Virginia alleging that the refusal to provide documents to citizens of other states violated the Constitution's privileges and immunities clause. In a unanimous decision, the Supreme Court explained that it has long "made clear that there is no constitutional right to obtain all the information provided by FOIA laws."[31]

To work around such restrictions, journalists may seek colleagues in the relevant states to file a request on their behalf, or use a service such as MuckRock, a fee-based service that files requests on behalf of its users and makes the documents available to not only the original requester but also its other users. You can learn more about MuckRock at www.muckrock.com. The Reporters Committee for Freedom of the Press has a similar project called iFOIA, which is available at www.ifoia.org.

An emerging issue in this area of law is the extent to which police body camera (body cam) footage is accessible through open records laws. Although such video footage would be very likely considered a government record under most conventional definitions, and therefore subject to disclosure under most states' laws, those laws also contain myriad exemptions that law enforcement agencies can use to withhold it.

---

28 C.R.S. § 24-72-201, *et seq.*
29 C.R.S. § 24-6-401, *et seq.*
30 R.S.A. Ch. 91-A
31 *McBurney v. Young*, 569 U.S. 221, 232 (2013)

The Los Angeles Police Department, for instance, has taken the position that body cam footage is evidence and therefore not disclosable under the California Public Records Act. Other agencies have withheld the footage on the basis that it is part of a personnel matter involving police misconduct, which is, of course, often exactly the reason that journalists seek the footage in the first place. Some have asserted privacy concerns as the reason for nondisclosure. For example, the Washington, DC Metropolitan Police Department has declined to release footage citing privacy concerns and being unable to properly redact it.

A number of states have enacted, or are considering enacting, specific exclusions for body cam footage. In 2016, Illinois enacted the Law Enforcement Officer-Worn Body Camera Act that specifically made police body cam footage exempt from disclosure under the Illinois Freedom of Information except if requested by the individual in the footage or the officer whose camera captured the footage.[32] North Carolina's law provides that body cam footage is simply not considered a public record, and Arizona's law is similar, except that footage is considered a public record if it involves deadly force, and even then, the law enforcement agency involved must consent to its disclosure.[33]

COVERING THE COURTS

Although the judicial branch is part of the government, which would suggest that its documents and records should be freely available to the public, just like those of other government agencies, covering court proceedings raises a unique tension between two conflicting constitutional provisions.

On one side is the First Amendment which requires, among other things, that the press be given access to information about the government and the ability to report freely on its affairs. On the other side is the Sixth Amendment to the constitution, which guarantees criminal defendants certain rights, such as the right to a speedy, public trial, an impartial jury, the right to understand the nature and cause of the charges against them, and the right to confront their accusers.

Sometimes, the rights of the First Amendment will conflict with an individual's rights under the Sixth Amendment. There are often legitimate and compelling

---

32 50 Ill. Comp. Stat. Ann. 706/10-20 (West 2022).
33 Jared Gans and Crawford Humphreys, *9 States with Some of the Strictest Rules on Releasing Body Cam Videos,* The Hill, May 10, 2021, available at https://thehill.com/homenews/state-watch/552665-9-states-with -some-of-the-strictest-rules-on-releasing-body-cam-videos#:~:text=Footage%20captured%20by %20body-worn%20cameras%20is%20not%20subject,may%20release%20the%20footage%20at%20their %20own%20discretion.

reasons why public and press access to trials and other court proceedings, or information about those proceedings, may need to be limited to ensure that a criminal
defendant receives a full, fair, and impartial trial.

ACCESS TO JUDICIAL INFORMATION

Generally speaking, court records are public documents. Although the federal judiciary is not subject to the Freedom of Information Act (and the same is true for most
state judicial branches under their respective state open records laws), court systems
make procedural information, dockets, and case filings available to the public, and
most major court systems now have web-based portals that make much of the court's
information available online.

The federal system is called PACER, available at www.pacer.gov, which serves as a
hub for all federal courts. There is no charge to have a PACER account, but access to
documents costs ten cents per page, although fees are waived for users that have $30
or less of charges in a given quarter.

There is a presumption that court documents are public and proceedings are open,
however, courts will sometimes **seal** documents because they contain sensitive, non-
public information. In civil cases, for instance, courts may seal filings if they contain
confidential business information. In criminal cases, requests for arrest warrants are
generally sealed until the target is in custody to avoid tipping them off so they can
evade capture. Information about crime victims and witnesses is also often kept
confidential, especially in highly sensitive crimes such as sexual abuse or assault cases,
where the victim or witness is a juvenile or where disclosure may jeopardize their
safety.

ENSURING IMPARTIALITY

Arguably, where the tension between the First and Sixth amendments is most pronounced is when courts seek to ensure that criminal defendants receive a fair, impartial trial. An essential part of that is making sure that the jurors selected to hear the
case come to it with an open mind and without any preconceived notions of what the
outcome should be. For routine cases, that is generally not especially difficult, but for
high-profile matters, it can be challenging to find jurors that have not been exposed
to the widespread media coverage that is typical of such cases.

The Supreme Court has acknowledged that "[q]ualified jurors need not ... be
totally ignorant of the facts and issues involved."[34] It is sufficient that a prospective
juror can set aside whatever preconceived notions they may have and judge the case
based on the evidence admitted in court. "The relevant question is not whether the

---

34 *Murphy v. Florida*, 421 U.S. 794, 800 (1975).

community remembered the case, but whether the jurors ... had such fixed opinions that they could not judge impartially the guilt of the defendant."[35]

JURY SELECTION

Courts have a number of tools available to help them assemble an impartial jury. The first is the routine jury selection process **voir dire**, known more colloquially as jury selection, which simply involves questioning each juror and asking them pointed questions about their exposure to media coverage of the case. Those who the court believes may have had excessive exposure to reports of the case, or who appear to have already drawn conclusions about the guilt or innocence of the defendant, may be dismissed.

CHANGE OF VENUE

If it is impossible to assemble an impartial jury in the community where the defendant has been charged, sometimes the court will order a **change of venue**, which essentially involves moving the trial to another community where there has been less media coverage and, by extension, where jurors are less likely to have been exposed to it.

That is what happened in 2004 when Scott Peterson stood trial for murdering his wife and unborn child. The judge in that case agreed with the defense attorney's argument that Peterson would not have been able to get a fair trial in Modesto, California, because of extensive local media coverage. The trial was moved to Redwood City, just south of San Francisco,[36] about 90 minutes west of Modesto.

SEQUESTRATION

In extreme cases, a court may order the jury to be **sequestered** – that is, isolated from the outside world so that they are not tainted by media coverage of the trial that might include inadmissible facts or other information that might improperly influence them. Sequestered jurors usually stay at a hotel with no access to newspapers, television, radio, or the internet, and are shuttled back and forth to court by law enforcement personnel.

Because sequestration is so onerous on the jurors, keeping them away from friends and family, it is done only sparingly. In some cases, the judge may restrict jurors only during key portions of the trial as opposed to the entirety of the proceedings. For instance, during the trial of Derek Chauvin, the Minneapolis Police Officer convicted of killing George Floyd outside a convenience store in May of 2020, the jurors were carefully monitored during the trial, but sequestered only during final arguments and while deliberating.[37]

---

35 *Patton v. Yount*, 467 U.S. 1025, 1035 (1984).

36 Petersen was ultimately convicted on two counts of murder and sentenced to death. In 2020, the death sentence was overturned because it was discovered that some potential jurors had been improperly dismissed during jury selection.

37 Laurel Wamsley, *Chauvin Trial Judge Denies Request for Jury Sequestration After Police Shooting*, NPR, April 12, 2021, available at https://www.npr.org/sections/trial-over-killing-of-george-floyd/2021/04/12/986444151/chauvin-trial-judge-denies-request-for-jury-sequestration-after-police-shooting.

GAG ORDERS

Another extreme remedy at courts' disposal is to issue an order restricting participants in the case from making public statements about the proceeding that could get back to members of the jury (or prospective members) and lead to a decision being made on evidence or information that was not admissible in court.

Such orders, sometimes referred to as **gag orders**, are disfavored because they constitute a prior restraint on speech. As a result, gag orders are relatively rare, and are typically imposed only in especially high-profile cases where there is significant press attention, or where there is a particular risk that trial participants may attempt to "litigate the case from the courthouse steps."

In *Nebraska Press Association v. Stuart*,[38] the Supreme Court observed that extensive pretrial publicity itself "does not inevitably lead to an unfair trial."[39] Rather, it "is in part, and often in large part, shaped by what attorneys, police's and other officials do to precipitate news coverage."[40] It went on to hold that a gag order is only appropriate where:

1. There is intense and pervasive publicity about a case;
2. No other measure, such as change of venue, a delay in proceedings to let publicity subside, voir dire, or clear instructions to the jury to not consider information presented outside of the courtroom, would effectively protect the defendant's Sixth Amendment rights; and
3. The gag order would effectively keep prejudicial information away from the jury.[41]

A growing issue for courts is the increase in jurors using social media to access, intentionally or otherwise, information about the case for which they are sitting as a juror. According to a recent survey, 94% of federal judges have had a situation where a juror has used social media either during the trial or in deliberations. Some judges reported that jurors attempted to "friend" participants in the case, or otherwise communicated or attempted to communicate with participants.

Jurors have been dismissed for their improper use of social media. For example, a New Jersey judge dismissed a juror on a murder case who had commented "Sitting on the jury LMAO" on a news article about the case. Making matters worse, one of the other jurors reached out to the dismissed juror via Facebook messenger, and the dismissed juror subsequently gave an interview on the same platform.[42]

38 427 U.S. 539 (1976)
39 *Id.* at 554.
40 *Id.* at 555.
41 *Id.* at 562–67.
42 Andrew J. Ennis and Catherine A. Green, *A Quick Guide to Social Media Litigation*, American Bar Association Practice Points, January 17, 2020, available at: https://www.americanbar.org/groups/litigation/committees/commercial-business/practice/2020/quick-guide-social-media-litigation.

As a result of recent issues, judges have begun including social media-specific language in their instructions to the jury, commanding them not only to not consume traditional media or to speak to anyone about the case but to specifically avoid the use of social media platforms that may expose them to prejudicial material.

CAMERAS IN THE COURTROOM

The tension between the First and Sixth amendments is perhaps most pronounced when it comes to the perennial question of whether court proceedings should be televised, or otherwise made available publicly. Although there had long been a strong presumption of press access to trials, the 1935 trial of Bruno Hauptmann, the man who abducted and murdered Charles Lindbergh's son, became such a media frenzy that it resulted in a backlash to the practice. The American Bar Association and a number of state courts took the position that cameras had no place in the courtroom because the potential harm to Sixth Amendment interests of criminal defendants outweighed the media's First Amendment right to cover the proceedings.

In 1981, the Supreme Court recognized that although cameras in courtrooms could be deleterious to a defendant's right to a fair trial, that was not necessarily always the case, and that a blanket prohibition on the practice was unnecessary, leaving it to individual courts and judges to make the determination on a case-by-case basis. "[T]he states must be free to experiment," the court said.[43]

The Florida trial of serial killer Ted Bundy was the first to be televised nationally, marking the beginning of what has become common practice today. In 1991, a new cable network called Court TV launched, bringing the public "gavel-to-gavel" coverage of high-profile trials, accented with commentary and analysis by a team of legal pundits. Among Court TV's greatest hits was the 1994 trial of Erik and Lyle Menendez, convicted of murdering their parents, and the 1995 trial of O.J. Simpson, in which he was acquitted of murdering his ex-wife and her friend.

The O.J. Simpson trial is often used as an example of why cameras should not be allowed in the courtroom. Although the term did not originate with the Simpson case, it was often characterized as a "media circus" because of the frenzy outside the courthouse during the trial. As one media scholar observed, "because the trial was on camera ... everyone involved in the courtroom was performing as if they were stars of the highest-rated miniseries ever."[44] Even the Los Angeles district attorney who

---

43 *Id.*

44 Greg Braxton, "*O.J. Trial of the Century" Revisits Murder Case as It Unfolded*, L.A. Times, June 14, 2014, available at https://www.latimes.com/entertainment/tv/la-et-st-oj-simpson-documentary-20140612-story.html.

oversaw Simpson's prosecution has since said that cameras in the courtroom were a "[h]orrible mistake."[45]

Federal courts have been more cautious about allowing cameras. Former Supreme Court Justice David Souter once famously quipped that the case against cameras in the courtroom "is so strong that I can tell you the day you see a camera come into our courtroom, it's going to roll over my dead body."[46] The Supreme Court, however, has long released audio of its oral arguments after they take place (but almost never live), and a number of appellate courts have either made audio recordings of their hearings available or allowed partial camera access in certain limited circumstances. Federal trial courts have sometimes allowed cameras in for key hearings and events, but it is much rarer than it is in state courts.

CHANGING TECHNOLOGY AND CHANGING ATTITUDES

The COVID-19 pandemic that began in late 2019 and led to widespread lockdowns in 2020 required courts (and many media enterprises for that matter) to rethink how they perform their work. As a result, the Supreme Court, for the first time in its history, conducted oral argument entirely by telephone and allowed the news media to broadcast them in real time.

Many courts began conducting hearings and other judicial business via phone or videoconference out of necessity, as courthouses were shut down, deemed unsafe because of the highly infectious virus. Yet, despite the transition to the remote administration of justice, many courts have attempted to apply the same rules pertaining to recording judicial proceedings in the remote, online environment that had applied in the pre-pandemic, live courtroom environment.

A federal trial court in Michigan, for example, suspended three *New York Times* reporters' access to online court proceedings for taking screenshots of an otherwise public hearing conducted by Zoom in June 2020.[47] The court threatened "broader sanctions and/or monetary penalties" against the individual reporters or the *New York Times*.[48] Numerous other courts have imposed similar restrictions and rules against the dissemination of online proceedings.

Media lawyer Matthew Schafer has argued that applying old rules to new ways of holding court is simply unnecessary and inappropriate given the underlying policy objectives of the rules:

---

45 Steven Zeitchik, *Ex-D.A. in O.J. Case Finally Talks: Gil Garcetti Has Kept Silent for 22 years. Now He's Telling All in 'Made in America,'* L.A. Times, June 15, 2016.

46 *On Cameras in Supreme Court, Souter Says, 'Over My Dead Body,'* N.Y. Times, March 30, 1996, https://www.nytimes.com/1996/03/30/us/on-cameras-in-supreme-court-souter-says-over-my-dead-body.html.

47 Emma Cueto, *NYT Staffers' Court Access Suspended Over Zoom Screenshot,* Law360, June 26, 2020, https://www.law360.com/articles/1287214/nyt-staffers-court-access-suspended-over-zoom-screenshot.

48 *Id.*

By and large, rules prohibiting recording while physically present in courtrooms are intended to preserve decorum, prevent distraction, and put a stop to potential juror bias as a result of media attention obvious from the presence of the press and cameras. Yet, these considerations do not obtain when a reporter records digital hearings, unknown to the participants, from the comfort of her home office.[49]

He goes on to observe that although courts may have the right to regulate the conduct of the media within the walls of the courtroom, dictating the media's conduct outside of that arena would be an unprecedented move that would "greatly expand courts' powers" over third parties.[50]

Some anticipate that even as the pandemic subsides, remote court proceedings will become more common, and perhaps the standard, for some proceedings. As courts, litigants, defendants, and other stakeholders in the judicial process become more familiar and comfortable with the practice, many in the media hope improved, if not universal, access to record and disseminate court proceedings will likewise become the standard.

For now, however, journalists should take care to fully understand the rules, policies, and practices of the courts upon which they report so as not to draw the ire of the court and end up like the three *The New York Times* reporters discussed above, or worse, be held in contempt of court.

IN THE NEWS: *MINNESOTA V. CHAUVIN*

An example of how remote technology helped advance the interests of justice as opposed to creating an unhelpful spectacle comes from Minneapolis where, in early 2021, former police officer Derek Chauvin was tried and convicted for the May 2020 murder of George Floyd. Floyd's murder led to widespread protests and marches championing racial equality and drawing attention to the problem of police brutality, particularly as it impacts racial minorities. The Chauvin proceedings were closely watched around the world and the high-profile nature of the case led some to fear that the trial, if televised, would become a "media circus," which is how the famous 1995 trial of O.J. Simpson is often characterized.

Over the State of Minnesota's objections, the trial judge granted the defense's motion to allow the trial to be broadcast, subject to specific rules pertaining to the number of cameras, their location within the courtroom (which was fixed for the duration of the trial), and what those cameras were and were not allowed to show. The cameras were to be operated by a single media organization. They were obligated to distribute

---

49 Matthew Schafer, *Lack of Access to Remote Court Proceedings Is Inexcusable*, Law360, November 16, 2020, https://www.law360.com/articles/1328481/lack-of-access-to-remote-court-proceedings-is-inexcusable.
50 *Id.*

the feed to any media organization who wanted it – a relatively common practice for high-profile events, where there is limited space for the media's equipment, which is called "pooling."

Under normal circumstances, cameras are allowed in Minnesota courtrooms only if all parties consent. Here, the state objected. So why did the court authorize the broadcast? Simply put, it had to because of COVID.

Due to social distancing restrictions, the courtroom could only hold a small handful of people, effectively closing the trial to the public, which arguably would have infringed Chauvin's Sixth Amendment right to a fair, public trial. The state argued that a more appropriate solution was to simply stream the trial into several "overflow courtrooms," but the judge recognized that even if every courtroom were devoted to showing the Chauvin proceedings, there would still be unreasonable limits on access to the trial, and those in the overflow rooms would be watching what was, essentially, a television broadcast in any event.

The court ultimately concluded that "the only way to vindicate the Defendants' constitutional right to a public trial and the media's and public's constitutional right of access to criminal trials is to allow audio and video coverage of the trial, including by broadcast in the media."[51]

The Chauvin trial broadcast arrangement was a success. Minnesota criminal defense attorney Earl Gray noted that the setup "doesn't interfere with the trial at all … After five minutes, you don't even realize they're there"[52] in stark contrast to the bulky, prominent cameras used in previous high-profile trials such as O.J. Simpson's. And the public was clearly interested in the trial. The Minneapolis *Star Tribune*'s YouTube channel had "garnered nearly 300,000 views in the first week of jury selection and the number of people watching at the same time hovered around 2,000."[53] According to Nielsen, which tracks television viewership, at least 23.2 million people watched the verdict.[54]

Media lawyers Leita Walker and Emmy Parsons, who represented a coalition of media organizations covering the trial, hope that the success of the Chauvin trial will serve

51 Order Allowing Audio and Video Coverage of Trial, *Minnesota v. Chauvin*, Case No. 27-CR-20-12646 (Nov. 4, 2020).
52 Rochelle Olson, *Chauvin Trial Puts Cameras Front and Center of the Hennepin County Courtroom*, Minneapolis Star Tribune, March 19, 2021, available at https://www.startribune.com/chauvin-trial-puts-cameras-front -and-center-of-the-hennepin-county-courtroom/600035860/.
53 Leita Walker & Emmy Parsons, *Chauvin Trial Shows Why Cameras Need to Be in Court*, Bloomberg Law, March 31, 2021, available at https://news.bloomberglaw.com/us-law-week/chauvin-trial-shows-why -cameras-need-to-be-in-court.
54 WCCO-TV, *Nielsen: At Least 23,2 Million Watched Verdict in Derek Chauvin Trial*, WCCO-TV, April 22, 2021, available at https://minnesota.cbslocal.com/2021/04/22/nielsen-at-least-23-2-million-watched -verdict-in-derek-chauvin-trial/.

as an example to other courts and "will encourage Minnesota, and jurisdictions that also do not allow cameras in courtrooms, to rethink their rules once they realize that cameras do not conflict with the goals of an orderly court proceeding."[55]

"Although courts should not move to audio–visual access in lieu of in-person access, perhaps it is time to decide that the digital 'courtroom' of the 21st century is akin the 100-person courtroom of the 20th century," write Walker and Parsons. "We should embrace today's technology, not reject it, and let the world watch. A commitment to transparency — and perhaps even the U.S. Constitution — demand it."[56]

KEY POINTS AND TAKEAWAYS

1. The right to record the police in the course of their official duties is among those protected by the First Amendment. Restrictions on the right to record must meet the constitutional test for a reasonable time, place, and manner restriction.
2. All 50 states and the Federal government have open records and meetings laws that afford the public, including journalists, access to certain government information and proceedings. The degree of access and scope of materials available varies by jurisdiction, but in its simplest form, a simple written request to a government agency is sufficient to yield a response. For more complex inquiries, there are free and low-cost services available to help journalists navigate the various legal issues that may arise.
3. Cameras in courtrooms, particularly for high-profile criminal trials, were traditionally disfavored for fear of creating a "media circus" of what should be a solemn proceeding. In the late 1970s and early 1980s, states began experimenting with allowing cameras into certain proceedings. Today, the practice has become commonplace in many state courts, but less so in federal courts. In any case, the practice is generally subject to tight controls by the presiding judge.

QUESTIONS FOR DISCUSSION

1. One of the arguments against making police body cam footage available to the public is that it could violate the privacy rights of third parties. For instance, suppose a police officer enters an individual's home because they are suffering a medical emergency. The body cam would capture not only the individual in an especially vulnerable situation but also their personal space and effects. Public disclosure of that footage might justifiably be considered a violation of the individual's privacy. How should policymakers balance the need for government transparency and, in particular, police transparency, with individual privacy considerations?

---

55 Walker & Parsons, *supra* n. 53.
56 *Id.*

2. Some states' freedom of information laws restrict access to material to state residents on the theory that state government accountability is most relevant to the state's own citizens. Critics of the practice have argued that the restrictions are unnecessary since they are so easily circumvented by services like MuckRock that can file requests on an out-of-state user's behalf. What do you think? How should policymakers think about the issue?

3. As remote, online court proceedings become more common, and camera equipment becomes smaller, less obtrusive, and more ubiquitous, how do you think policymakers and courts should think about "cameras in the courtroom?" Do the traditional concerns about a high-profile trial becoming a "media circus" still hold in the modern environment? How should courts think about the balance of First Amendment and Sixth Amendment imperatives in today's courtrooms (in-person or remote)?

8

CHAPTER 8
COMMERCIAL SPEECH AND ADVERTISING

In what ways are advertisements different than other types of content that a media enterprise might produce and distribute? Which regulatory agencies oversee advertising issues and what laws and regulations must media enterprises be mindful of when determining which ads to accept (and vetting the content of those ads)?

This chapter considers the constitutional and regulatory environment of commercial speech, including various disclosure laws, restrictions on certain types of advertising, and the like.

WHAT IS COMMERCIAL SPEECH?

In simple terms, commercial speech means "advertising" and like Justice Potter Stewart famously said about pornography: one knows it when they see it.[1] Although it may seem obvious, the Supreme Court has nevertheless defined it a bit more precisely to mean any speech that proposes a commercial transaction, and the Court has further held that it is entitled to First Amendment protection.[2]

Recognizing that although commercial speech is different than that which the First Amendment was originally intended to protect, the court has observed that commercial speech is important and worthy of protection because it promotes "intelligent and well informed … private economic decisions" that are central to our free enterprise economy.[3] "The free flow of commercial information," the Court said, "is indispensable."[4]

The case that gave rise to this conclusion, *Virginia State Board of Pharmacy v. Virginia Citizens Consumer Council*, involved a Virginia law that prohibited pharmacies from advertising prescription drug prices. The Court determined that the state's purported interest in the prohibition, to maintain professionalism in its licensed pharmacists, could be achieved in other, less restrictive ways and that it did not justify the complete ban on price advertising.

1 *See Jacobellis v. Ohio*, 378 U.S. 184, 197 (1964) (Stewart, J., concurring).
2 *Virginia State Board of Pharmacy v. Virginia Citizens Consumer Council, Inc.*, 425 U.S. 748, 762 (1976).
3 *Id.* at 765.
4 *Id.*

DOI: 10.4324/9781003197966-8

The Court also observed that whatever state interest may exist, it was outweighed by the public's right to receive information about prescription drugs: "When drug prices vary as strikingly as they do, information as to who is charging what becomes more than a convenience. It could mean the alleviation of physical pain or the enjoyment of basic necessities."[5]

WHAT COMMERCIAL SPEECH IS NOT

Just as important as understanding the definition of commercial speech is understanding what is excluded. The mere fact that speech may be undertaken for commercial purposes – that is, produced and distributed for the purpose of making money – is not sufficient to make it "commercial speech" for constitutional purposes. We saw this concept previously, in the context of rights of publicity and misappropriation (see Chapter 5), where an expressive use could not give rise to a misappropriation of an individual's right of publicity, because such uses are protected by the First Amendment.

The same is true more generally. The mere fact that speech may be undertaken for the primary purpose of making money does not render such speech "commercial." Most media producers intend to make money on their productions, either through direct sales (e.g., selling movie tickets or copies of a book), subscriptions (e.g., streaming services), or advertising (e.g., podcasts, traditional broadcasting, and some ad-supported streaming services), but that does not mean they are commercial.

The advertising announcements contained within ad-supported media may be commercial speech, but the expressive content itself typically is not, and it is therefore entitled to broad First Amendment protection.

THE SPECTRUM OF FIRST AMENDMENT PROTECTION

With *Virginia State Board of Pharmacy*, we start to see a spectrum of First Amendment protection for speech emerge. At one end of the spectrum is speech that is nearly absolutely protected – the type of speech that falls squarely within what the framers of the Constitution sought to protect – political and expressive speech. On the other side of the spectrum is speech that receives no protection – obscenity, child pornography, and, as we will see later in this chapter, false or misleading advertising. In the middle sits commercial speech, which is entitled to some protection, but not as much as those categories of core First Amendment speech.

Put differently, the government has more latitude to regulate commercial speech than it does political or expressive speech, but it cannot ban it outright, as it can with categories of speech that receive no First Amendment protection.

5 *Id.* at 764–65.

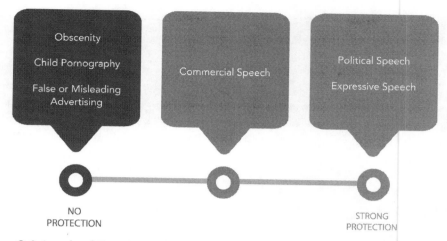

Figure 8.1 Levels of First Amendment protection for certain types of speech.

REGULATING COMMERCIAL SPEECH

Several years after *Virginia Board of Pharmacy*, the Supreme Court decided *Central Hudson Gas & Electric v. Public Service Commission*,[6] in which it was called upon to determine whether New York State could ban electric utilities from advertising to promote the use of electricity.

In concluding that the New York regulation violated the First Amendment rights of the electric utility, it articulated a four-part test, essentially modeled on the general intermediate scrutiny test,[7] to determine whether a particular restriction on commercial speech passes constitutional muster. Such a regulation is constitutional if:

1. The speech involves a lawful activity and the speech is not misleading;
2. The government has a substantial government interest in regulating the speech;
3. The regulation must directly advance the government's purported interest; and
4. The regulation must be no more extensive than necessary to advance the interest.[8]

For example, in 2020, a federal appeals court invalidated a Colorado town's ordinance that prohibited door-to-door solicitation after 7 pm.[9] The town of Castle Rock asserted that the ordinance was necessary to advance the government's interest in ensuring the privacy and safety of its citizens on the theory that a significant amount

---

6 447 U.S. 557 (1980).

7 Some courts have subsequently determined that the *Central Hudson* test is appropriate only where the regulation at issue is content neutral. Where the regulation is content based, the ordinary strict-scrutiny test would apply. *See, e.g., Reed v. Town of Gilbert*, 576 U.S. 155, 173 (2015).

8 *Id.* at 566.

9 *Aptive Environmental, LLC v. Town of Castle Rock*, 959 F.3d 961 (10th Cir. 2020).

of crime was perpetrated by people posing as door-to-door solicitors, and that such crimes often happen at night.[10]

The court didn't buy it, finding that the town failed to establish that the curfew on door-to-door solicitation directly advances its stated interest because there was no evidence to suggest that there was a correlation between evening solicitation and crime, nor any evidence that solicitation infringes on the privacy of Castle Rock's citizens, much less in the evening specifically. The court therefore struck the law as unconstitutional.[11]

COMPELLED COMMERCIAL SPEECH

Central Hudson deals with circumstances where the government seeks to regulate commercial speech that is made voluntarily by its speaker, but recall that the First Amendment not only guarantees the right to speak freely, but also the right to not speak or to be free from compelled speech. Since there is less protection given to commercial speech than other types of speech, does that mean there are circumstances where the government may be able to force those engaging in commercial speech to say certain things?

In short, yes. The Supreme Court has held that regulations requiring the placement of warnings, disclosures, or other verbiage intended to protect consumers are generally constitutional so long as the content is factual, uncontroversial, and reasonably related to the state's interest in consumer protection.[12]

Where the mandated content is considered controversial, courts apply the *Central Hudson* test.

WHO REGULATES COMMERCIAL SPEECH?

When it comes to commercial speech, there is no shortage of government agencies eager to impose their oversight.

FEDERAL REGULATION

Perhaps the most widely known agency with authority over advertising, and certainly the one with the broadest authority, is the **Federal Trade Commission** (FTC), an independent agency with five commissioners, which has authority under the Federal

---

10 *Id.* at 966.
11 *Id.* at 999.
12 *Zauderer v. Office of Disciplinary Counsel of the Supreme Court of Ohio*, 471 U.S. 626, 651 (1985).

Trade Commission Act to regulate, investigate, and impose civil penalties for a broad array of conduct, including false and deceptive practices and related consumer protection concepts.

Depending on the nature of the commercial speech, there may be other federal agencies in the mix as well, imposing obligations that go beyond the basic standards set forth in the FTC Act.

For instance, the Food and Drug Administration regulates advertising of prescription drugs, while airline advertising is overseen by the Department of Transportation. Food advertising and labeling is the province of the Department of Agriculture. Alcohol ads are regulated by the Bureau of Alcohol, Tobacco, Firearms, and Explosives. A host of agencies have jurisdiction over ads for banks and other financial services, including the Securities and Exchange Commission, the Federal Deposit Insurance Corporation, the Consumer Financial Protection Bureau, and others.

STATE REGULATION

State governments also play a considerable role in the regulation of advertising within their borders, especially for licensed professionals such as lawyers, doctors, insurance agents, real estate brokers, general contractors, and the like.

Moreover, most state attorneys general have an office of consumer protection that operates akin to the Federal Trade Commission, investigating and prosecuting general affronts to consumer protection through false or deceptive practices.

The principal distinction between state and federal regulations is that state regulations, as you might expect, apply only to activities and advertising that take place within the state, whereas federal enforcement agencies have jurisdiction throughout the entire United States.

FALSE OR DECEPTIVE ADVERTISING

Under the Federal Trade Commission Act, at a minimum, advertising must be truthful, non-deceptive, and fair. In addition, any claims made in the advertising must be backed up by appropriate evidence.

DECEPTIVE ADVERTISING

The FTC describes a deceptive advertisement as one that contains a statement that is likely to mislead consumers acting reasonably under the circumstances, and that the statement is material, that is, it is a key part of the consumer's desire to buy the product or service.

The phrase "acting reasonably under the circumstances" means that the consumer is expected to perform a reasonable degree of diligence or have a reasonable amount of knowledge about the product or service that they are buying given the nature of that product or service. For example, it is reasonable to expect a consumer to spend more time learning about and evaluating her options when buying a car as opposed to when buying laundry detergent. The standards for deceptiveness are therefore variable based on the nature

When the FTC evaluates whether an ad is deceptive, it considers the totality of the message in context, taking the text, images and graphics, voiceover, and the like as a whole, as well as how a reasonable consumer would respond to it and what they would believe to be true about the product or service based on the ad.

Note that just as important as what an advertisement says is what it does not say. Omitting key details or features of a product or service in an advertisement can be considered deceptive if the details might have reasonably informed a customer's purchasing decision. For example, suppose an advertisement for a portable media device did not disclose that to use the device the consumer must also buy a monthly subscription for an additional fee. Such an omission would likely be material since some consumers would likely choose to not purchase the device if they had known of the required subscription.

The prohibition on deceptive advertising is why in advertisements and product packaging for food, you will sometimes notice the phrase "serving suggestion." For example, an advertisement for ice cream may feature a photograph of an ice cream sundae, complete with whipped cream, chocolate syrup, nuts, and a cherry. Because the advertiser is selling only the ice cream, but not the accouterments, without a "serving suggestion" disclaimer, one could argue that the ad is deceptive because it creates the impression that the seller is offering the full sundae or ingredients sufficient to make it.

Similarly, some food advertising, such as ads for breakfast cereals, include close-up photos of the product, and carry a disclaimer noting that the photo is "enlarged to show texture" so as not to mislead consumers.

Incidentally, cereal ads often carry the "serving suggestion" disclaimer as well because the cereal is usually shown served with milk, perhaps alongside a serving of fruit or orange juice, none of which are included in the box of cereal.

ADVERTISING UNFAIR BUSINESS PRACTICES

According to the FTC, the technical definition of an unfair business practice is one that causes (or is likely to cause) substantial injury to consumers that the consumer could not reasonably avoid, and the benefit to the consumer does not outweigh the harm. In most cases, "substantial injury" means financial harm or harm to an individual's health or safety.

The most common types of practices that have been held to be unfair are things like aggressive sales tactics used to pressure consumers into buying things they do not really want, or before they have had an opportunity to fully investigate and evaluate their options, for example, time-share vacation rentals.

Another category of unfair practices is known as "negative option arrangements," which is where a consumer receives regular deliveries of particular goods unless they specifically decline a delivery. Such practices can be beneficial to consumers because they provide for routine deliveries of something they may want or need, but they can become unfair when the seller makes it unreasonably difficult to cancel or ignores a consumer's cancellation request.

EVIDENCE-BASED REQUIREMENT

Finally, the FTC requires that advertisers have a "reasonable basis" for the explicit and implicit claims made in their advertising. An explicit claim is a claim that the advertiser affirmatively makes, for example, "this product cures COVID-19." An implicit claim is where the advertiser makes a statement that infers a fact but does not state it directly, for example, "this product boosts antibodies known to fight COVID-19." The nature of the evidence required varies significantly based on the nature of the product or service being advertised and the specificity of the claims.

At a minimum, the claims must be true. If an advertiser states that "four out of five doctors" recommend something, or that something is rated "best in class," there must be some survey evidence to support that statement. If an advertisement makes health or safety claims, the FTC typically requires that an advertiser has "competent and reliable scientific evidence" such as studies that have been reviewed by other professionals in the field.

FTC ENFORCEMENT TOOLS

Although the FTC does not handle consumer complaints directly, it does use such complaints to determine its enforcement priorities. That is, if the FTC receives many complaints about a particular advertiser, it is more likely to investigate.

The FTC has a number of enforcement tools at its disposal. The first and most common is the issuance of a cease-and-desist order that mandates the errant advertiser stop engaging in the false or deceptive practices and can sometimes require that the advertiser takes certain proactive steps in the future, such as presenting evidence of claims made in the ads to the FTC before buying advertising.

The FTC also has the authority to levy civil penalties which, depending on the violation, can amount to millions of dollars. The agency can also mandate that false or deceptive advertisers refund consumers' money either partially or entirely. Sometimes the FTC will order advertisers to buy corrective advertising that includes specific statements or disclosures intended to correct the misrepresentations made in the original advertising.

SPECIAL CATEGORIES OF ADVERTISING

The basic FTC rules against false and deceptive advertising apply to all commercial activities but certain types of advertisements or certain types of claims in ads often draw special regulatory attention.

ADVERTISING TARGETED AT CHILDREN

The FTC looks especially closely at advertising targeted at children or advertising that promotes products and services aimed at children. The FTC reviews such ads using the ordinary principles of false and deceptive advertising, but from the perspective of a child, as opposed to an adult, which effectively heightens the standard since children cannot reasonably be expected to have the same level of knowledge or understanding as an adult.

Online services targeted at children under 13 that collect personal information from their users must separately be sure to comply with the Children's Online Privacy Protection Rule, often referred to as COPPA. The law applies broadly to websites, apps, and even "connected" toys, and "personal information" is defined similarly broadly, including things as simple as the child's name, to more intrusive information such as social security numbers or geolocation data.

Those services subject to COPPA's rules must have a clear and conspicuous privacy policy that identifies the nature of the personal information collected, how it is used, and a description of the parent's rights with respect to their child's personal information.

Perhaps most importantly, COPPA requires that such services get the child's "verifiable parental consent." Although the law provides little guidance on what that means, some common methods include requiring the use of a debit or credit card (simply for age verification, even if there is no charge for the service) or requiring the parent to call the service to confirm consent.

WEIGHT LOSS, DIETARY SUPPLEMENTS, AND RELATED PRODUCTS

The weight loss, physical fitness, nutrition, and wellness markets are massive and are frequent advertisers in virtually all media. Like all other advertisements, claims made in ads for weight loss and related products and services must be fair, accurate, and not deceptive, but because claims in this category are susceptible to exaggeration, the FTC has identified this area for special attention.

In 2003, the agency released a report describing seven claims that were scientifically infeasible, yet appeared in various ads, including products that claim to result in weight loss of two pounds or more per week, for a month or more, without dieting or exercise, products that claim to block the absorption of fat or calories, and products that claim to cause permanent weight loss even after the consumer stops using the product.

"GREEN" PRODUCTS AND SERVICES

Growing categories of claims that have led to increased scrutiny are those that purport to be "green" or "eco-friendly." According to FTC guidance, advertisers should avoid making broad, generalized claims about the environmental friendliness of their products and services because such claims are difficult to substantiate to FTC standards. Advertisers should take care, and ensure they have adequate evidence to support their claims, when making representations about carbon offsets, the degree to which products may be biodegradable, compostable, recyclable, nontoxic, or free from certain chemicals or other substances.

SPONSORSHIP IDENTIFICATION RULES FOR BROADCASTERS

Radio and television broadcasters have an additional layer of regulation when it comes to commercial speech. The FCC's regulations require that when an advertiser provides money, services, or other consideration (essentially anything of value) to the radio or TV station in exchange for anything that appears on the air, the station must identify the content as being sponsored and identify the sponsor.

The regulations also provide that where the station broadcasts a commercial that is clearly a commercial from its context, for example, it identifies the sponsor's name and/or the name of the sponsor's product or service, it means that routine ads placed in normal commercial breaks – the type we're all accustomed to seeing – do not need an explicit notice that they are paid for by an advertiser since it is clear from the context.

The FCC's sponsor identification regulations apply most prominently to programs that feature **product placement** or **product integration**, where an advertiser pays to have their product or service integrated into the narrative of the story, in the case of scripted programming, or where an advertiser pays for coverage during news or lifestyle programming that looks like editorial (news) content. Such programs typically include a sponsor disclosure during the end credits.

Failing to disclose the fact that a particular product reference or appearance is sponsored would not only constitute a violation of FCC rules for licensed broadcasters but could also be considered a deceptive business practice under the FTC's rules.

Online media such as streaming services, podcasts, and websites are not subject to the FCC's jurisdiction, but they are subject to the FTC's rules if they operate in the United States or target U.S. consumers. As more consumers turn to such services as their primary source of news and entertainment, the FTC has increased its attention on them. Accordingly, online media outlets would be well advised to consider whether any of their practices could trigger obligations under the FTC's rules.

ENDORSEMENTS AND SOCIAL MEDIA INFLUENCERS

A related practice that has recently drawn significant attention from the FTC is the use of paid endorsers to hawk products and services on behalf of an advertiser.

The use of endorsers, particularly celebrities, is not a new phenomenon. Major brands have used celebrities to endorse their products for decades, particularly sports personalities such as Michael Jordan who has done dozens of commercials over the years for various brands, including Nike, Gatorade, and Hanes.

The FTC's endorsement guidelines provide that endorsements, by celebrities, customers, or otherwise, are generally acceptable provided that:

1. The endorsement reflects the honest opinions, findings, beliefs, or experiences of the endorser;
2. The endorsement accurately reflects the extent to which the endorser is a user of the product or service being advertised (that is, the ad cannot represent that the endorser is a user of the product if they are not in fact using it);
3. The endorsement does not contain any representations, express or implied, that would constitute false or deceptive advertising if made by the advertiser directly;
4. The advertiser discloses any material connections between the seller and endorser that might materially affect the weight or credibility of the endorsement – for example, if the endorser was paid or given the endorsed product or service for free in exchange for the endorsement – if it is not obvious from the context that the endorser was paid (such as an ad that runs during an obvious commercial break or the endorser is widely known to the public).

In the past, it was relatively easy for advertisers and paid celebrity endorsers to comply with the rules because the endorsers were almost always celebrities, well known to the public as actors, musicians, sports figures, and the like, and the endorsements they offered almost always appeared in ads that were clearly identified as ads. Recently, however, the nature of those paid to endorse products and services has changed.

SOCIAL MEDIA INFLUENCERS

Owing to the rise of social media as a marketing tool, a new form of endorser has emerged: the **social media influencer**. Although some influencers are known outside of their role on social media, most have become popular by virtue of their social media presence, as their audiences grow, brands have begun to hire social media influencers to help promote their wares through sponsored posts.

There is fundamentally nothing wrong with the practice – it is, after all, no different than the traditional celebrity endorsement model – but advertisers and the influencers they hire can get into trouble if they do not properly and effectively disclose the relationship or the sponsored nature of the post.

That is true with any endorsement, but the risk of running afoul of the law is particularly pronounced in the social media context because often the sponsored posts look and feel very similar to the type of posts that influencers might make even without a sponsorship relationship.

For example, a social media influencer who has built her following on offering physical fitness and nutrition tips might regularly post about her workouts or her diet. A photographer might make posts about the camera gear and post-processing software he used to make a certain image.

Such posts are entirely reasonable and entirely lawful, provided that they were made independently by the influencer. But if the influencer begins making posts about particular products or services in exchange for compensation, which could be money, but it also could be simply providing the influencer with a complimentary product or service, then it triggers the FTC's disclosure obligations since, without them, the average social media user would be unable to distinguish between the two.

In contrast, traditional celebrity endorsements are widely understood to have compensation flowing from the advertiser to the endorser, and the advertisements featuring the endorser usually appear in contexts where it is obvious that it is a commercially motivated announcement.

Moreover, most celebrity endorsers and the brands that they represent are well advised by agents, managers, and lawyers, and have become familiar with the law's requirements. Although some online influencers are similarly represented, many are not, and are unfamiliar with the rules of the endorsement marketing road.

Because of the rapidly growing role that social media influencers play in modern marketing, and the corresponding rise in influencer posts that blur the lines between the influencer's own posts and those that are motivated by commercial intent, the FTC issued special guidance in late 2019 specifically aimed at social media influencers.

Regarding *when* to disclose, the FTC recommends:

- Disclose when you have any financial, employment, personal, or family relationship with a brand.
  - Financial relationships aren't limited to money. Disclose the relationship if you got anything of value to mention a product.
  - If a brand gives you free or discounted products or other perks and then you mention one of its products, make a disclosure even if you weren't asked to mention **that** product.
  - Don't assume your followers already know about your brand relationships.
  - Make disclosures even if you think your evaluations are unbiased.
- Keep in mind that tags, likes, pins, and similar ways of showing you like a brand or product are endorsements.
- If posting from abroad, U.S. law applies if it is reasonably foreseeable that the post will affect U.S. consumers. Foreign laws might also apply.
- If you have no brand relationship and are just telling people about a product you bought and happen to like, you don't need to declare that you don't have a brand relationship.

Regarding *how* to disclose, the FTC offers the following guidance:

- Place it so it's hard to miss.
  - The disclosure should be placed with the endorsement message itself.
  - Disclosures are likely to be missed if they appear only on an "About Me" or profile page, at the end of posts or videos, or anywhere that requires a person to click "More."
  - Don't mix your disclosure into a group of hashtags or links.
  - The disclosure should be in the same language as the endorsement.
  - Don't assume that a platform's disclosure tool is good enough, but consider using it in addition to your own, good disclosure.
- If your disclosure is in written form, use simple and clear language.
  - Simple explanations like "Thanks to Acme brand for the free product" are often enough if placed in a way that is hard to miss.
  - Using terms such as "advertisement," "ad," or "sponsored" are also often sufficient.
  - On a space-limited platform like Twitter, the terms "Acme Partner" or "Acme Ambassador" (where "Acme" is the brand name) may be sufficient.
  - It is acceptable, but not necessary, to include a hashtag with the disclosure, such as #ad or #sponsored.

- Avoid using vague or confusing terms such as "sp," "soon," or "collab," or stand-alone terms like "thanks" or "ambassador," and stay away from other abbreviations and shorthand when possible.
- If your endorsement is in picture form on a platform such as Instagram Stories or Snapchat, superimpose the disclosure over the picture and make sure viewers have enough time to read it.
- If your endorsement is in video form, the disclosure should be in the video and not just in the description that appears alongside the video. Viewers are more likely to notice disclosures made in both audio and video. Some viewers may watch without sound and others may not notice superimposed words.
- If making an endorsement in a live stream, the disclosure should be repeated periodically during the stream so that viewers who only see part of the stream will also see or hear the disclosure.[13]

One way that advertisers and endorsers can run afoul of the law is through the use of fake reviews to tout products and services. According to a recent FTC press release: "the rise of social media has blurred the line between authentic content and advertising, leading to an explosion in deceptive endorsements across the marketplace. Fake online reviews and other deceptive endorsements often tout products throughout the online world." The director of the FTC's consumer protection bureau further observed that "[f]ake reviews and other forms of deceptive endorsements cheat consumers and undercut honest businesses."[14]

To help combat this issue, the FTC recently issued a notice to more than 700 U.S. companies warning them about the illegality of using fake reviews and other unfair or deceptive practices, including:

- Falsely claiming endorsements by third parties;
- Misrepresenting whether an endorser is an actual, current, or recent user;
- Using an endorsement to make deceptive performance claims;
- Failing to disclose an unexpected material connection with an endorser; and
- Misrepresenting the experience of endorsers as representing consumers' typical or ordinary experience.

Although the notice and associated press release were clear that recipients, which included some of the largest, most powerful companies and brands in the United States, were not singled out or identified because they had violated the law, it is clear that online endorsement marketing is among the FTC's top priorities for the future.

13 Federal Trade Commission, *Disclosures 101 for Social Media Influencers*, November 2019, https://www.ftc.gov/system/files/documents/plain-language/1001a-influencer-guide-508_1.pdf.
14 Federal Trade Commission, Press Release, *FTC Puts Hundreds of Businesses on Notice about Fake Reviews and Other Misleading Endorsements*, October 13, 2021.

IN THE NEWS: COVID-19

In the early days of the COVID-19 pandemic in the spring of 2020, many state and local governments issued executive orders imposing severe restrictions on businesses. In many cases, businesses selling products or offering services deemed not to be "essential" were required to close, and those that could stay open had to follow strict capacity and social distancing guidelines.

In Michigan, Governor Gretchen Whitmer's "Stay Home, Stay Safe" order mandated, among other things, that retailers with more than 50,000 square feet, selling a mix of items deemed essential and nonessential were allowed to stay open, but must close off those areas of the store devoted to selling nonessential items. In addition, the order required that those retailers "should not advertise or promote goods that are not groceries, medical supplies, or items that are necessary to maintain the safety, sanitation, and basic operation of residences."[15]

The Association of National Advertisers (ANA) responded by urging Whitmer to rescind the advertising ban, arguing that it violates the First Amendment because the government failed to justify why it only applies to large retailers, and because "items that are necessary to maintain the safety, sanitation, and basic operation of residences" was not defined.[16] Just several days later, the governor reversed course and removed the advertising ban, a move that was applauded by the ANA.[17]

The pandemic has kept the federal government busy as well, and in more ways than just the obvious ones.

The Federal Trade Commission has pursued a number of enforcement actions aimed at scammers who took advantage of the fear and uncertainty surrounding COVID-19. In July 2020, the FTC sued a California pharmaceutical company for deceptively advertising a $23,000 treatment plan that the company claimed was "uniquely qualified to treat and modify the course of the Coronavirus epidemic in China and other countries" and that it would cause COVID symptoms to subside within two to four days.[18] The company had also promoted various dietary supplements – composed primarily of herbs and spices – claiming that they were effective against cancer and Parkinson's disease, among others. The FTC alleged that the company falsely represented that its treatments had been reviewed by the Food and Drug Administration and that they were safe and effective.[19]

---

15 Michigan Executive Order 2020-42, April 9, 2020.
16 Press Release, Association of National Advertisers, *ANA Calls on Michigan Governor to Rescind Advertising Restrictions*, April 10, 2020.
17 Press Release, Association of National Advertisers, *ANA Applauds Michigan Governor for Not Continuing Advertising Limitation*, April 24, 2020.
18 Press Release, Federal Trade Commission, *Company falsely claimed its "Emergency D-Virus" treatment is "FDA Accepted,"* July 31, 2020.
19 *Id.*

A year later, the medical director of the pharmaceutical company settled the claims by agreeing to not make health-related product misrepresentations in the future and prohibiting him from falsely claiming a product or treatment has been FDA approved when it has not been. He was also ordered to pay a civil judgment of just over $100,000 that could be used to compensate defrauded consumers.[20]

In an April 2021 report, the FTC explained that the case described above was one of 13 enforcement actions brought against companies for making false COVID-19 treatment or prevention claims, or for accepting orders for personal protective equipment and cleaning supplies, such as masks, hand sanitizer, and disinfectants, and either never delivering them or delivering them weeks later.[21] According to the report, since the beginning of the pandemic, the FTC directed more than 350 companies to remove deceptive claims from their marketing materials for products and services, including purported COVID-19 prevention and treatment products and financial relief programs for small businesses and students suffering from pandemic-related economic hardship.[22] During that same period, the FTC received more than 436,000 reports pertaining to COVID-19-related issues, in which consumers reported nearly $400 million in fraud losses.

The report serves as a cautionary tale that there is no shortage of people willing to use tragic events or circumstances as a way to fleece consumers, and those in the media industry should take care to ensure that they do not unwittingly aid and abet them

KEY POINTS AND TAKEAWAYS

1. Commercial speech has been defined by the Supreme Court as "speech that proposes a commercial transaction."
2. The mere fact that speech is produced for the purpose of some commercial advantage – for example, a television show that is supported by advertising or a film that appears on a paid streaming service – is not enough to make the underlying speech "commercial."
3. Commercial speech is protected by the First Amendment, but it enjoys less protection than political or expressive speech.
4. As a result of having less First Amendment protection, it is easier for the government to regulate commercial speech. The limits of such regulation are prescribed by the Supreme Court in the four-factor *Central Hudson* test.
5. The government may also compel commercial speech in appropriate circumstances, such as requiring consumer protection disclosures on products and their packaging.

---

20 Press Release, Federal Trade Commission, *Promoter of $23,000 COVID-19 "Treatment" Plan Barred from Making Bogus Health Claims*, June 14, 2021.
21 Federal Trade Commission, *Protecting Consumers During the COVID-19 Pandemic: A Year in Review* 1 (2021).
22 *Id.*

6. The Federal Trade Commission (FTC) Act prohibits false and misleading advertising at the federal level, which is enforced by the FTC. Many states have their own, similar consumer protection laws that are enforced by state attorneys general or appropriate regulatory agencies.
7. Beyond the FTC's and states' general prohibitions on false or deceptive advertising, there are also a number of regulatory agencies that oversee advertising practices in particular industries, including airlines, financial services, drugs, and food.
8. Endorsement marketing has been used by advertisers for years, but social media has made it more difficult for consumers to readily identify sponsored content. The rules that apply to traditional celebrity endorsers also apply to social media influencers, and the FTC has recently suggested that online endorsements will be an enforcement priority going forward.
9. When in doubt, disclose relationships that may alter the public's opinion or impression of a sponsorship, endorsement, or a particular piece of content.

QUESTIONS FOR DISCUSSION

1. What constitutional principle that we learned about in Chapter 2 is the reason the FTC shares authority with the states over consumer protection and false or deceptive advertising?
2. What do you think about the Michigan governor's attempt to regulate the advertising of "nonessential" items during the early days of the COVID-19 pandemic? The ban was quickly reversed after an industry group suggested it may be unconstitutional, but had the ban been challenged, who would have prevailed? Why? Is it appropriate to apply standard constitutional rules or tests when confronted with something as momentous as a global pandemic?
3. Although the FTC's endorsement rules apply broadly to all types of advertising, the FCC's sponsorship identification rules apply only to broadcast media (outlets licensed by the FCC – essentially only radio and television stations). Should a similar rule be imposed for streaming media?
4. A common theme in the law is that the regulatory framework is often several steps behind technology. In the realm of commercial speech, we have seen the FTC assert that its advertising rules apply to social media, and the agency has issued guidance specifically aimed at social media influencers. Is that appropriate? Is there a case to be made that the FTC's advertising, endorsement, and disclosure regulations should not apply to streaming or the online media space? Why or why not?

9

CHAPTER 9
RADIO AND TELEVISION

The U.S. broadcasting, cable, and satellite industries are subject to a complex regime that governs virtually all aspects of their operation. What are the policy objectives behind the regulatory structure and how well do those fare in an environment where, thanks to the internet, virtually anyone can be the equivalent of a "broadcaster" with the click of a mouse or the swipe of a finger?

This chapter focuses on the Federal Communications Commission and the regulatory framework that governs broadcast radio and television stations and, to preview Chapter 10, looks at recent attempts to expand the FCC's authority into regulating the internet.

TRADITIONAL BASES FOR REGULATION

Although this book is primarily focused on the law of "digital media," it is useful to look at how so-called "traditional" or "legacy" media is regulated so that we can better understand how and why digital media is regulated differently. Moreover, as discussed earlier, many digital media services are, in fact, simply new-technology manifestations of traditional media services. For instance, the CBS News streaming service offers 24/7 news and public affairs programming derived primarily from the CBS broadcasting network and its television stations. Similarly, the iHeartRadio app features streaming audio derived primarily from iHeartMedia's 700+ broadcast radio stations.

BROADCASTING AND THE FIRST AMENDMENT

The Supreme Court has acknowledged that broadcasters are entitled to First Amendment protection but has also recognized that certain characteristics of the medium justify less protection than other forms of communication, which means it is subject to more regulation, just as we saw with commercial speech in Chapter 8.

The Supreme Court has articulated two rationales for regulating broadcasting: spectrum scarcity and pervasive presence.

SPECTRUM SCARCITY

In a 1969 case, *Red Lion Broadcasting v. FCC*,[1] the Court explained that "because of the scarcity of radio frequencies, the Government is permitted to put restraints on licenses in favor of others whose views should be expressed on this unique medium."[2]

1 395 U.S. 367 (1969).
2 *Id* at 390 (1969).

DOI: 10.4324/9781003197966-9

Radio frequencies – which can carry both radio and television signals – are scarce because they make use of the naturally occurring electromagnetic spectrum which is, by definition, limited, and has been deemed to belong to the public. In addition to broadcasting, that same spectrum must accommodate uses such as public safety two-way communications, air traffic control, military applications, radio astronomy, and myriad others. To help manage everyone wanting to use the airwaves, the government has stepped in to keep the spectrum organized and to ensure that parties do not attempt to use the same portion of the spectrum in a way that might conflict with one another.

One of the most foundational ways the FCC regulates broadcasting is by issuing licenses to broadcasters to use small portions of the spectrum that have been specifically allocated for radio and television use. In *Red Lion Broadcasting*, the Court affirmed that the government's authority extends even to broadcasters, despite the fact that their speech is entitled to First Amendment protection.

The Court noted that while broadcasters have First Amendment rights of their own that warrant protection, more important are the First Amendment rights of their viewers and listeners, which include the right to receive information and participate in the marketplace of ideas. Those rights, said the court, are well served by ensuring that broadcasters, who play a central role in the dissemination of news and information about public affairs, are free from unnecessary government intrusion.[3]

PERVASIVE PRESENCE

Several years after *Red Lion Broadcasting*, the Supreme Court decided another seminal case about the scope of broadcasters' First Amendment rights. In *FCC v. Pacifica Foundation*, the Court considered whether the FCC violated the First Amendment rights of a radio broadcaster when it threatened to sanction it for airing George Carlin's "Filthy Words" monologue that, as the name implies, contained profane material.

In concluding that the FCC was within its rights to regulate indecent or profane material on broadcast platforms, the Court explained that "the broadcast media have established a uniquely pervasive presence in the lives of all Americans" and that "material presented over the airwaves confronts the citizen, not only in public, but also in the privacy of the home, where the individual's right to be left alone plainly outweighs the First Amendment rights of an intruder."[4]

The Court also noted that merely requiring broadcasters to warn people in advance of an indecent or profane broadcast – as opposed to banning the broadcast outright or requiring it to be broadcast during a particular time – was insufficient "[b]ecause the

3 *Id.* at 390.
4 *FCC v. Pacifica Foundation*, 438 U.S. 726, 748 (1978) (citations omitted).

broadcast audience is constantly tuning in and out, prior warnings cannot completely protect the listener or viewer from unexpected program content."[5]

Finally, the Court was especially concerned about the extent to which children could obtain access to broadcast material, observing that "broadcasting is uniquely accessible to children, even those too young to read" and that "[t]he ease with which children may obtain access to broadcast material … amply justify special treatment of indecent broadcasting."[6]

THE FCC AND THE COMMUNICATIONS ACT

As we saw in *Red Lion Broadcasting* and *Pacifica*, the **Federal Communications Commission** (FCC) is the federal agency that has broad authority to regulate broadcast and telecommunications in the United States. Like the Federal Trade Commission that we discussed in Chapter 8, the FCC has five commissioners and is independent, that is, it is not directly associated with any of the three branches of government, though the Commissioners are appointed by the President and confirmed by the Senate.

In 1927, Congress passed the Radio Act, which created the Federal Radio Commission, and was the law that established the guiding principle for the licensing and regulation of broadcasters. To maintain their licenses, broadcasters must show, and the FCC must conclude, that their programming and other actions serve the "public interest, convenience, and necessity."

The Radio Act and the commission it established were soon replaced by the more expansive Communications Act of 1934 and the Federal Communications Commission which, owing to the new law, enjoyed regulatory authority over a broader set of communications technologies, including telephone, telegraphy, and broadcasting.

Although the Communications Act has been amended over the years, the most significant overhaul in recent memory came in 1996 when President Bill Clinton signed the Telecommunications Act into law. The overarching principle of the law was to promote competition in and among communications services, largely by focusing on allowing providers in one market, such as a local telephone company, to compete in another market, such as long-distance phone service, or cable television.

Among the law's more controversial provisions was a significant relaxing of the regulations around broadcasters, including increasing caps on the number of stations

5 *Id*. at 748.
6 *Id*.

any one broadcaster could own, and changing the way broadcasters' licenses were renewed, eliminating the previous competitive licensing process and replacing it with what essentially amounts to presumptive renewal, which means that once somebody has an FCC license to operate a radio or television station, it is very difficult to lose it.

Still, the FCC does have broad authority to enforce its rules. The most common approach is for the FCC to levy fines on broadcasters that violate its rules. The agency may also order corrective measures be taken. In extreme cases, particularly those where there is a pattern of bad conduct, the FCC may seek to revoke a broadcaster's license.

The FCC manifests its authority over broadcasters in a number of ways: through the imposition of regulations on certain types of content, limits on the number of broadcast stations an individual person or company can own, and certain technical considerations and limitations.

BROADCAST CONTENT REGULATION

The Communications Act states plainly that it is not intended to give the FCC "the power of censorship" over radio or television broadcasts and that the FCC is not empowered to do anything that will violate broadcasters' First Amendment rights.[7] But we know from *FCC v. Pacifica*, that although broadcasters do have First Amendment rights, they are limited, which effectively gives the FCC some significant latitude to regulate the content of television and radio broadcasts.

INDECENT AND PROFANE MATERIAL

One area that has been particularly fraught for the FCC over the years is its regulation of indecent and profane material. Recall from Chapter 3 that obscenity receives no First Amendment protection and is therefore unlawful on radio, television, or otherwise. Indecent and profane material is entitled to some First Amendment protection and is therefore sometimes allowed on radio and television, subject to certain rules.

The FCC recognizes indecent material as that which portrays sexual or excretory organs or activities in a way that is patently offensive but does not rise to the level of obscenity. Profane content is that which includes "grossly offensive" language.[8] Indecent and profane material is generally prohibited on radio or television from the hours of 6 am to midnight because it is more likely that children may be in the audience during those hours.[9]

---

7 *See* 47 U.S.C. § 326.
8 Federal Communications Commission, *Obscene, Indecent and Profane Broadcasts*, https://www.fcc.gov/consumers/guides/obscene-indecent-and-profane-broadcasts.
9 Recall that one of the reasons that the *Pacifica* court articulated for justifying limits on broadcasters' First Amendment protection was that broadcasting is so pervasive that children may easily access it.

Despite the general prohibition on indecent and profane material during daytime hours, the FCC has long recognized that there may be occasional slip-ups, particularly during live events such as breaking news or sports coverage, that make it on the air despite the broadcasters' best intentions. Historically, the FCC took the position that it would not levy penalties against broadcasters that inadvertently aired so-called **fleeting expletives** or isolated, brief, unexpected moments of indecency or profanity.

But in 2004 the agency abruptly changed course, assessing a then-record fine against CBS for a widely publicized "wardrobe malfunction" in which Super Bowl XXXVII halftime show performer Justin Timberlake tore off part of co-performer Janet Jackson's clothes, revealing her breast (conveniently timed to coincide with the final line of Timberlake's performance: "Gonna have you naked by the end of this song").[10] That same year, the FCC fined NBC for a Golden Globes telecast in which U2's Bono exclaimed that winning an award was "really f*cking brilliant."[11]

In 2006, the FCC levied fines against Fox for two live broadcasts of the *Billboard Music Awards*, one in 2002 and one the following year. In 2002, the broadcast featured a speech by Cher in which she said: "I've also had critics for the last 40 years saying that I was on my way out every year. Right. So f*ck 'em." The following year's awards telecast featured socialites Nicole Richie and Paris Hilton discussing their Fox show *The Simple Life*. At the beginning of the exchange, Hilton admonished Richie to watch her language, but Richie then went on to talk twice about "cow sh*t," observing that cleaning it out of a Prada purse is "not so f*cking simple," despite the title of their show.[12]

In its order levying the fine against NBC, the FCC noted simply that its prior practice – that moments of isolated or fleeting indecency or profanity would not be enforced by the FCC – was "no longer good law" without additional elaboration.[13]

CBS and Fox challenged the fines and sued the FCC. The cases become procedurally complex, but ultimately the Supreme Court determined that the fines against Fox were unconstitutional because the change in the FCC's enforcement practices, without advance notice to broadcasters, constituted a violation of Fox's due process rights.[14] An appeals court determined that the fine against CBS was improper on similar grounds, though its rationale was rooted in administrative procedure law as opposed to constitutional law.[15]

The FCC's current enforcement guidance provides that when evaluating whether to bring an enforcement action for indecent material, the agency considers the specific

---

10 *CBS Corporation v. FCC*, 535 F.3d 167, 171–72 (3d Cir. 2008).
11 *FCC v. Fox Television Stations, Inc.*, 556 U.S. 502, 508-09 (2009).
12 *Id*. at 510.
13 *Id*. at 517.
14 *FCC v. Fox Television Stations, Inc.*, 567 U.S. 239, 259 (2012).
15 *FCC v. CBS Corporation*, 567 U.S. 953, 953 (2012) (denying certiorari).

nature of the content under review, the time of day it was broadcast, and the context in which the broadcast took place.

CHILDREN'S PROGRAMMING

As we have seen, a common theme in broadcast regulation is the extent to which children may be exposed to inappropriate material. In the Children's Television Act of 1990, Congress mandated that television broadcasters proactively serve the needs of children by offering a minimum amount of children-focused programming.

The FCC's rules implementing the CTA, known unofficially as the "KidVid" rules, require television stations to broadcast at least three hours per week of "educational and informative" (E/I) programming aimed at children 16 years old or younger. Stations must document their E/I programming efforts and the FCC must consider stations' E/I performance when considering whether to renew a station's license.

CLOSED CAPTIONING AND AUDIO DESCRIPTION

Closed captions are textual representations of the audio portion of a television broadcast, superimposed on the screen, intended to benefit individuals who are deaf or hard of hearing. Audio description involves a special audio track on which a narrator describes the major features of the visual portion of the programming, intended to benefit individuals who are blind or have visual disabilities.

Empowered by various federal statutes, the FCC requires that most broadcasters offer closed captions on all English or Spanish-language programming, and to include such captions on any subsequent distributions of the programming, such as on streaming services. The FCC also maintains quality standards for closed captioning to ensure they are accurate, properly placed on screen, and correctly timed to coincide with the corresponding words or sounds that they represent.

Larger broadcasters are required to offer audio description for a portion of their programming, with the expectation that the portion will increase over time such that all programming is covered.

Notably, the FCC's closed captioning and descriptive video rules apply only to broadcast programming. Although the closed captioning rules extend to streaming services, they apply only when the programming was first prepared for broadcast use.

Still, other legal regimes may compel streaming services and other non-broadcast players to provide closed captions and descriptive audio. In particular, the

Americans with Disabilities Act (ADA) requires that places of "public accommodation" take steps to avoid discriminating against individuals with disabilities. Some have asserted that streaming services constitute a place of "public accommodation" and must therefore offer closed captioning and audio description to be compliant with the ADA.

LOUD COMMERCIALS

For years, television viewers had complained about commercials being significantly louder than the programs that they accompanied, a technique that many believed was intentional, to make the commercials stand out and more difficult to ignore. Broadcasters denied the practice.

In 2010, Congress passed the Commercial Advertisement Loudness Mitigation (CALM) Act, directing the FCC to establish rules that require broadcasters and their distributors (cable companies and satellite providers) to apply industry-standard methods to ensure that broadcast programming, including its commercials, are distributed at a consistent average volume.

FALSE INFORMATION, HOAXES, AND NEWS DISTORTION

It may seem fairly obvious, but it is illegal for a broadcaster to knowingly distribute false information, participate in or perpetrate hoaxes, or distort the news. The FCC's prohibition on hoaxes prohibits the broadcast of false information concerning a "crime or catastrophe" if the broadcaster knows the information is false, if it is reasonably foreseeable that the broadcast of the material will cause substantial public harm, and if the public is in fact harmed. As documented by broadcast lawyer David Oxenford, the hoax rule came about in the early 1990s following several high-profile incidents:

> including one case where the on-air personalities at a station falsely claimed that they had been taken hostage, and another case where a station broadcast bulletins reporting that a local trash dump had exploded like a volcano and was spewing burning trash. In both cases, first responders were notified about the non-existent emergencies and emergency teams responded to the fake events after listeners called. Thus, these crucial emergency personnel were temporarily not available to respond to real emergencies.[16]

---

16 David Oxenford, *Plan April fools' Day On-Air Stunts With Care – Remember the FCC Hoax Rule*, Broadcast Law Blog, March 30, 2021, available at https://www.broadcastlawblog.com/2021/03/articles/plan-april-fools-day-on-air-stunts-with-care-remember-the-fcc-hoax-rule/.

Broadcasters that violate the hoax rule can be fined and may have their licenses challenged during the next renewal cycle.

Beyond the hoax rule, the FCC also has a policy against intentionally rigging or slanting the news (news distortion), which, says the Commission, "is a most heinous act against the public interest."[17] Despite the forceful statement, news distortion is not expressly restricted in its regulations. Rather, the FCC looks into whether a broadcaster's actions have deceived the public on some matter of public importance.[18]

CANDIDATE ACCESS RULE

The FCC's candidate access rule requires that broadcasters give candidates for federal office "access" to "use" their facilitates, which essentially means that the stations cannot decline to sell candidates airtime for their commercials. The access rule does not apply to state or local candidates, or to "issue" advertisers or political action committees.

EQUAL-TIME RULE

The equal-time rule requires that if a station sells time to a candidate for *any* office – federal, state, or local – it must offer an equal opportunity to opposing candidates to buy time as well. In this context, an equal opportunity means an opportunity to buy a comparable amount of time, to reach a comparable audience, at the same (or less) cost than the initial candidate.

The equal-time rule is not triggered by coverage of a candidate on a bona fide newscast, interview program, documentary (where the candidate is not the central subject), or on-the-spot news coverage that happens to involve the candidate. That means if a broadcaster features coverage of a particular candidate, or broadcasts a documentary that includes a brief mention of a particular candidate, the broadcaster is not obligated to offer equivalent access to opposing candidates.

The equal-time rule is similar to the candidate access rule, but the key distinction between the two is that the candidate access rule applies only to federal candidates. The equal-time rule applies to any qualified candidate, provided that the station has offered time to an opposing qualified political candidate.

FAIRNESS DOCTRINE

The equal-time rule is sometimes confused with the now-defunct **fairness doctrine**, a law that was abolished in 1987. The regulation required broadcasters to dedicate a

---

17 *In re Complaints Covering CBS Program "Hunger in America,"* 20 F.C.C.2d 143, 151 (1969).
18 *See* Chad Raphael, *The FCC's Broadcast News Distortion Rules: Regulation by Drooping Eyelid*, 6 Comm. Law & Pol'y 485, 496 (2001).

certain amount of airtime to covering controversial matters of public importance and give airtime to each side of a particular debate. For example, if a broadcaster spent time discussing an anti-abortion measure, the fairness doctrine would require that the broadcaster also present a pro-choice perspective on the same measure.

But in practice, issues are rarely as binary as the equal-time rule would suggest. Indeed, abortion is a good example of the complexity inherent in administering and enforcing the doctrine. Some believe abortion should be prohibited entirely, while others believe it is the mother's choice. Still others believe that there should be no limits, others believe late-term abortions should be prohibited, while others believe the procedure should be reserved for when it is necessary to protect the life of the mother or where the mother is a victim of sexual assault.

The various "shades of gray" in the abortion debate illustrate the challenges of enforcing the fairness doctrine. Under the doctrine, should each of those positions be given equal time?

Despite the practical challenges of enforcing the law, in recent years, in the wake of the increasingly polarized political climate, and growing accusations of "fake news," some have called for restoring the doctrine as a way to bring the media back to being an instrumentality of the marketplace of ideas, thereby advancing democratic ideals.

OWNERSHIP LIMITS

In addition to its limited authority over broadcast content, the FCC has rules that limit the number of radio and television stations any one company or entity can own. Those rules were significantly relaxed in 1996 following the passage of the Telecommunications Act, but in exchange, the FCC was obligated to review its rules every four years to see if they continue to serve the public interest. Specifically, the FCC looks into whether its rules foster increased competition among broadcasters, the development of local programming, and diverse programming, viewpoints, and minority-controlled broadcast outlets.

The 1996 changes to the ownership laws led to a momentous shift in the structure of the industry. Prior to 1996, most radio and television stations were run by small or mid-sized operators that owned perhaps a handful of stations, and outside of a few hours per week that were devoted to national programming, the stations were operated and programmed locally.

Today, most local broadcast stations are owned by one of a handful of major broadcast conglomerates and much of the programming originates from a handful of major stations in the larger markets.

Table 9.1 Top five U.S. radio groups.

Broadcaster	Station count	Number of markets
iHeartMedia	745	149
Cumulus Media	355	85
Townsquare Media	224	52
Audacy	217	47
Educational Media Foundation	201	137

Table 9.2 Top five U.S. television groups.

Broadcaster	Station count	Number of markets
Gray	182	112
Nexstar	179	116
Sinclair	125	84
Scripps	105	75
TEGNA	67	52

TELEVISION OWNERSHIP LIMITS

There are no specific limits on the number of television stations a single individual or company can own, but no one entity may own more than 39% of all U.S. television households. As a result, someone owning a number of stations in large, densely populated markets may effectively own fewer stations than someone owning stations in smaller, less populous markets.

Within a single market, a person may own up to two television stations, provided that one of them is not among the top four. As a practical matter, in most markets this means that one entity cannot own more than one of the network-affiliated stations (e.g., ABC, CBS, FOX, or NBC), so the pairings typically involve a single network-affiliated station plus an independent station or one of the smaller networks, such as the CW. When one entity owns two stations in a market, it is called a **duopoly**.

RADIO OWNERSHIP LIMITS

There are no national radio ownership limits, however, the limits on local ownership are more complex than they are in television. The number of radio stations any one individual or entity depends on the total number of stations in the market, and the "service band" of those stations – that is, whether they are on AM or FM. For example, in a large market with 45 or more stations, an entity may own up to eight, but no more than five may be in the same service band. The following chart summarizes the rules for each market size.

Table 9.3 Radio ownership caps.

Station count	Total cap	Service cap
45+	8	5
30–44	7	4
15–29	6	4
<14	5	3

"CROSS-OWNERSHIP" RULES

For many years, the FCC prohibited a single entity from owning both a broadcast station and a newspaper in the same market. Separate rules also prohibited the same entity from owning radio *and* television stations in the same market, unless there was a certain number of other "independently owned media voices" in the market, as determined by a formula in the FCC's rules.

In 2017, the FCC abolished both rules, finding that they were outdated given the rapid rise in the number of new sources through which people could access news and information. The FCC's action was challenged in court by several media watchdog organizations, but ultimately the FCC prevailed, and the cross-ownership rules were formally abolished in June 2021.

PAY TV REGULATION

The FCC also has the authority to regulate cable and satellite providers, sometimes called **pay tv providers** or, in the industry, they are known as **multichannel video programming distributors** or **MVPDs**. The term MVPD encompasses both **cable operators**, such as Comcast and Spectrum, that distribute programming by wires that enter customers' homes, and **direct broadcast satellite services**, such as Dish Network and DIRECTV, that distribute programming to consumers by way of small satellite dishes attached to a consumer's house. Today, a growing number of MVPDs distribute content via the internet using apps, a class of distributor sometimes called a **virtual MVPD**, which includes providers like YouTube TV and Sling TV.

The precursor to today's MVPDs, known as community antenna television (CATV) systems, began in the 1940s when they were used to distribute broadcast television signals to areas that could not receive them over the air due to various geographic constraints, such as mountainous terrain, that made the signals difficult to receive. The CATV system would mount an antenna somewhere where the signals could be received and then distribute them over wires to each household in the affected area.

Over time, the technology advanced, and enterprising broadcasters recognized that cable-based distribution could be a business unto itself, charging a monthly fee to consumers for access to programming that was not available through over-the-air broadcasters. Programmers began to create channels of programming that would be distributed only by way of cable transmission as opposed to traditional over-the-air broadcasting. Early cable networks, distributed solely by way of a cable system, included TBS, TNT, and CNN. As technology continued to evolve, the industry developed new business models, which led to premium channels such as HBO and Showtime and pay-per-view movies and sporting events.

Today, most MVPD lineups have dozens of channels featuring subject-specific programming on a range of topics including news, public affairs, sports, general entertainment, lifestyle, science and technology, history, and children's programming.

THE REGULATORY ENVIRONMENT OF PAY TV

Recall that the two principles that justify the regulation of broadcasting are spectrum scarcity (*Red Lion Broadcasting*) and pervasiveness (*Pacifica*).

Neither applies to MVPDs.

Cable operators do not use the public electromagnetic spectrum. Instead, they build their own wire-based networks by burying cables (or stringing them from telephone poles). DBS providers use some electromagnetic spectrum, just like broadcasters, but the portion of the spectrum they use is not nearly as limited as the traditional broadcast spectrum.

Satellite or cable providers do not have the same pervasive presence as broadcasters. To receive pay tv content, a consumer must pay for it, and in some cases, a representative of the MVPD visits the house to install equipment and authorize the service. Put simply, MVPD programming is essentially "invited into the home."

On account of those differences, the Supreme Court has acknowledged that the degree of First Amendment protection that MVPDs are entitled to is greater than broadcasters, but it is not absolute. In *Turner Broadcasting System v. FCC*,[19] the Court was called upon to determine whether a 1992 law requiring cable systems to carry local broadcasters' signals was a violation of the cable companies' First Amendment rights against speech. The court concluded that the state's interest in ensuring access to local broadcast signals outweighed the harm to cable companies' rights and allowed the law to stand.

19 512 U.S. 622 (1994).

THE BROADCAST-CABLE SPECTRUM OF PROTECTION

As we have seen elsewhere in this book, the principles of First Amendment protection articulated by Congress and the courts allow us to infer a spectrum of protection for broadcast and MVPD-distributed programming.

On the far left is broadcasting, which receives the least amount of protection, and is therefore the most regulated, on account of spectrum scarcity and pervasiveness. To the right of broadcasting are cable and satellite, which we can infer from *Turner Broadcasting*, and the reasoning in *Pacifica* and *Red Lion Broadcasting*, are afforded more protection (and the government is even less entitled to regulate it) because it does not use public spectrum. It is also not pervasive in the same way broadcasting is, since one has to subscribe to it.

Although the Court has not decided a case specifically on this issue, we can infer that premium cable is afforded a bit more protection than even regular MVPD programming. That's because it's even less pervasive – not only do you have to have an MVPD subscription, but you have to have to separately subscribe to the premium channel. That's why the programming on premium cable networks can be more liberal with indecent or profane material.

That leads us to the internet. What degree of protection should the internet be afforded under the First Amendment? The spectrum scarcity principle might suggest that the First Amendment should be unbounded on the internet because there is today an abundance of bandwidth. Virtually anyone who wants a presence on the internet can have one. The pervasiveness principle might counsel the opposite though. The internet has become so ubiquitous, and accessible through so many devices today, that it has become practically impossible to avoid.

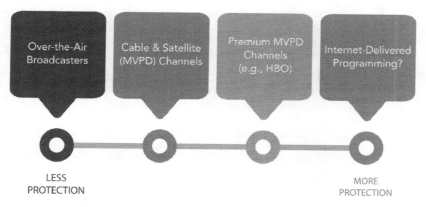

Figure 9.1 Levels of First Amendment protection afforded to different types of electronic media.

As we will see in the rest of this chapter and into the next, the questions surrounding whether and, if so, to what extent the internet should be regulated have no easy answers, and are still very much the subject of fervent debate.

NEW TECHNOLOGIES

In *Red Lion Broadcasting*, the Supreme Court wrote that "although broadcasting is clearly a medium affected by a First Amendment interest … differences in the characteristics of new media justify differences in the First Amendment standards applied to them."[20]

Putting aside the quaintness of the Court referring to broadcasting as "new media," the Court made a sage observation: new technologies sometimes require changes to the regulatory environment.

THE EVOLUTION OF PAY TV

MVPDs have become best known for selling a bundle of channels for a single monthly price, often divided into various packages, with costlier packages offering more programming than cheaper packages. Although some consumers found the bundle convenient, as prices climbed, many began to believe that the bundle had grown too big and bloated to be worth the money.

Seeking to capitalize on changing consumer preferences, and the growth of fast internet connections, some cable programmers began to devise direct-to-consumer services that offered content through the internet as opposed to traditional MVPDs. Such offerings have become known as **over the top** or **OTT** services because they go "over the top" of existing television services. Of course, the MVPDs were resistant to OTT at first because such services threatened their bottom line: if people could subscribe to "cable television" without a cable company, there would soon be no need for cable companies.

To appease the MVPDs, programmers devised a plan to provide OTT services only to paid MVPD subscribers. The approach, sometimes called a **walled garden** or **authenticated viewing**, required consumers to sign in to the OTT platform using their MVPD credentials. Only if a viewer had access to a particular channel or suite of channels through their MVPD subscription would they have access to the OTT service.

Among the earliest OTT services was HBO GO, which allowed consumers who had an HBO subscription through their MVPD to access the various HBO channels, plus

---

20 *Red Lion Broadcasting v. FCC*, 395 U.S. 367, 388 (1969).

HBO's rich library of past programming, from a variety of devices, without being tethered to their television.

MVPDs eventually grew more comfortable with the OTT approach, in part because they began to see themselves as broadband providers as opposed to just video distributors. Reduced demand for traditional MVPD services has resulted in increased demand for bigger, faster internet connections to allow consumers to stream all of that content from OTT services.

Slowly, the market evolved, and OTT services began to be made available to those who were not already MVPD subscribers. HBO Now, for instance, represented HBO's expansion of HBO Go to those who did not already have an HBO subscription. Both services have since been subsumed by HBO Max, which is available to anyone for a monthly fee, as well as bundled with traditional MVPD subscriptions.

Indeed, each of the major networks is now affiliated with at least one corresponding streaming service; the same is true for most cable networks as well, whose content is available either through a dedicated OTT platform or a platform that aggregates content from multiple sources.

Many consumers today have done away with a traditional MVPD subscription, opting instead for broadband service and one or more streaming services. In the industry, these people are referred to as **cord cutters** because they have "cut the cord" of traditional cable. Those who have never had an MVPD subscription are called **cord nevers**.

Table 9.4 Major media enterprises and their corresponding production and distribution entities.

Parent company	Studio	Traditional network	Streaming service
Disney	Disney Television; Twentieth Century Television	ABC	Disney+
Paramount Global (formerly ViacomCBS)	CBS Studios; Paramount	CBS; Showtime	Paramount+; Showtime Anytime
Comcast	Universal	NBC	Peacock
Fox Corporation	Fox Entertainment	FOX	Tubi
Comcast + Disney	Various	Various	Hulu
Warner Bros. Discovery	Warner Bros.; HBO; Turner	HBO; Turner Networks (e.g., CNN, TBS, TNT).	HBO Max

DO EVOLVING BUSINESS MODELS REQUIRE EVOLVING RULES?

As we have seen, our legal system justifies regulating broadcasters on the basis of spectrum scarcity and pervasive presence. MVPDs are regulated less than broadcasters because they are not as pervasive and do not use any public electromagnetic spectrum.

If streaming services have essentially become replacements for traditional broadcasting and MVPDs, should we regulate streaming services the same way we regulate traditional media? Streaming services use the public internet which is, for all practical purposes, limitless, and does not present the same spectrum scarcity issues that broadcasting does. Moreover, although the internet has become ubiquitous, it is not as pervasive as broadcasting, in that one must subscribe to an internet service provider to connect to it and have an internet-enabled device to access it.

So, on the one hand, as a replacement for traditional media, there is a justification for regulating it just as we regulate traditional media. On the other hand, the traditional bases for regulating media suggest that internet-delivered media should be unregulated, or at least less regulated than broadcasters and MVPDs.

A number of broadcasters affiliated with the major television networks recently argued that vertically integrated streaming services – that is, those owned by companies that also own studios or television networks, such as Disney+ or NBC's Peacock – should be subject to certain FCC rules that allow local broadcast stations to force MVPDs to carry their signals and require equal-access to certain programming so that it may be distributed across different platforms. Those in favor of such regulation point to the fact that streaming services are quickly becoming the predominant mechanism by which people consume news and entertainment. Those opposed, primarily the operators of such OTT services, assert that subjecting a new technology to regulations of yesterday's technology will burden the development of advancement and dissuade others from investing in new technologies.

IN THE NEWS: STREAMING WARS

Many readers will remember Netflix as one of the earliest streaming services. When Netflix first launched its streaming offering, pivoting from its original business as a DVD-by-mail movie rental house, the service featured popular content from traditional studios and networks, such as *Friends*, *The West Wing*, *Parks and Recreation*, and *The Office*. At the time, the studios found Netflix's offer of significant upfront cash payments for their library content too good to refuse. And for Netflix, having popular, marquee programming was key to driving consumers to sign up for the fledgling service.

As its subscriber base grew, Netflix amassed a significant amount of data about its viewers — what they liked to watch, how long they watched it, and so on — information that traditional broadcasters and MVPDs generally did not have. Eventually, Netflix used that information to begin its own foray into programming, first by commissioning content to be exclusive to Netflix, and later building its own studio operation to create original content wholly in-house.

Around the same time, the traditional studios who had been licensing content to Netflix, and enjoying the payday that came with it, began to question whether they should continue to do so, as Netflix evolved from merely a distributor of their content into a formidable competitor by using data it garnered from the distribution of studio content to help guide its decisions about which original productions to pursue.

The traditional studios and networks responded by launching their own streaming offerings, aimed at not only competing with Netflix, but also as a way to develop a direct relationship with their audiences and, in turn, begin to build a treasure trove of data about viewing patterns that might inform future programming and business decisions.

The business model that underlies most streaming services is fundamentally different from traditional media. In the traditional sphere, the goal was to get audiences to watch as much content as possible for as long as possible to maximize advertising revenue. Although there are some advertising-supported streaming services, it is far more common for such services to charge a monthly fee from subscribers. The goal, then, is to get as many subscribers as possible, regardless of whether they actually watch the content on the platform. To do that, streaming services focus on maximizing the amount of content they have available, hoping that there is something that is a "must have" for as many people as possible.

The shift to streaming-first business models is believed to be the motivation behind a wave of consolidation that has ripped through the entertainment industry over the past ten years or so. In 2011, one of the nation's largest MVPDs, Comcast, acquired NBCUniversal. AT&T, which owned satellite-based MVPD DIRECTV announced in 2016 that it would acquire Time Warner, the parent company of Warner Bros. studios, HBO, and various cable networks such as CNN, TNT, and TBS. The following year, Disney announced it would pay a staggering $71 billion to acquire the Twentieth Century Fox movie and TV studios as well as a host of popular networks including FX and National Geographic. In 2019, CBS and Viacom merged back together (the two had been combined in 2000, then split apart in 2006), and in 2022, Discovery, the parent company of networks such as the Discovery Channel, Animal Planet, and the Travel Channel, combined with WarnerMedia to create Warner Bros. Discovery, in a deal said to be worth $43 billion.

Today, the "streaming wars" are raging, with Netflix fighting to maintain its first-mover advantage over the traditional studios, which have been busy building massive content libraries through unprecedented industry consolidation, and each launching their own streaming services. Meanwhile, new, well-resourced players such as Apple have been getting into the space, leveraging their dominance in hardware to promote subscriptions to their Apple Music and Apple TV+ content services.

Be careful what you wish for.

One of the major criticisms of traditional MVPD offerings is that the packages offered had become large and bloated, with prices to match. Many complained that to get the channels they wanted, they also had to pay for channels they didn't even watch. Many consumer advocates saw direct-to-consumer streaming services as the solution to their bundling problems.

But now some consumers have become frustrated that they must subscribe to a battery of streaming services just to get the shows they want to watch. *Squid Game* is exclusive to Netflix, *The Good Fight* is only on Paramount+, while *The Mandalorian* is a Disney+ show, and so on. According to one industry study, 82% of U.S. households pay for at least one streaming service, while the average subscriber has four.[21] The study found that "[p]eople are finding it increasingly difficult to manage subscriptions, find the entertainment they're looking for, and balance costs against their tolerance for advertising."[22]

Industry insiders believe that the massive industry consolidation that is now afoot will result in a wave of re-bundling. For example, now that Discovery and WarnerMedia have combined to form Warner Bros. Discovery, many analysts expect the company will offer a combined streaming platform (or at least a special "bundle" price) for HBO Max and Discovery+. Indeed, Disney recently announced that it would package together Hulu Live – an OTT-delivered MVPD service – with its Disney+ and ESPN+ services.

KEY POINTS AND TAKEAWAYS

1. Broadcasters have First Amendment rights, but they receive less protection than other speakers, which allows the government to regulate broadcasting more than it might with other types of speech.

---

21 Deloitte, Digital Media Trends, April 16, 2021, https://www2.deloitte.com/us/en/insights/industry/technology/digital-media-trends-consumption-habits-survey/summary.html (last visited February 5, 2022).
22 *Id.*

2. The two principles upon which the Supreme Court has justified the regulation of broadcasting are spectrum scarcity, that is, a limited amount of electromagnetic spectrum requires a licensing mechanism to allocate portions of bandwidth for particular uses; and pervasive presence, meaning that broadcast signals are all around us, intrude our homes, and are capable of reaching children.

3. The FCC has implemented its authority over broadcasters through various content- and structure-based regulations, including restrictions on the broadcast of profane or indecent material, and various restrictions on the number of broadcast stations a single entity may own, among others.

4. Programming distributed through MVPDs – traditionally referred to as "cable television" but is today distributed through a number of methods including satellite and the internet – is subject to less regulation owing to the fact it is less pervasive (that is, a consumer has to "invite" it into the home) and it does not make use of the public electromagnetic spectrum.

5. Today, internet-based "over-the-top" streaming services, such as Netflix, Disney+, and Tubi, are beginning to replace traditional broadcast and MVPD offerings by providing low-cost or free ad-supported content delivered to virtually any internet-enabled device. Although such services are largely unregulated, there has been some interest among certain industry stakeholders to consider subjecting them to additional regulation.

QUESTIONS FOR DISCUSSION

1. The FCC's position on indecent and profane material, and particularly "fleeting expletives," has changed over time. Should the FCC have the authority to regulate such speech in the first place? If so, where should it draw the line? How should it go about drawing that line?

2. Some have criticized the relaxation of the FCC's ownership rules, asserting that it has led to exactly the opposite of the FCC's stated goals – less diverse programming and less competition among broadcasters – while others have asserted that the rule should be further relaxed because traditional broadcasting is simply not as important as it once was due to new distribution technologies such as streaming, and the laws are no longer required to serve their stated purpose. What do you think? Should we maintain restrictions on how many outlets a broadcaster can own?

3. Online streaming services are fast replacing traditional broadcast outlets as many consumers' primary source of news and entertainment. Should the FCC have jurisdiction over such services? How do the rationales of spectrum scarcity and ubiquity apply to internet-based streaming? Are those two principles still the correct lenses through which to evaluate media regulation?

CHAPTER 10
THE INTERNET

As compared with the broadcast industry, the internet is virtually unregulated. There are even several laws that grant internet broadcasters immunities that are simply not applicable to traditional media. As internet platforms become more pervasive and, in some cases, effectively serve as a replacement for traditional media enterprises, what changes may need to be made to the regulatory environment? What are the policy arguments for and against making changes?

NETWORK NEUTRALITY

One area where the FCC has attempted to insert itself into the regulatory framework of the internet is called **network neutrality** (or **net neutrality**, sometimes referred to as **internet openness**) – and its attempts have not been without controversy.

Network neutrality means different things to different people, but generally speaking, and in simple terms, network neutrality is the principle that no internet service provider (ISP) should discriminate based on the nature of the content being transmitted, the application or software being used, the type of user, or the platform or website that is engaged in a particular communication. In short, network neutrality means that the internet should offer a level playing field for everyone. Some characterize a neutral internet as a "dumb pipe" – that is, nothing more than a conduit that carries digital traffic, without regard to what it is, where it's going, and who it's going to and from.

CONCEPTS IN NETWORK NEUTRALITY

Broadly speaking, there are four key concepts in network neutrality that are important to understand.

PROTOCOL DISCRIMINATION

Protocol discrimination occurs when an ISP blocks or slows traffic based on the nature of the communication. For instance, instant messaging applications use certain protocols that can be identified by ISPs, and if one desired, could block or slow down all messenger-related traffic.

Why might an ISP block certain types of traffic? Net neutrality experts fear ISPs may do it to gain a competitive advantage over their competitors for other services. For example, when internet-based voice call services such as Skype entered the scene, allowing people to make long-distance voice calls without the use of a traditional

DOI: 10.4324/9781003197966-10

phone carrier (and, by extension, without running up high long-distance phone bills), a number of mobile carriers that offered both voice and data service reportedly began blocking the protocols used by the various voice call apps in an apparent attempt to force their users to place traditional long-distance calls that are more lucrative for the carrier.

IP ADDRESS DISCRIMINATION

An **internet protocol address** or **IP address** is a unique numeric identifier assigned to every device on the internet. Your laptop, tablet, and smartphone each have a unique IP address. Using IP addresses, or ranges of IP addresses, ISPs have the ability to identify the source or destination of traffic flowing across their network. IP address discrimination, then, is exactly what it sounds like: it is when an ISP accelerates or decelerates traffic destined to or from particular people or services. An ISP might, for example, offer to accelerate traffic from a particular video streaming service (or even decelerate traffic from a competing streaming service) in exchange for a fee paid by the streaming service to the ISP.

Net neutrality advocates fear that IP address discrimination will make it difficult for new internet services to get a foothold in the market because they cannot afford to pay for priority, putting them at a significant disadvantage over the larger, well-resourced incumbent services that could pay to have their traffic delivered faster which, in turn, leads to improved streaming quality, and the like.

PRIVATE NETWORK ACCELERATION

Closely related to IP address discrimination is the concept of **private network acceleration**, which occurs when an ISP agrees to accelerate or otherwise prioritize traffic to and from certain sources. For instance, an ISP might agree to guarantee certain transmission speeds for certain services, such as streaming media services. Another approach is to allow such traffic to flow without counting toward the data caps that the ISP imposes on its consumers, effectively de-prioritizing content that is not favored by the ISP.

For instance, in 2012, Comcast was accused of prioritizing content streamed through its own Xfinity app on the Xbox 360 by not counting such traffic against its customer's data caps, while traffic from competing streaming services, such as HBO Go, Hulu, and Netflix, did count. In response, Comcast explained that it was not prioritizing traffic on its network but rather, the Xbox traffic was carried on a separate network that was "above and beyond, and distinct from, the bandwidth a customer has for his or her regular Internet access service."[1] Accordingly, says Comcast, it made sense not to count the traffic against the user's ordinary usage cap.

----

1 Tony Werner, *The Facts about Xfinity TV and Xbox 360: Comcast Is Not Prioritizing*, Comcast Corporate Blog, https://corporate.comcast.com/comcast-voices/the-facts-about-xfinity-tv-and-xbox-360-comcast-is-not -prioritizing (last accessed February 5, 2022).

PEERING

Peering refers to the practice of locating internet servers at a physical location where they can connect directly to an ISP network, reducing the number of steps that the traffic must go through before reaching the end user which, in turn, improves speed and reliability.

Netflix, for example, has been known to enter into peering arrangements with internet service providers, which allows the streaming service to place its servers in the same data centers where the ISP has its equipment. This allows the ISP to tie directly into Netflix, which is intended to, in its own words:

> enable ISPs to provide a great Netflix experience for our mutual customers ... by localizing Netflix traffic as close as possible to our members, limiting the network and geographical distances that our video bits must travel during playback. This of course benefits Netflix members, but it also benefits ISPs and internet users in general.[2]

NETWORK NEUTRALITY IN THE UNITED STATES

Ensuring network neutrality was a major policy initiative for President Obama's administration, and in 2010, helmed by Obama-appointee Chairman Tom Wheeler, the FCC issued its Open Internet Order which, broadly, contained three key provisions:

1. **No blocking**. The order prohibited ISPs from blocking any lawful content, applications, services, or nonharmful devices from their networks. Mobile providers were specifically prohibited from blocking services that competed with their voice services.
2. **No unreasonable discrimination**. Under the order, ISPs were prohibited from unreasonably discriminating against lawful network traffic. The rule permitted ISPs to engage in reasonable "network management" practices, such as throttling people who use an excessive amount of bandwidth.
3. **Transparency**. Underlying the entire order is the principle of openness and transparency. The order required ISPs to publicly disclose their network management practices and the terms and conditions of their service so that consumers could make informed decisions about their ISP.

Just a few weeks after the FCC released its order, Verizon sued the FCC to challenge the law, arguing that the FCC lacked authority under the law to issue the order. In 2014, the court agreed in part, vacating the prohibitions on blocking and unreasonable discrimination.

---

2 Netflix, Open Connect Overview, https://openconnect.netflix.com/Open-Connect-Overview.pdf (last accessed February 5, 2022).

The court's reasoning was based on the fact that the FCC classified ISPs as "information services" as opposed to "telecommunications services," which were subject to more regulation and over which the FCC had more authority. The court acknowledged that the FCC had established a case for its rules and suggested that the outcome might be different if the FCC reclassified ISPs as "telecommunications services."[3]

The FCC picked up on the hint and reclassified ISPs in 2015 so that they could be regulated the same way traditional phone companies had been regulated for decades. The FCC then reissued its net neutrality rules, this time with prohibitions on blocking, throttling traffic, and paid prioritization, and an enhanced version of the transparency rules from the 2010 order. The rules were again challenged in court, but they were ultimately upheld.

Then in January 2017, President Donald Trump assumed office and appointed a new FCC chair, Commissioner Ajit Pai. Chairman Pai's first order of business was to reverse the prior regime's network neutrality rules. A year later, in early 2018, the FCC issued its "Restoring Internet Freedom" order that essentially reversed the FCC's prior decision and classified ISPs as information services, effectively killing the net neutrality laws. Advocates of network neutrality challenged the ruling by suing the FCC, but the court upheld the FCC's decision, though it also suggested that states might be able to pass their own network neutrality laws.

In response, a number of states did just that, including California, New Jersey, and Oregon. The Trump administration sued California over the measure, but when President Biden took office, the new administration dropped the lawsuit.

THE COMMUNICATIONS DECENCY ACT

In the years since the internet became commercialized there have been two significant legislative attempts at regulating the content that flows over it. One is the Digital Millennium Copyright Act (the DMCA), which will be discussed later in this book, and the Communications Decency Act (CDA), which was among the various parts of the Telecommunications Act of 1996 discussed earlier.

In brief, the CDA was an attempt to prevent minors from accessing pornographic or other indecent material on the internet. The law imposed criminal sanctions on anyone who knowingly gives, solicits, or displays to anyone under 18 years of age any comment, request, suggestion, proposal, image, or other communication that, in context, depicts or describes, in terms patently offensive as measured by contemporary community standards, sexual or excretory activities or organs. The law also criminalized providing "obscene or indecent" materials to people known to be under 18.

---

3 *Verizon v. FCC*, 740 F.3d 623, 650 (D.C. Cir. 2014).

The law was quickly challenged by free speech advocates and ultimately struck down in *Reno v. ACLU*.[4] In *Reno*, the Supreme Court concluded that the law was a content-based restriction on speech that failed to satisfy the exacting strict scrutiny test. Specifically, the Court held that although protecting minors from indecent material is a valid governmental interest, the CDA was overbroad, because it would likely affect speech aimed at adults,[5] and vague because it did not properly define "indecent" or "patently offensive."[6]

Following the demise of the CDA, Congress responded with the Child Online Protection Act (COPA), which imposed criminal sanctions on those who knowingly posted, for commercial purposes, material that could be harmful to minors.[7] The Supreme Court held that the law was unconstitutional because the government failed to establish that less-restrictive methods, such as using filtering or blocking software, would not be as effective.[8]

SECTION 230

Although the bulk of the CDA was struck by the Supreme Court, a small portion of it was allowed to stand and remains in the law today and in recent years has become a significant political issue.

Referred to as **Section 230**, because the relevant provision of the CDA was codified at Section 230 of the Communications Act, 47 U.S.C. § 230, the law grants **interactive computer services** broad immunities from the conduct of their users. An "interactive computer service" is what we today call an internet platform – a website or service that allows users to upload or post their own content. Section 230 refers to the party uploading the content as an **information content provider**.

Section 230 gives platforms two key protections. First, it states unambiguously that no platform "shall be treated as the publisher or speaker of any information" provided by someone other than the platform. For example, a social media platform cannot be held responsible for defamatory statements posted by a user on its platform. Traditional media do not enjoy such immunities. If that same user were to have made the defamatory comments on television or in a newspaper, the television station or newspaper publisher would be responsible to the defamed party under the republication rule discussed in Chapter 4.

The other protections that Section 230 gives platforms are from liability for engaging in any action to remove or limit access to obscene, violent, harassing, or otherwise

---

4 512 U.S. 844 (1997).
5 *Id.* at 879.
6 *Id.* at 871–72.
7 *See Ashcroft v. ACLU*, 542 U.S. 656, 656 (2004).
8 *Id.* at 666–67.

objectionable content, regardless of whether such material is protected by the First Amendment. Put differently, merely removing or attempting to remove objectionable content does not make a platform a "publisher."

EXCEPTIONS

Section 230 is very broad, but it does contain several exceptions. Section 230 is no defense for a platform that is accused of breaking a criminal law. Likewise, Section 230 does not insulate platforms from intellectual property infringement claims because the DMCA provides a separate procedure for such claims.

In 2018, Congress updated Section 230 with a new exception for sex trafficking, creating potential liability for platforms that support or facilitate such activity. The change in the law was motivated by an investigation into Backpage, an online classified ad service that had been accused of accepting ads that supported or facilitated sex trafficking, but which was likely immune from civil or criminal liability because of Section 230.

It might seem hard to believe that anyone would be opposed to a measure that would make it more difficult to facilitate sex trafficking, but free speech and open internet advocates argued that creating an exemption for Section 230 would simply lead to even more regulation in the future. And they argue that more regulation would stifle innovation by unreasonably placing a burden on platforms for conduct it may not even know about, stifling innovation or causing those already in the market to exit.

Indeed, shortly after the anti-sex trafficking amendments were signed into law, Craigslist shuttered its "Personals" section, asserting that continuing to operate it was too risky given the potential liability exposure.

GROWING FRUSTRATIONS WITH ONLINE PLATFORMS

Although Section 230 has been in the law since 1996, it was largely something that only people in tech and internet circles knew or cared about – it received relatively little public attention. But as the internet and social media services have become increasingly central to daily life, the impact of such services, and by extension, the regulatory environment in which they operate, have begun to receive more scrutiny.

Frustration with the broad immunities of Section 230 had been brewing in certain circles for some time, but issues with the law came to the fore in the months leading up to the 2016 election and have grown ever since as we learned more about the extent to which Russia interfered with that election by buying divisive ads on social media platforms to influence the vote.[9]

In 2019, a video of House Speaker Nancy Pelosi giving a speech, altered to make it appear as though she was inebriated, surfaced on Facebook and quickly became an internet sensation. Despite the verifiable inauthenticity of the video, Facebook refused to remove it, explaining that the company does not "have a policy that stipulates that the information you post on Facebook must be true."[10]

Beyond election interference and political issues, there have been concerns that social media services were responsible for fueling the rapid spread of misinformation about the COVID-19 pandemic and, in particular, the legitimacy and efficacy of vaccines.[11] President Biden accused the platforms of "killing people,"[12] though he later backed off that statement, clarifying that according to one study, just 12 online personalities, with a combined following of 59 million people, were responsible for the majority of the COVID-19 misinformation on the internet, much of it distributed and amplified by Facebook.[13]

In addition to the concerns over intentional manipulation of such platforms, some have grown weary of the impact that social media has on social discourse and society generally. In 2021, former Facebook employee Frances Haugen came forward to publicly challenge the company's practices. In testimony to the UK Parliament, Haugen explained that Facebook's own internal research recognized the addictive nature of social media to young people, and the difficulties they experience when they try to stop using such services despite how they might feel when they do. Haugen explained: "The last thing they see at night is someone being cruel to them. The first thing they see in the morning is a hateful statement and that is just so much worse."[14]

9 See, e.g., U.S. House of Representatives, Select Committee on Intelligence, Exposing Russia's Effort to Sow Discord Online: The Internet Research Agency and Advertisements (https://intelligence.house.gov/social-media-content) (last visited February 5, 2022).

10 Drew Harwell, Faked Pelosi Videos, Slowed to Make Her Appear Drunk, Spread across Social Media, The Washington Post, May 24, 2019, available at https://www.washingtonpost.com/technology/2019/05/23/faked-pelosi-videos-slowed-make-her-appear-drunk-spread-across-social-media.

11 Daniel E. Slotnik, Whistle-Blower United Democrats and Republicans in Calling for Regulation of Facebook, The New York Times, October 5, 2021, updated October 26, 2021, https://www.nytimes.com/live/2021/10/05/technology/facebook-whistleblower-frances-haugen.

12 Cecelia Kang, Facebook Tells Biden: "Facebook Is Not the Reason" Vaccination Goal Was Missed, The New York Times, July 17, 2021, updated August 31, 2021, https://www.nytimes.com/2021/07/18/technology/facebook-vaccine-misinformation.html.

13 Daniel E. Slotnik & Cecelia Kang, "Facebook Isn't Killing People": Biden Softens His Attack over Vaccine Misinformation, The New York Times, July 19, 2021, https://www.nytimes.com/2021/07/19/world/biden-facebook-misinformation.html.

14 Jim Waterson & Dan Milmo, Facebook whistleblower Frances Haugen calls for urgent external regulation, The Guardian, October 25, 2021, available at https://www.theguardian.com/technology/2021/oct/25/facebook-whistleblower-frances-haugen-calls-for-urgent-external-regulation.

ATTEMPTS TO CHANGE SECTION 230

Until recently, most social media services have given short shrift to concerns about false or misleading information on their platforms, or more generally, the impact that their platforms have on society. Historically, when questioned about such issues, the platforms deflect, noting that they merely provide a forum for users and cannot be held responsible for the actions of those users. When pressed, they cite Section 230 as the reason they don't have to do anything about it. And they're right.

Although some social media services have recently begun to implement policy changes that aim to neutralize or outright prohibit false or misleading information, they are doing so largely in response to increasingly credible threats that Congress may seek to change Section 230. Such attempts have been fraught in the past, but the growing chorus of bipartisan support for measures to reign in the major internet platforms means that the threat of a changed regulatory environment is more real today than it ever has been in the past.

One such attempt is the Justice Against Malicious Algorithms Act, which would create a new exception to Section 230 for platforms that knowingly or recklessly use algorithms to feed information to users that ultimately cause physical or severe emotional injury.[15] But algorithms are at the heart of most social media platforms. They serve up content that they believe their users are most likely to engage with, with the goal of keeping users on the platform as long as possible. According to *The Washington Post*, since 2009:

> Facebook has used software that predicts which posts each user will find most interesting and places those at the top of their feeds while burying others. That system, which has evolved in complexity to take in as many as 10,000 pieces of information about each post, has fueled [Facebook's news feed] into a dominant information source.[16]

According to Haugen, the reliance on algorithms is the whole problem with social media today because, it "systematically amplifies and rewards hateful, divisive, misleading and sometimes outright false content by putting it at the top of users' feeds."[17] Because users are served information that is likely to keep them engaged with the platform as long as possible, users tend to see content that supports and amplifies their existing views, which some believe has led to increased divisiveness in political and social discourse.

---

15 H.R. 5596, 117th Cong., 1st Sess. (2021).
16 Will Oremus, *Why Facebook Won't Let You Control Your Own News Feed*, The Washington Post, November 15, 2021, https://www.washingtonpost.com/technology/2021/11/13/facebook-news-feed-algorithm-how-to-turn-it-off.
17 *Id.*

In an attempt to combat this issue, several members of Congress have introduced the Filter Bubble Transparency Act, which would require internet platforms to disclose whether they use algorithms or artificial intelligence (AI) to determine what posts their users see and to offer users a version of the service that is not influenced by algorithms or AI.[18]

The debates around Section 230 are peculiar as far as legislative debates go. They are, on the one hand, bipartisan, in that each side thinks something ought to be done to reign in the big social media platforms, but the right and left are sharply divided as to which portions of Section 230 are most problematic. Those on the left believe that by providing immunities to social media platforms, they lack an incentive to do more to stop the proliferation of false or misleading information, bullying, abuse, and the like. Those on the right accuse the social media platforms of censorship whenever they label or remove content, as they are empowered to do, without liability, under Section 230.

DE-PLATFORMING

Although many of the complaints about social media platforms center on their refusal to remove or moderate content, the platforms are criticized when they do take content down, ban consistently problematic users, or otherwise identify user-posted content as false or misleading. A platform removing a user, thereby cutting off access to their audience, has become known as **de-platforming**.

For instance, following years of misrepresentations, deceptive posts, and at times, outright lies tweeted by President Trump throughout the years of his candidacy and much of his presidency, Twitter suspended his account in early 2021 following the January 6 insurrection. Facebook, Snapchat, YouTube, Twitch, and Reddit had previously either banned or limited Trump's access to their platforms.[19]

In response to the Twitter ban, President Trump issued a statement railing against Twitter: "Twitter is not about FREE SPEECH. They are all about promoting a Radical Left [sic] platform where some of the most vicious people in the world are allowed to speak freely."[20]

---

18 S. 2024, 117th Cong., 1st Sess. (2021).

19 Kate Conger & Mike Isaac, *Twitter Permanently Bans Trump, Capping Online Revolt*, The New York Times, January 8, 2021, updated, January 12, 2021, https://www.nytimes.com/2021/01/08/technology/twitter-trump-suspended.html.

20 *Id.*

In 2020, several social media platforms drew the ire of the conservative right when Facebook, Twitter, and other social media platforms either limited or blocked the distribution of a *New York Post* article that contained unsubstantiated assertions about then presidential candidate Joe Biden's son Hunter Biden.[21] Twitter even temporarily suspended the White House press secretary's account for posting the story.[22]

In response, President Trump referred to Facebook as "terrible" and "a monster," while Senator Marsha Blackburn, a Tennessee Republican, called Twitter "despicable," likened its action to the Russian interference with the 2016 election, and described the two company's actions as "silencing media that go against their political beliefs."[23]

There are myriad other examples.

But recall that the First Amendment guarantees not only the right to speak but the right to be free from compelled speech. As such, the social media platforms have strong arguments that they cannot be forced to disseminate content that they do not agree with, or simply do not want to perpetuate, nor can they be forced to allow President Trump to use their platform (even if he was, at the time of his suspension, the President of the United States).

But given how important social media has become to modern social discourse, some have begun to question whether Facebook and other social media services have become a *de facto* public square of modern times and, by extension, whether we should treat the platforms like public forums, subjecting their actions to heightened First Amendment scrutiny.

In 2018, a federal trial court in New York concluded that President Trump engaged in unconstitutional viewpoint discrimination when he blocked certain users with whom he disagreed from seeing posts he made to his public Twitter account, @RealDonaldTrump.[24] The Second Circuit agreed, explaining that although Twitter was owned and operated by a private company, the president's Twitter account was a public forum because Trump used it as a vehicle for announcing policy and made its interactive features – commenting, retweeting, liking, or replying to his tweets – available for public use.[25]

The court went on to hold that because the Twitter account was a public forum, the First Amendment protected other users' rights to use it to express their views, and

21 Katie Glueck, Michael S. Schmidt & Mike Isaac, *Allegation on Biden Prompts Pushback from Social Media Companies*, October 14, 2020, updated October 26, 2020, https://www.nytimes.com/2020/10/14/us/politics/hunter-biden-ukraine-facebook-twitter.html.

22 *Id.*

23 *Id.*

24 *Knight First Amendment Institute at Columbia University v. Trump*, 302 F. Supp. 3d 541, 580 (S.D.N.Y. 2018).

25 *Knight First Amendment Institute at Columbia University v. Trump*, 928 F.3d 226, 237 (2d Cir. 2019).

barred Trump from discriminating against speech based on a user's point of view.[26] The court explained that replying and retweeting are "undeniably speech" for First Amendment purposes, and that liking a tweet "conveys approval or acknowledgment … and is therefore a symbolic message with expressive content."[27] The court ultimately concluded that Trump violated certain users' First Amendment rights by blocking them from his Twitter account.[28]

We know, then, that social media accounts or posts made by government actors may be considered public forums, subjecting them to the principles and limitations of the First Amendment. Courts have yet to consider what other circumstances may give rise to similar outcomes, or whether there are circumstances when an entire platform, or portion of a platform, may be designated as a public forum. Given the rapid rise of social media platforms as a hub for discourse about politics and other matters of importance, it is difficult to imagine that the courts will avoid it for long, bringing to the fore complex questions of how to balance First Amendment interests of the public at large with those of the private companies that have invested in and operate the platforms.

Indeed, as Justice Thomas observed:

> [t]oday's digital platforms provide avenues for historically unprecedented amounts of speech, including speech by government actors. Also unprecedented, however, is the concentrated control of so much speech in the hands of a few private parties. We will soon have no choice but to address how our legal doctrines apply to highly concentrated, privately owned information infrastructure such as digital platforms.[29]

VIOLENT CONTENT IN VIDEO GAMES

An example of a once-new technology that the law had to figure out how to handle came in the late 1990s and early 2000s when a spate of violent incidents perpetrated by children led some to question whether violent video games were to blame. In the wake of one of the tragic mass shooting at Columbine High School in 1999 near Denver, several of the victims' families sued various video game publishers alleging that the games the shooters had played had desensitized them to violence.[30] The game publishers in those cases ultimately prevailed, but it led to various attempts at putting more responsibility on video game manufacturers.

26 *Id.* at 237–38.
27 *Id.* at 237.
28 *Id.* at 239.
29 *Biden v. Knight First Amendment Institute at Columbia University*, 141 S.Ct. 1220, 1221 (2021).
30 *See, e.g.,* Greg Toppo, *Do Video Games Inspire Violent Behavior*, Scientific American, July 1, 2015, https://www.scientificamerican.com/article/do-video-games-inspire-violent-behavior.

One such attempt came from California, where the state legislature passed a measure that made it illegal to sell or rent "violent video games" to minors and required that the packaging for such games indicate that they are intended for individuals 18 and older.[31]

Under the statute, a "violent" video game was one that gives players the option of "killing, maiming, dismembering, or sexually assaulting an image of a human being" and that allows players to "inflict serious injury … in a manner which is especially heinous, cruel, or depraved" in a manner that "[a] reasonable person, considering the game as a whole, would find appeals to a deviant or morbid interest of minors," that is "patently offensive to prevailing standards in the community as to what is suitable for minors," and that "causes the game, as a whole, to lack serious literary, artistic, political, or scientific value for minors."[32]

The video game industry sued to block the law from being enforced, alleging it violated the First Amendment. The Supreme Court agreed, acknowledging unequivocally that video games are entitled to some measure of First Amendment protection: "Like the protected books, plays, and movies that preceded them, video games communicate ideas — and even social messages — through many familiar literary devices … and through features distinctive to the medium."[33]

Having concluded that video games are entitled to full First Amendment protection, the Court went on to evaluate whether the law was constitutional. Because the law was a content-based regulation on speech, to prevail, the state would have to show that it satisfies the strict scrutiny test.

It didn't.

Characterizing the measure as "the latest episode in a long series of failed attempts to censor violent entertainment for minors,"[34] the Court concluded that the state had failed to establish that the law was narrowly tailored to achieve a compelling government interest. Specifically, it determined that the state failed to establish that youth access to violent video games was connected to real-world violent behavior, or that parents needed help in preventing their children from accessing such games (the purported state interests).

Even if the state had established a compelling interest, the Court found the law both over- and under-inclusive. It was under-inclusive because it restricted only portrayals of violence in video games, as opposed to other forms of media, and over-inclusive

31 Cal. Civ. Code. § 1746, *et seq.* (2009).
32 *Id.* at 1746.
33 *Brown v. Entertainment Merchants Ass'n*, 564 U.S. 786, 790 (2011).
34 *Id.* at 804.

because it adversely affects access to such games to those children "whose parents (and aunts and uncles) think violent video games are a harmless pastime."[35]

> If the last part of the California statute seems familiar to you, you aren't imagining things. The language was largely borrowed from the Supreme Court's test for obscenity articulated in *Miller v. California*, discussed in Chapter 3, in an apparent attempt to insulate the law from constitutional scrutiny. hoping that applying a well-known standard would insulate the law from constitutional scrutiny. The Supreme Court disagreed, however, explaining that the familiar Miller standard applied only to "sexual conduct," not "whatever a legislature finds shocking," such as violence.[36] In short, speech about violence cannot be obscene under current law.

We know, then, that video games are afforded full First Amendment protection, and that state attempts at regulating them must meet the same high standard required of other forms of speech regulation.

DEEPFAKES

The video of House Speaker Nancy Pelosi that had been edited to make it appear as though she was intoxicated is an example of how easy it has become to manipulate videos and images to create new "versions" of reality. It was relatively easy to figure out that the Pelosi video was fake because a real, unadulterated version of the same press conference had been readily circulated.

But what if it were possible to create videos or images that were entirely fake but nearly impossible to detect? For better or worse, that technology is here today, and the result of it are called **deepfakes** – videos, photos, or audio recordings that are *so* fake, they have no grounding in reality whatsoever.

Deepfakes are the result of rapidly advancing artificial intelligence technologies and faster more powerful computing technology. The ability to make deep fakes has existed for years and has been used by professionals in the motion picture industry, for example, but only recently has the technology been accessible to the masses using consumer-grade equipment. Only with the advent of the internet has it been possible to send the results around the world at the push of a button for no cost.

Deepfakes are fueled by a type of artificial intelligence known as machine learning, in which a computer is fed a significant volume of legitimate media from which it learns

---

35 *Id.* at 805.
36 *Brown v. Entertainment Merchants Ass'n*, 564 U.S. 786, 793 (2011).

the unique visual and speech patterns of a particular individual. Once the computer has ingested enough source material, it is capable of rendering footage that is entirely fake, but also entirely believable.

Deepfakes are especially feared among public figures, and particularly politicians, because they can be used to place people in offensive situations or say incendiary things. For instance, one could easily create deepfake pornography using the likeness of a famous actor, leading their career into a tailspin, a video in which a head of state says provocative things about an unstable foreign power, potentially leading to a diplomatic crisis, or one where a candidate for office makes inappropriate remarks about his or her opponent.

Many of the major internet platforms have policies against deepfakes and will remove them when identified. But identifying deepfakes is easier said than done because of how convincing they are. To help combat the issue, computer scientists from academia, the government, and many of the major internet platforms have been developing technology that uses the same machine learning techniques employed by those who make deepfakes, with the hope of eventually making them easier to find and either remove or identify as fake.

In 2019, as part of a defense spending authorization bill, Congress directed the Director of National Intelligence to study and monitor the deepfake issue, and to establish an incentive program to encourage the commercialization of deepfake detection technology.[37] Other proposed measures are at various stages of the legislative process.

At the state level, several jurisdictions have considered legislation to address the issue, including California, which passed two new laws in late 2019.

One of the California laws makes it unlawful to distribute "materially deceptive" media of a candidate for elected office within 60 days of an election if done with "actual malice." Candidates whose voice or likeness appears in a deepfake can seek an injunction to have the video removed and to seek damages from the person or entity that created the deepfake if they can be identified.[38]

Another makes it unlawful to create and intentionally disclose sexually explicit material without the consent of the person depicted in it,[39] which includes people that appear "as the result of digitization, to be giving a performance they did not actually perform or to be performing in an altered depiction."[40]

---

37 National Defense Authorization Act for Fiscal Year 2020, Pub. L. No. 116-92 § 5709 (2019).
38 Cal. Elec. Code § 20010.
39 Cal. Civ. Code § 1708.85(b).
40 Cal. Civ. Code § 1708.86(a)(4).

Of course, deepfakes are a form of speech, and it is likely that at some point, the deepfake statutes will be challenged on constitutional grounds even though the legislature included various provisions that attempt to limit the reach of the laws and protect bona fide news reporting and the like.

Indeed, free speech advocates called for the California governor to veto the two bills over First Amendment concerns,[41] arguing that the prohibition on election-related deepfakes would bar reenactments of true events, which ostensibly would make the law overbroad (and therefore not narrowly tailored), while the prohibition on sexually explicit material does not address situations where a person creates such material but does not distribute it.

Whether the laws are narrowly tailored enough to pass constitutional muster will eventually be a question for the courts – and perhaps ultimately the Supreme Court – to decide.

NONCONSENSUAL PORNOGRAPHY ("REVENGE PORN")

Revenge pornography (or simply **revenge porn**), increasingly called **nonconsensual pornography** refers to when someone posts sexually explicit images or videos – typically of a former romantic partner – to a public internet website with the intent of shaming or embarrassing the person featured in the image. In some cases, the images were captured and distributed without consent. In others, the images were captured with the consent of the other party but shared without consent.

PUNISHING PERPETRATORS

Although some existing laws can be used by victims or prosecutors to go after those that create and post revenge porn, most of the current legal doctrines are an imperfect fit. Wiretapping laws may be useful tools to prosecute those who create explicit material without consent, but it is much more difficult to prosecute those who improperly post material that was *created* with the consent of the victim, even if the victim never consented to the *distribution*.

To address this issue, nearly every state has passed a revenge porn law intended to enhance criminal penalties for engaging in the practice. In California, for instance, it is a misdemeanor, punishable by up to six months in jail and a fine of up to $1,000, for distributing an image where the victim is identifiable, with the intent to cause

---

41 *See* K.C. Halm, et al., *Two New California Laws Tackle Deepfake Videos in Politics and Porn*, Davis Wright Tremaine, https://www.dwt.com/insights/2019/10/california-deepfakes-law (October 11, 2019).

serious emotional distress, and the victim actually suffered such distress.[42] In Illinois, intentionally publishing an image of another person who is engaged in a sexual act or whose intimate parts are exposed, and whose identity is discernible from the image, could result in up to three years in prison and a fine of up to $25,000.[43] In addition, the Illinois statute allows victims to recover damages from the offender.

Although most would agree that revenge porn laws are generally good for society, those charged with violating the laws may seek to invalidate them by arguing that they are an unconstitutional restriction on speech. Indeed, because most revenge porn laws target specific types of content – for example, "intimate" images – there is a reasonable argument to be made that they constitute a content-based restriction on speech and must therefore meet the high bar of strict scrutiny.

A number of state courts have confronted the issue and come to diverging opinions. For instance, the Illinois Supreme Court reviewed the law discussed above and concluded that the law was a content-neutral time, place, and manner restriction, subject to the less onerous intermediate scrutiny test, and ultimately found that it passed constitutional muster.[44]

Contrast that result with a decision from a Texas intermediate appellate court that struck down that state's revenge porn law, holding that it was a content-based restriction on speech that did not use the least-restrictive means of achieving the state's interest in protecting its citizen's privacy.[45] The state's highest court for criminal matters overruled the appellate court, holding that the law's provisions were sufficiently specific that it was appropriately narrowly tailored.[46]

The diverging opinions, among states and courts within states, illustrate that the question of whether revenge porn statutes comport with the constitution is still open, and if state courts render inconsistent decisions, it is likely that the Supreme Court will ultimately take up the issue.

REMOVING OFFENSIVE MATERIAL

In many cases, more important than the ability to recover damages from an offender, or see that the offender is punished for his or her actions, is getting the offensive material off of the internet. Unfortunately, the law provides little support.

Revenge porn, though vile, rarely rises to the level of obscenity, so it is not per se unlawful, and it is rarely used in a commercial manner, so it does not implicate the

---

42 Cal. Penal Code § 647(j)(4).
43 720 Ill. Comp. Stat. Ann. 5/11-23.5 (West 2022).
44 *People v. Austin*, 155 N.E.3d 439 (Ill. 2019).
45 *Ex parte Jones*, 2018 WL 2228888, *7 (Texas App. May 16, 2018).
46 *Ex parte Jones*, 2021 WL 2126172 (Texas Crim. App. May 26, 2021).

victim's right of publicity. Moreover, generally, the victim of revenge porn does not own the copyright in the images or videos that they created, so they cannot use copyright law to have the images removed.

Fortunately, most of the major internet platforms have beefed up their terms of use to effectively prohibit revenge porn and to provide an avenue to have it removed. For example, Facebook, Instagram, Reddit, Tumblr, Twitter, and Yahoo all specifically prohibit nonconsensual pornography, and most reputable file storage and sharing tools such as Google Drive and Microsoft's OneDrive have policies against hosting it and will remove it when asked.

NONFUNGIBLE TOKENS (NFTS)

There has recently been a lot of hype surrounding a new form of digital asset called a **nonfungible token** or, more commonly referred to by its acronym, an **NFT**. An NFT is a digital asset whose ownership is recorded on a **blockchain**, which is essentially a list of transactions, stored electronically and on a distributed basis, meaning that copies of the blockchain record exist on various internet-connected servers located all over the world. As a result, every transaction on a blockchain is recorded in multiple, disparate locations, making the technology relatively tamperproof. Each transaction is stored on a "block." When a subsequent transaction takes place, it is written to a new block that is "chained" to the old one, thus a blockchain.

There is no shortage of entrepreneurs, and even large, well-established businesses, looking for ways to apply blockchain technology to existing business models or to develop new ones. And that has led to the rapid rise of NFTs, which are essentially digital collectibles, the existence and ownership of which are recorded, and therefore verifiable, on a blockchain. The blockchain record serves as a digital certificate of authenticity for the digital asset because every transaction since the inception of the NFT is traceable. Because the blockchain allows an NFT's creator to precisely control the number issued, they can create scarcity in the marketplace, which can lead to high prices if the underlying content asset is popular.

Although the rights that an NFT buyer receives vary depending on the specific NFT and the policies set by the person or company that issued it, the most common approach is that the NFT grants its owner limited rights to display or perform the underlying work in certain internet-based contexts, and bragging rights associated with being able to say they own an NFT of a particular work.

Some artists, musicians, and other creatives have been testing the waters by issuing NFTs for their digital works. Although NFTs can be issued for any type of media asset, they have become most commonly used for digital art. By issuing a single NFT for a particular work, they can mimic the effects of the traditional art market, where a single person or company buys an individual piece and the new owner has exclusive control over it. An artist might also issue a limited number of NFTs for a particular work – a digital limited edition. Using another blockchain technology called **smart contracts**, the original issuer can even set up the NFT so that they get a portion of the proceeds every time the NFT is sold to a new owner, something that does not exist in traditional markets, leaving individual artists without any way to reap the benefits as their work appreciates in value over time.

Beyond individual artists, NFTs have exploded in the past year or two as traditional media organizations and personalities look to launch their own to capitalize on their existing media libraries. The National Basketball Association, for example, recently launched NBA Top Shot, which allows users to buy, sell, and trade highlights or "moments" from NBA games. As one commentator explains, "[t]hey're basically virtual sports cards, but instead of a picture of a player with statistics on the back, you get a video highlight of a play like a LeBron James dunk or a Steph Curry 3-pointer."[47] Prices range from a few dollars to hundreds of thousands of dollars, depending on the player and how rare the moment is.[48]

Other major players in the entertainment space are getting into the field as well. Fox Entertainment and its animation production company, Bento Box Entertainment, recently launched Blockchain Creative Labs to provide content creators "computer ecosystem solutions to build, launch, manage and sell [NFT] content and experiences,"[49] and NFL superstar Tom Brady recently co-founded Autograph .io which, in its words, "brings together the most iconic brands and legendary names in sports, entertainment and culture to create unique digital collections and experiences."[50] *Business Insider* recently observed that Disney, a company with a massive library of valuable creative content, was looking for a business development manager to "lead Disney's efforts in the NFT space."[51]

Despite all the excitement, the NFT space remains fraught with open legal issues, unanswered questions, and uncertainty in the marketplace. It is often not clear to buyers, and sometimes to sellers, what rights are included in a particular NFT transaction. In most cases, the NFT will permit the buyer to display or perform the work in certain limited contexts, but it will not confer any rights to the underlying content, such as the copyright (we discuss copyrights in much more depth in Chapter 11). Still, people may not understand that and aim to sell rights in works to which they have no

47 Weston Blasi, *What is NBA Top Shot? Everything You Need to Know about the Digital Asset with over $230 Million in Transactions*, MarketWatch, February 28, 2021, https://www.marketwatch.com/story/what-is -nba-top-shot-everything-you-need-to-know-about-the-digital-asset-with-over-230-million-in-transac- tions-11614287023.

48 *Id.*

49 Erik Pedersen, *Fox & Bento Box Enter NFT Market with Blockchain Creative Labs,* Deadline, June 15, 2021, https://deadline.com/2021/06/nft-fox-bento-box-blockchain-creative-labs-1234775579.

50 www.autograph.io.

51 Stephen Jones, *Disney Is Hiring Experts to Spearhead Its NFT Ambitions*, Business Insider, February 8, 2022, https://www.businessinsider.com/disney-is-hiring-experts-to-leads-its-investment-in-nfts-2022-2.

legal rights. The platform that sold an NFT of Twitter co-founder Jack Dorsey's first tweet for nearly $3 million had to halt trading at one point because people were selling content without appropriate authorizations. The founder of the platform called it a "fundamental problem" of the digital assets market.[52]

In addition, despite the fact that the NFT landscape is largely unregulated for now, some lawyers believe that certain aspects of the blockchain ecosystem may be susceptible to banking or securities regulations, which could complicate matters for those who seek to issue NFTs.

INFORMATION PRIVACY AND DATA SECURITY

Earlier, we discussed privacy from the perspective of an individual's right to control how their likeness is used for commercial purposes. Those rights apply on the internet just as they do in the "real world," but the widespread use of internet-based platforms has led to a new breed of concerns centered around what the platforms can do with the treasure trove of information they have amassed about their millions of users.

Nearly every aspect of our online life is recorded in some way or another. Social media platforms track how often we use the platform, the type of content that we look at while we're using it, the type of content that we most commonly engage with, the people we most frequently interact with, the ads we click on, and even where we are located when we connect to the service.

Websites that facilitate commercial transactions such as Amazon.com have data about the types of products that we buy and how often we buy them. Brick-and-mortar retailers track what we buy using loyalty programs, and credit card companies also track such information. Using sophisticated processing techniques, data brokers have the ability to take the information from these various sources and combine it into a comprehensive dossier that can be used to more effectively target advertising to consumers.

Although businesses have been gathering data about their consumers for marketing purposes for decades, the pervasiveness of the internet and the breadth and depth of information now available to them has led to consumer and privacy advocates calling for more oversight of the services and platforms that gather and use information for advertising.

---

52 CNN (Reuters), *NFT Marketplace Suspends Most Sales, Citing "Rampant" Fakes and Plagiarism*, February 13, 2022, https://www.cnn.com/2022/02/13/tech/nft-marketplace-plagiarism/index.html.

NEW PRIVACY REGULATIONS

Among the most dramatic changes to privacy law, aimed squarely at bringing big tech into check, came on May 25, 2018, the date that the General Data Protection Regulation (GDPR), a massive overhaul of Europe's consumer privacy scheme, went into force in the European Union. You may remember when this happened because virtually every major website sent its users an email advising that it had made updates to its privacy policy, and most websites began featuring new, more robust warnings about the use of "cookies" – digital tracking devices – on their sites. Operators of some sites found the new rules so onerous that they simply shut down or blocked visitors from Europe.[53]

The guiding principle of the GDPR is that consumers, as opposed to the big tech players, should have control over how their data is obtained, collected, used, and stored, concepts that are beginning to appear in U.S. laws as well. Although there is not yet a comprehensive federal data privacy law in place, in 2018, California became one of the first states to enact significant privacy legislation, the California Consumer Privacy Act (CCPA) that aims to achieve some of the same objectives as the GDPR, including the right to know what information a business collects (and to get a copy), the right to have that information deleted, and the right to opt-out of having that information sold to other businesses. Just two years later, the law was amended by the California Privacy Rights Act (CPRA), which adds additional protections for consumers, such as the right to correct inaccurate information and the right to restrict access to or use of personal information, among others.

Other states have followed suit in the years since the CCPA was enacted, including Colorado, Hawaii, Maryland, Massachusetts, New York, North Dakota, and Virginia, with no doubt more to come, as data privacy continues to be a key issue for consumers, regulators, and elected officials.

One issue that has started to raise concerns among privacy advocates and some regulators is the practice of **"doxing"** (or **"doxxing"**), which involves releasing and publicizing personal information, usually on the internet, about individuals for the purpose of shaming or intimidating them. Often, the information is obtained from public sources and simply aggregated in a way that makes it easier to disseminate for nefarious purposes. In more extreme cases, certain confidential information may be obtained by hacking into secure computer systems. The practice has been used to intimidate abortion providers, journalists, political adversaries, and high-profile members of the media, among others.

53 *See, e.g.,* Alex Hern and Jim Waterson, *Sites Block Users, Should Down Activities and Flood Inboxes as GDPR Rules Loom,* The Guardian, May 24, 2018, https://www.theguardian.com/technology/2018/may/24/sites-block-eu-users-before-gdpr-takes-effect.

There are no laws that explicitly prohibit doxing. Instead, authorities must rely on related laws that criminalize conduct around the access or use of an individual's sensitive information. Hacking may be charged under the Computer Fraud and Abuse Act, for instance, while using the disclosed information to intimidate someone may violate various laws against stalking or harassment. Other laws may apply depending on the circumstances.

In 2018, Democratic Party staffer Jackson Cosko was arrested for doxing several members of the Republican Party who had been especially supportive of then Supreme Court nominee Judge Brett Kavanaugh by posting their names and phone numbers to Wikipedia. Cosko was convicted of violating the Computer Fraud and Abuse Act and disclosing restricted personal information and sentenced to four years in prison.[54]

Not all doxing cases are as egregious as Cosko's, however, and yet they can be just as frightening to the individuals whose information is disclosed. A number of states are considering anti-doxing laws that would either make it a crime to engage in the practice or give victims a private right of action against those who do.

WHAT DOES ALL THIS HAVE TO DO WITH THE MEDIA?

As traditional media enterprises evolve, they have become increasingly reliant on direct connections with their consumers through streaming services, in part, to gather data about their viewing patterns to better compete with the streaming-first operators.

Such data is useful to a media company in two ways: First, it can be used to help predict what audiences want to see so producers can deliver more of it. For example, in writing about the success of the *House of Cards* remake in 2013, one media critic observed that:

> Netflix, which has 27 million subscribers in the nation and 33 million worldwide, ran the numbers. It already knew that a healthy share had streamed the work of [*House of Cards* director] [David] Fincher, the director of "The Social Network," from beginning to end. And films featuring [Kevin] Spacey had always done well, as had the British version of "House of Cards." Within those three circles

---

54 *United States v. Cosko*, Criminal No. 18–00303 (D.D.C.), Judgment in a Criminal Case, ECF No. 54 (July 5, 2019).

of interest, Netflix was able to find a Venn diagram intersection that suggested buying the series would be a very good bet on original programming.[55]

Put simply, Netflix's bet on *House of Cards* was a pretty safe one since they had data sufficient to show that it would likely be successful. The same treasure trove of data that helped Netflix make that decision is also what drives Netflix's recommendation feature that suggests new movies or television shows to watch based on your prior viewing history, with the goal of keeping you on the platform for as long as possible.

The second way media companies harness the power of their data is by selling targeted advertising. Although not all of the popular streaming services sell advertising, those that do are able to harness the information they have about their users to target advertising much more specifically than traditional media ever could.

In the past, advertisers had to make educated guesses about the likelihood that their ads would reach their target customers based on the broad demographic profiles of the audience. Today, thanks to the massive amounts of data that streaming services have about their users, advertisers are able to target their messages to very specific groups of people and, in some cases, to specific individuals. That has made online advertising much more effective and, in turn, much more lucrative for media enterprises with ad time to sell.

All of this is to say that as media enterprises evolve and develop new distribution channels for their content, they will inevitably become more reliant on data, subjecting them to the rapidly changing landscape of privacy regulation. Media enterprises looking to develop or expand targeted digital offerings will need to carefully consider consumer privacy interests more than they likely have in the past.

IN THE NEWS: *NUNES V. LIZZA, ET AL.*

We know that Section 230 immunizes platforms from the actions of its users, but to what extent is the users' conduct subjected to the traditional legal doctrines such as those we have discussed elsewhere in this book?

Take, for example, a recent Eighth Circuit decision, which held that a reporter who retweeted a link to an article could have been acting with actual malice when he posted a link to a story he wrote that was the subject of a lawsuit. In that case, the reporter had published an article that suggested California Congressman Devin Nunes operated a family farm in Iowa (as opposed to California, as he had claimed), and suggested that the farm made use of undocumented labor, which was inconsistent with political positions that Nunes had taken in the past.[56]

---

55 David Carr, *Giving Viewers What They Want*, The New York Times, February 24, 2013, https://www .nytimes.com/2013/02/25/business/media/for-house-of-cards-using-big-data-to-guarantee-its-popular- ity.htm.

56 *Nunes v. Lizza, et al.*, 12 F.4th 890, 894 (8th Cir. 2021).

Nunes sued reporter Ryan Lizza and the parent company of *Esquire*, the magazine in which the article appeared, for defamation.[57] Because Nunes is a public figure, to prevail on his claim, he had to show that Lizza acted with actual malice when he published the story. The court determined that he failed to meet that exacting standard and dismissed the claim.[58]

However, it let stand a separate-but-related defamation claim on a tweet that Lizza had sent in which he linked to the article. The court determined that the tweet could be plausibly construed as a "republication" of the original story and therefore subject to its own separate analysis, which could shake out differently.

Specifically, the Eighth Circuit observed that because Lizza sent the tweet after the lawsuit about the article had been filed, Lizza could have acted with actual malice with respect to the tweet, even though the court concluded that he had not, at least with respect to the article itself.[59] The court reasoned that the underlying purpose of the republication rule is to recognize the fact that a subsequent publication may reach a new audience, and explained that in this case, it appeared Lizza had intended to do just that with his tweet.[60]

Notably, the court considered the matter at the motion to dismiss stage, which means that its ruling simply means that Nunes said enough in his lawsuit to make his actual malice claim "plausible." To ultimately prevail against Lizza and the publisher, Nunes will still have to establish that Lizza did, in fact, act with actual malice when he tweeted a link to the article.

Note that Nunes did not name Twitter as a defendant, even though it supplied the platform on which Lizza ostensibly "republished" the defamatory statement from the article.

Why not?

As we learned earlier, Section 230 immunizes platforms such as Twitter from liability for the actions of its users by expressly providing that no platform shall be considered "the publisher or speaker" of any information supplied by a user. Any attempt at bringing suit against Twitter for the statements made by its users would be swiftly met by an easily granted motion to dismiss.

---

57 *Id.* at 895.
58 *Id.* at 899.
59 *Id.* at 900–1.
60 *Id.*

Although nobody has ever seriously suggested that defamation law simply should not apply online, many of the new internet-enabled ways people communicate, such as the short snippets posted on Twitter, raise questions about how certain doctrines, such as the republication rule, should apply in the online space when it is easier than ever to redistribute and amplify statements made by other people.

KEY POINTS AND TAKEAWAYS

1. The extent to which the internet should be regulated has been a political flash-point since the beginning of the commercial internet. Technologists and entre-preneurs argued that regulating the internet or holding internet companies and platforms responsible for the actions of their users will dissuade investment in the technology and hamper further development. Those who believe the internet should be subject to more regulation believe that internet companies and plat-forms should share the burden of maintaining order online.

2. The Communications Decency Act of 1996 was largely struck down by the Supreme Court as an unconstitutional restraint on free speech, but a small yet powerful portion of it remains in the law. Specifically, Section 230 of the Communications Act provides that internet platforms cannot be held responsible for the actions of their users or for taking action to moderate content on their platforms.

3. Many policymakers and members of the public have become frustrated with the internet platforms' lackadaisical approach to the growing abuse of their plat-forms – for example, the dissemination of false or misleading information – and have called for changes to Section 230 and related laws to put more responsibility onto the platforms. Platforms argue that burdening them with more responsibility would chill innovation.

4. With every new technology, or new use of an existing technology, often comes new questions about the extent to which the technology should be regulated and, where speech or expression is involved, the extent to which the new forms are entitled to First Amendment protection and, by extension, the extent to which they may be regulated. The Supreme Court has recognized that video games are entitled to the same degree of protection as other expressive works but has yet to consider whether regulation of deepfakes and nonconsensual pornography comports with the First Amendment.

5. Beyond First Amendment considerations, the business models of the major plat-forms – gathering large amounts of data about their users and then either selling that data or simply using it to target ads to its users – raise significant questions about the privacy of that information. Some jurisdictions, such as the European Union and most notably in the United States, California, have enacted sweeping legislation aimed at giving the power over how such information is used to the individual internet users about whom that information pertains.

QUESTIONS FOR DISCUSSION

1. What's your take on net neutrality? Advocates of net neutrality laws argue we need legislation to ensure a level playing field. Opponents argue that regulation is unnecessary and that ordinary market forces will result in an internet that best serves the needs of its users.

2. Should social media platforms be considered "publishers" for purposes of Section 230 or are they merely conduits for their users' posts? How should we think about the fact that these platforms use algorithms to decide what you do and do not see? Does the use of a platform-managed algorithm change your view about whether such platforms are properly designated as publishers?

3. Some lawmakers have proposed statutes that would either criminalize doxing or empower victims to sue those who release their personal information. Do such laws comport with the First Amendment? What standard of scrutiny should a court use to evaluate the constitutionality of such restrictions?

4. In *Nunes v. Lizza*, we saw a court conclude that tweeting a link to an article, when the person sending the tweet was aware that the subject matter of the article was in dispute, might constitute "actual malice" for purposes of defamation law. Did the court get it right? What if the person tweeting a link to an article was not the author of the piece, but was still generally aware that the article was disputed by Rep. Nunes? What if someone retweeted the author's link to the article (as opposed to posting an entirely new tweet)? Should that constitute a "publication" for purposes of applying defamation law?

5. What role should internet platforms play in identifying deep fakes and other forms of "fake news." Some platforms have invested heavily in artificial intelligence technology that aims to identify and remove deep fakes from their services; others have hired fact checkers to check news stories and other posts so that the false information can be removed or at least identified as such. Is it appropriate to put that burden on the platform? What about smaller platforms, or new entrants, that may not be able to handle the significant investment required to implement such practices?

6. To what extent should internet users have control over the data that platforms and other businesses collect about them? On the one hand, as the subject of the data, it stands to reason that he or she would have some control over how it is used. On the other hand, the platforms that gather such information are generally offered without cost to the users, and the information gathered is, in some ways, the *quid pro quo* for that access. How should policymakers balance the interests of the internet platforms and the interests of internet users and consumers?

11

CHAPTER 11
INTELLECTUAL PROPERTY: MEDIA AS IP USER

What issues do media enterprises face when ensuring that their news reports, entertainment properties, and other programming are properly cleared for distribution? What should lawyers advising media companies look out for when advising journalists, producers, and other creative professionals? How can media organizations minimize their exposure to liability for infringement?

This chapter looks at intellectual property issues that arise in the context of journalism and media production and offers practical guidance on evaluating fair use and how to avoid or minimize the risk of infringement liability.

A BRIEF INTRODUCTION TO IP

Intellectual property or **IP** refers to a class of intangible property that is granted certain legal protections. Broadly, IP can be divided into four categories: patents, trade secrets, copyrights, and trademarks.

PATENTS

Patents give inventors the exclusive right to make, use, sell, or offer to sell certain inventions, methods, systems, and processes. Once a patent is granted, only the patent owner can make, use, sell, or offer to sell the patented invention. Patents are granted to inventors by the government only after a rigorous examination process to confirm that the invention is sufficiently innovative and does not simply restate common scientific or industrial knowledge.

An inventor's exclusive rights typically run 20 years from the date the patent is filed, after which anyone is free to make and sell the invention. In exchange for the exclusive period of protection, the inventor must disclose in the patent itself the best way to construct the patented invention known at the time of filing.

A common example of how patent protection works can be found in the pharmaceutical industry. A drug manufacturer will typically seek patent protection on a new drug and enjoy the exclusive rights to make and sell that drug for the life of the patent. When the patent expires, other companies are free to manufacture and sell the same drug. These so-called "generic" versions of the original product are often available to consumers at a fraction of the cost of the patented version because of the increased competition in the marketplace.

DOI: 10.4324/9781003197966-11

Patent infringement occurs when someone makes, uses, sells, or offers to sell a patented invention without a license from the patent owner before the patent has expired. Because patents are highly technical, patent infringement litigation can be enormously expensive and time consuming. Accordingly, most patent claims settle relatively quickly.

US009648385B2

(12) **United States Patent**
Park et al.

(10) **Patent No.:** **US 9,648,385 B2**
(45) **Date of Patent:** *May 9, 2017

---

(54) **ADAPTIVE STREAMING FOR DIGITAL CONTENT DISTRIBUTION**

(71) Applicant: **NETFLIX, INC.**, Los Gatos, CA (US)

(72) Inventors: **Anthony Neal Park**, San Jose, CA (US); **Wei Wei**, Fremont, CA (US)

(73) Assignee: **NETFLIX, INC.**, Los Gatos, CA (US)

(*) Notice: Subject to any disclaimer, the term of this patent is extended or adjusted under 35 U.S.C. 154(b) by 30 days.

This patent is subject to a terminal disclaimer.

(21) Appl. No.: **14/152,705**

(22) Filed: **Jan. 10, 2014**

(65) **Prior Publication Data**

US 2014/0189771 A1   Jul. 3, 2014

Related U.S. Application Data

(63) Continuation of application No. 12/509,365, filed on Jul. 24, 2009, now Pat. No. 8,631,455.

(51) **Int. Cl.**
H04N 7/173	(2011.01)
H04N 21/44	(2011.01)
H04N 21/442	(2011.01)
H04N 21/6373	(2011.01)
H04N 21/61	(2011.01)

(52) **U.S. Cl.**
CPC . *H04N 21/44004* (2013.01); *H04N 21/44209* (2013.01); *H04N 21/6175* (2013.01); *H04N 21/6373* (2013.01)

(58) **Field of Classification Search**
CPC H04N 21/44004; H04N 21/6175
USPC 725/116, 96
See application file for complete search history.

(56) **References Cited**

U.S. PATENT DOCUMENTS

5,414,455 A	5/1995	Hooper et al.	
5,608,732 A *	3/1997	Bestler et al.	370/474
6,438,630 B1 *	8/2002	DeMoney	710/56
6,453,114 B2 *	9/2002	Schultz et al.	386/351

(Continued)

FOREIGN PATENT DOCUMENTS

EP	0515101 A2	11/1992
EP	1298938 A2	4/2003

(Continued)

OTHER PUBLICATIONS

Extended European Search Report for application No. PCT/US2011/063564 dated Sep. 11, 2014.

(Continued)

Primary Examiner — Pankaj Kumar
Assistant Examiner — Franklin Andramuno
(74) *Attorney, Agent, or Firm* — Artegis Law Group, LLP

(57) **ABSTRACT**

One embodiment of the present invention sets forth a technique for adapting playback bit rate to available delivery bandwidth in a content delivery system comprising a content server and a content player. A content player periodically estimates whether a given playback bit rate can feasibly provide complete playback for a given title assuming currently available bandwidth. If playback becomes unfeasible at a current bit rate assuming currently available bandwidth, then the content player adapts the bit rate downward until a feasible bit rate is achieved. If playback is feasible using a higher bit rate, then the content player may adapt the bit rate upward.

22 Claims, 12 Drawing Sheets

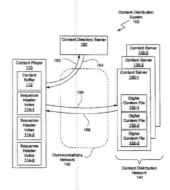

Figure 11.1 The first page of U.S. patent 9,648,385 granted to Netflix for a media streaming technology.

TRADE SECRETS

A **trade secret** is a commercially valuable, non-public piece of information that is generally difficult to reverse engineer. Trade secret protection persists for as long as the information is maintained in secrecy, which could be far longer than the 20 years of protection granted by a patent. Because of this, sometimes businesses will seek to protect their proprietary methods, systems, processes, or recipes by claiming trade secret protection instead of patent protection. To maintain trade secret protection, an owner must take reasonable efforts to keep the information confidential. The Coca-Cola formula, the recipe for KFC's famous "11 herbs and spices," and the Google search algorithm are all examples of trade secrets.

It is generally not unlawful to attempt to reverse engineer a trade secret or to develop the subject matter of the trade secret independently. Trade secret **misappropriation** occurs when someone obtains a secret through improper means (e.g., stealing it or inducing someone else to steal it) or when it is misused by someone who is entrusted with it for a legitimate purpose, such as an employee who has access to a secret for use in his or her job and then uses it to compete with their employer.

COPYRIGHTS AND TRADEMARKS

Although there are no doubt patent and trade secret issues in the context of the media and entertainment industries, the majority of intellectual property concerns that arise relate to two other forms of intellectual property: copyrights and trademarks. Because these two legal doctrines are so prominent in the media industry, we discuss them in more depth below.

COPYRIGHT

Copyright provides authors of creative works with the exclusive right to exploit those works for a limited period of time, on the theory that creatives will be more likely to create if they are given a period of time during which they can control – and make money from – the fruits of their creative labors.

Copyright applies broadly to any original work of authorship fixed in a tangible medium of expression, which includes literary works (books, articles), musical works (music and lyrics), dramatic works (plays, screenplays, teleplays), choreographic works, motion pictures and audiovisual works (films and television shows), sound recordings, and visual art. Copyright does not protect ideas or concepts, only specific expressions of those ideas.[1]

---

1 17 U.S.C. § 102.

In some ways, "copyright" is a misnomer because a copyright actually gives the owner a "bundle" of several rights. Among them is copyright's namesake, the right to reproduce (or *copy*) the work, but copyright owners also enjoy the exclusive right to distribute the work, and in some cases, the right to publicly perform or display it. The copyright owner also has the exclusive right to prepare **derivative works**, such as translations or adaptations.[2] When a book is adapted into a movie, the resulting movie (and the screenplay that likely preceded it) are considered derivative works of the original book.

Only the copyright owner has the right to exploit the exclusive rights or the power to license others to do so.

DURATION

Copyright protection begins upon the creation of a qualifying work. Unlike patents, which require the government to affirmatively grant them, copyright arises automatically upon creation. The law does provide some additional benefits for those who choose to register their works with the government, but it is not necessary for protection.

Copyright protection lasts a relatively long time. For works created by individuals, it lasts for the life of the person plus an additional 70 years. For works created by employees, as part of their job, for the benefit of their employer, the copyright lasts either 120 years from the year of creation or 95 years from the year of first publication, whichever comes first.[3]

Works whose copyright has expired are said to be part of the **public domain** and are free for use by anyone without permission.

LIMITATIONS AND EXCEPTIONS

Copyrights are not absolute. In addition to the exclusive rights granted to authors discussed previously, the law also contains a number of carefully crafted limitations and exceptions to those rights, aimed at achieving certain objectives that policymakers have determined to be socially desirable. Some of the exceptions are very specific, such as the provision that allows for certain qualifying organizations to make Braille reproductions of certain literary works for individuals with visual impairments,[4] while others are more broadly applicable, such as the various exceptions for public performance or display in the course of classroom teaching.[5]

---

2 *Id.* at § 106.
3 *Id.* at § 302.
4 *Id.* at § 121.
5 *Id.* at § 110.

INFRINGEMENT AND DAMAGES

Copyright infringement occurs when someone exploits one of the exclusive rights of copyright without the permission of the copyright owner and the exploitation does not fall within the scope of a limitation or exception. To prove infringement, the copyright owner must show two elements: (1) that the defendant had access to the original work; and (2) that the defendant's work is **substantially similar** to the copyright owner's original.

If the copyright owner succeeds, the defendant could be liable to pay money damages in the amount of either actual damages that the copyright owner suffered, or the profits that the infringer gained, as a result of the infringement. In either case, the plaintiff must provide evidence of the amount sought from the defendant.

If the copyright was registered before the infringement, or within three months of when the work was first published, the defendant may be liable for statutory damages, and the court may order the defendant to pay the plaintiff's attorney's fees and costs associated with litigating the matter. Statutory damages are granted at the discretion of the court and can range anywhere from $200 to $150,000 per work infringed depending on the circumstances surrounding the infringement.

In addition to money damages, a prevailing copyright owner may seek injunctions against future or continued infringement and order the destruction of any remaining infringing copies.

Although copyright protection does not extend to ideas, only the original expression of those ideas, it is not uncommon for prominent media enterprises to be sued by people who believe they originated the idea for popular films, television shows, or songs.

For example, in 2015, the producers of the hit TV show *Empire* were sued by a writer claiming to have originally conceived of the show as King Solomon which, like *Empire*, was centered around a Black-owned record label. The court granted the producers a motion to dismiss because the writer had failed to even allege that the producers had seen the proposal for his show, and did not identify any particular elements that had been copied, beyond the basic premise and general plot points, which are not protected by copyright.[6]

Similarly, in 2017, a child development expert sued Disney claiming that its 2015 film *Inside Out* was based on her film idea, in which she represented five emotions using different colors. The trial court and Ninth Circuit sided with

6 *Astor-White v. Strong*, 817 Fed. Appx. 502, 503–4 (9th Cir. 2020).

Disney, concluding that "[d]eveloping a character as an anthropomorphized version of a specific emotion is not sufficient, in itself, to establish a copyrightable character,"[7] and that she "cannot copyright the idea of colors or emotions, nor can she copyright the idea of using colors to represent emotions where these ideas are embodied in a character without sufficient delineation and distinctiveness."[8]

REGISTRATION

As already mentioned, copyright arises automatically upon the creation of a copyrightable work, but the law provides some additional benefits to those who register their work with the U.S. Copyright Office. For works made in the United States, registration is required before a copyright owner may file suit to enforce their copyright. Timely registration also permits the copyright owner to recover statutory damages and attorney's fees. In addition, registration creates a public record of the copyright claim in the database of the U.S. Copyright Office.

FAIR USE

Perhaps the most widely known (and also mis-cited and misunderstood) limitation in copyright law is fair use and is also likely the most commonly encountered among media professionals. Fair use is something of a "catch-all" provision that allows for certain limited uses of copyrighted works that do not have a significant impact on the original market or intent of the work without the permission of the copyright owner.

Fair use was designed to be a "safety valve" to ensure that copyright law, which is a type of restriction on speech, does not run afoul of First Amendment values by allowing people to use copyrighted works without permission of the copyright owner for purposes of criticism, comment, news reporting, certain teaching activities, scholarship, or research. To determine whether a particular use is fair, courts consider four factors:

1. The purpose and character of the use. Commercial uses are less likely to be fair than editorial uses.
2. The nature of the copyrighted work. Fictional works are generally afforded more protection (and their use less likely to be fair) than works composed primarily of facts or real-life accounts.

---

7 *Daniels v. The Walt Disney Co.*, 958 F.3d 767, 773 (9th Cir. 2020).
8 *Id.* at 772.

3. The amount and substantiality of the portion used in relation to the copyrighted work as a whole. The shorter the portion taken, the more likely the use is to be fair, taking into consideration the scope of the underlying work. Taking a few lines from a novel is likely to be fair but taking that same amount from a haiku poem is less likely to be fair. Note that sometimes even using a small portion may not be fair use if that portion can be considered the "heart" or essence of the work.
4. The effect of the use upon the potential market or value of the copyrighted work if the use is likely to have an adverse impact on the market for the original, including any ancillary markets such as licensing or merchandizing. Of course, like all things in fair use, context is key: Using a 30-second clip of a two-hour film in the context of a movie review is likely fair, even if the review is bad and results in fewer people going to see the movie. Using a 45-minute clip of that same movie in a positive review would likely not be considered a fair use.

You may have noticed that the explanations above, and in the examples that follow, regularly use the word "likely." That's because determining whether something is fair use is an inexact science. The principles in the statute were designed to be flexible, which means that what is or is not fair use can sometimes be ambiguous, and unless a court has decreed a specific use to be fair, we have to make educated guesses based on the outcome of the cases that have come before.

Fortunately, in the nearly 50 years since the current formulation of fair use was written into the law, courts have considered many of the most common use cases, and lawyers with extensive expertise in fair use analysis have been able to come up with some basic rules of thumb to help guide day-to-day decisions. Table 11.1 offers some examples.

> Because fair use analyses are inherently uncertain, most large media enterprises have their own guidelines and practices that have been developed by their lawyers, taking into account the company's own tolerance for risk. If you work for one of those companies, you should familiarize yourself with those guidelines and know who to contact if questions arise.

GETTING PERMISSION

Generally, to make use of a copyrighted work, where that use does not fall within a limitation or exception such as fair use, you need the permission of the copyright owner. In copyright, that permission is called a **license**.

Because copyright can be divvied up into various rights, which can be exploited at different times by different parties, in different places, licenses can often become very complex. Getting a license from the copyright owner, or its authorized agent, is the safest way to avoid running into trouble with copyrighted work.

Table 11.1 Examples of fair and not fair uses.

Likely fair use	Likely not fair use
Using a few sentences of a 400-page autobiography in a book review.	Using the few sentences of a novel in which the author reveals the identity of the murderer in a podcast episode about the book's release.
Using a short clip of a commercially released popular song to accent a news report about the performer's recent concert tour being canceled.	Using a short clip of a commercially released popular song as the theme to a weekly television show that also appears on YouTube.
Showing the front page of the local newspaper (or its website) to illustrate the newsworthiness of a local story.	Using the photograph from the front page of the local newspaper (or its website) to illustrate your own coverage of the same story because you didn't get a good shot.
Using a short clip of a movie or clips of a few songs from an album in connection with a review of the movie or album.	Playing or posting full-length copies of the album or songs on a website or other public place to accompany the album.
Using a photo or video from a social media post to illustrate the popularity or virility of a particular phenomenon.	Using a photo or video from a social media post to illustrate or accent a report or production with little or no connection to the social media post.

Although this chapter is primarily concerned with the needs of media organizations to avoid copyright issues as a user of intellectual property, it is worth noting here that licensing is the lifeblood of the creative industries, including the media industry. Copyright licensing is the mechanism by which most media organizations make money and distribute their work. Film and television studios license the public performance rights to their productions to theaters, broadcasters, and streaming services, record labels and music publishers license the performance rights to their music to streaming services, book publishers license distribution rights to various e-book distributors, and so on. Even when a user uploads a video to YouTube, that user is granting YouTube a license to distribute it to the public.

COMMERCIAL LICENSING

The easiest way to ensure that you have the rights necessary to incorporate something into a production is to formally license it through traditional channels. Stock photography and footage archives can license footage to producers, and similarly, traditional record labels and music publishers will license most major commercial releases, though they can be expensive. For more cost-conscious producers, there are scores of production music libraries eager to license music from virtually any genre and for virtually any use.

Licensing from a commercial distributor is useful because they generally stand behind the works that they make available. If a copyright owner shows up later claiming that you are infringing on their work, the company from which you licensed it will typically step in and handle it on your behalf.

SOCIAL MEDIA

Using media from social media posts presents a unique set of problems. Generally, with few exceptions, it is generally not permissible to take images, videos, or other media from social media posts and use them for your own purposes unless you have permission from the copyright owner. The only exceptions are where there may be a strong fair use defense (see above), or where you are sharing or amplifying the post within the social media platform itself (e.g., retweeting).

So before using media from social media posts, it is usually prudent to get permission. But there is a wrinkle: There is no guarantee that the person who posted an image or video to social media is the person who owns the copyright. Other than asking directly, there is no sure-fire way to avoid this issue, and even then, a user may be misrepresenting their ownership, which could lead to a copyright claim if it turns out that the person who posted it to social media is not the copyright owner.

Still, it has become common practice for many media enterprises to seek permission by simply asking some simple questions and relying on the user's response as the license. Depending on the intended use, it may sometimes be desirable to ask the user to sign a more formal license agreement.

At a minimum, you should ask the poster:

1. Whether they created the content you want to use;
2. If so, whether they consent to your intended use (which you should describe clearly, but as broadly as possible);
3. Whether they have granted rights to anyone else and, if so, on what terms; and
4. Whether you need to obtain permission from anyone else to use the content.

Note that there has recently been an alarming increase in the number of cases where a media enterprise will obtain permission on a social media platform only to find that the copyright owner has separately granted exclusive rights to another party – usually a licensing agency that specializes in "viral" social media content – which then attempts to extract a license fee from those who had been previously granted permission, claiming that the prior permission was either ineffective or had been revoked. Although the ethics of the practice are questionable, it is likely legal in most cases, and the licensing agency typically seeks a modest payment of just a few hundred dollars, often making such claims easier to pay and move on, rather than fight over.

Asking whether the poster has granted rights to anyone else, and whether you need to obtain permission from anyone else, should help minimize the risk of this type of claim, but there is no way to eliminate it entirely, short of simply not using material posted to social media.

CREATIVE COMMONS

In recent years, new licensing models have begun to emerge that are intended to recognize the fact that not all authors of creative works necessarily want to pursue traditional distribution and licensing models for their works, but also do not necessarily want to give them away without any strings attached.

The most common alternative licensing framework is known as **Creative Commons** (**CC**), which offers a series of structured licenses intended to allow people to make use of the work without financial remuneration but subject to certain standardized license terms.

1. **Attribution**. All CC licenses require that the user provide credit in the way that the author requests.
2. **Share Alike**. Grants the right to use an author's work only if the user makes their own work available on the same CC terms.
3. **No Derivatives**. Allows use of an author's work but does not permit modifications.
4. **Noncommercial**. Allows use of an author's work, but only for noncommercial purposes.

The four terms can be mixed and matched to create six specific licenses.

You can identify works offered under a CC license because they are often identified by a statement such as "CC BY-NC" (Creative Commons, Attribution, Noncommercial) in lieu of the familiar copyright symbol (©).

Many popular media-sharing sites now allow authors to make their content available under a CC license and allow users to search specifically for content assets that come with such license terms. In addition, the Creative Commons organization maintains its own database of CC-licensed works – available at www.creativecommons.org.

Beware that many websites that offer works that are available under a CC license, or simply purport to be available for free, may sometimes contain content that was placed there without the permission of the copyright owner. For instance, there have been a number of cases where photographers have found their copyrighted images available either for free, or offered under a CC license, on sites to which they had never provided their images. Instead, a nefarious actor stole the images from the photographer's website and re-uploaded them, without permission, identifying them as free or CC-licensed when they are not. Because the copyright owner had not granted the appropriate permission, any subsequent use of that material would likely constitute an infringement, subjecting the user to potential money damages, even if they were not aware their use was infringing.

MUSIC LICENSING

One area of copyright licensing that bears special mention is music, an area which is complicated by the fact that there are two separate copyrights at issue: One in the musical work, or composition, and the other in the sound recording. In most cases, the rights are owned by separate entities, and even where they are owned by the same entity, the licensing practices around each are entirely different.

The other reason music licensing is so complex is that different uses of music often require different licenses, and each has its own licensing nomenclature. For instance, if you are using a recording of a popular song in a podcast, you will need a **master recording license** from the record label to use the recording and a **synchronization** (or **synch**) **license** from the publisher of the underlying composition. Both licenses are effectively granting the user the right to make a reproduction of the song in the context of the podcast.

If that same podcast were broadcast over traditional radio or television, it would require a public performance license for the composition, which is issued by one of several **performance rights organizations (PROs)** – ASCAP, BMI, SESAC, and GMR. PRO licenses are generally granted on a blanket basis, meaning that a license from, say, ASCAP includes the rights to publicly perform anything in the ASCAP catalog. If the podcast were to be broadcast online, through a streaming platform, the streamer would need not only a PRO license but also a license from SoundExchange to cover the performance of the sound recording. SoundExchange operates in a similar fashion to the PROs, but it represents owners of sound recordings, as opposed to owners of the musical work.

Because of an oddity in U.S. copyright law, copyright owners of sound recordings only get paid performance royalties when the work is performed by way of a digital transmission, which is why traditional radio and television stations do not need a license from SoundExchange unless they also stream their content online.

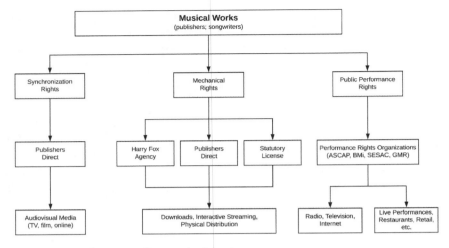

Figure 11.2 Music licensing for musical works.

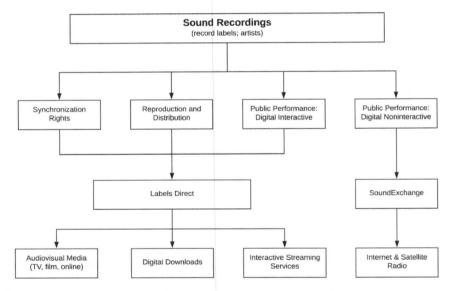

Figure 11.3 Music licensing for sound recordings.

As you can see, music licensing is sufficiently complex that warrants its own book (and indeed, there are a number of good ones). One of the easiest ways to avoid complicated music issues is to use music from libraries specifically marketed for use in productions, such as those offered by companies like APM Music, Warner/Chappell Production Music, and Universal Production Music. Those libraries typically are able to offer one-stop licensing (except for the performance rights, which are licensed through the PROs).

Licensing popular music by well-known artists has traditionally been reserved for sophisticated, well-resourced players in the media industry, but recently some publishers and labels have begun making certain music available to smaller producers in response to market demand.

TRADEMARKS

Trademarks are likely already quite familiar to you because they are so central to much of modern commerce. In its simplest form, a trademark is any word, name, symbol, or device that is used on a product or service to distinguish its source. Among the most obvious examples are words, logos, and slogans. For instance, the word McDonald's, the golden arches logo, and the slogan "I'm Lovin' It" are all registered trademarks of McDonald's Corporation.

Less obvious are what the law refers to as "devices," which include sounds, colors, or even the unique nature of a product's packaging. For instance, the three-note NBC chimes, the roar of the MGM lion, and the orchestral 20th Century Fox fanfare are all registered sound marks. Colors can also serve as trademarks, such as UPS's signature brown color, Tiffany & Co.'s powder blue, or Home Depot's vibrant orange.

TRADEMARK PROTECTION

Trademark rights arise automatically when a particular mark is "used in commerce." The hallmark of a trademark is that it is **distinctive**, which means that it identifies the origin of particular goods or services as distinguished from others' goods or services. Delta Air Lines, Inc., for instance, owns the trademark "Delta" in connection with air transportation services, but it can peacefully coexist with Delta Faucets, because consumers are not likely to confuse the two as they are in entirely separate industries.

Trademarks vary in their degree of distinctiveness depending on the mark and the context in which it is used. Courts have developed a spectrum of distinctiveness, sometimes known as the Abercrombie Classification after the Second Circuit case from which it derives.[9] At one end of the spectrum are **fanciful marks**, which receive the strongest protection, because they are completely made-up words, such as Kodak or Pepsi. At the other end of the spectrum are **generic marks** – marks that do nothing more than describe the product or service to which they are applied.

In the middle are **descriptive marks**, which are just slightly above generic in the sense that they describe the product or service but have acquired some degree of distinctiveness over time.

9 *Abercrombie & Fitch Co. v. Hunting World, Inc.*, 537 F.2d 4 (2d Cir. 1976).

Next up are **suggestive marks**, which allude to but do not directly describe characteristics of the product or service to which they are affixed. Netflix, which is suggestive of movies ("flicks") delivered via the internet, or Greyhound, which is suggestive of fast movement, are examples of suggestive marks.

Finally, **arbitrary marks** are real but are applied in a context that is entirely unrelated to the normal meaning of the word. For example, "Apple," if applied to a brand of fruit, would be descriptive, but when applied to computers, phones, and related services, it is arbitrary. Similarly, "Shell," if applied to something related to the ocean or coastline might be descriptive or even suggestive, but when applied to gasoline, it is arbitrary.

LOSING TRADEMARK PROTECTION

A trademark persists indefinitely until it is no longer used in commerce, or until it loses its distinctiveness.

A trademark might lose its distinctiveness if the mark becomes so commonly associated with the product or service to which it is affixed. Trademark lawyers call this phenomenon **genericide**.

Aspirin is an oft-cited example of genericide. Once a trademark of Bayer for its brand of acetylsalicylic acid, it had become so widely associated with the painkiller in the United States that it was declared generic.

To avoid genericide, trademark lawyers encourage companies to identify their products with not only the trademark but also a generic identifier to differentiate the product description from the trademark. For instance, a trademark lawyer might have counseled Bayer to refer to its product as Aspirin-brand acetylsalicylic acid. Concerns about genericide are presumably why Johnson & Johnson updated its familiar Band-Aid jingle from the original "I'm stuck on Band-Aid because Band-Aid's stuck on me" to "I'm stuck on Band-Aid *brand* because Band-Aid's stuck on me."

Because trademarks can become generic over time simply because of the way people use them in common conversation, many trademark owners spend a lot of resources working to make sure the media properly identify their products and brand, hopeful that it will stick in the mind of consumers. Among the most famous is an ad aimed at journalists from Xerox, whose trademark is often used as a shorthand for photocopiers (or the act of making a photocopy). Its headline reads: "When you use 'Xerox' the way you use 'aspirin,' we get a headache."

REGISTRATION

Like copyright, trademarks can be registered, but they don't have to be. Trademark rights arise upon use – as soon as a mark is used in a way that identifies a good or service, it receives a limited amount of protection. Registering the trademark with the U.S. Patent and Trademark Office can provide additional protections, such as a legal presumption that the registrant has the right to use the mark nationwide, and puts others on notice of the trademark claim. Federally registered marks may use the ® symbol, while unregistered marks may only use the ™ symbol.

Most states also have a trademark registration scheme but it is typically used only for marks whose goods or services are made available only within the state (that is, they are not in interstate commerce, as is required for federal trademark protection). State-registered marks may only use the ™ symbol.

INFRINGEMENT

Trademark infringement occurs when one party uses a trademark in a way that is likely to confuse consumers as to the source or sponsorship of a particular product or service. In determining whether one party has infringed on another party's trademark, courts will typically look at the similarity of the marks involved and the similarity of the goods or services with which they are associated. Marks that are very similar, and goods or services that are in the same class, are generally more likely to lead to consumer confusion than cases where there are more distinguishing characteristics.

Courts may also look at the distribution channels for the relevant products or services, and the extent to which consumers research and evaluate their options before making the decision to purchase. The theory is that even where marks or products may be relatively similar, consumers are less likely to be confused where consumers undertake a careful examination of their options (e.g., buying a car) versus something that tends to be bought more routinely or on impulse (e.g., shampoo).

Finally, courts will look for evidence of actual confusion in the marketplace. Sometimes the parties to a trademark infringement case will conduct a consumer survey to establish whether consumers are actually confused about the source of a particular product or service.

DILUTION

There is another form of trademark infringement known as **trademark dilution**, which occurs when a mark is not used on directly competing goods or services, but on *unrelated* goods or services, either by **blurring**, which lessens the distinctiveness of the trademark – for example, using the McDonald's trademark on motor oil — or **tarnishment** – for example, associating an erectile dysfunction drug with adult entertainment services.

Only "famous" marks can be diluted. A **famous mark** is not well defined in the law, but it is generally understood to mean that the mark is widely recognized by the

general public and would be considered "famous," in the conventional sense of the
word, by most people.

AVOIDING TRADEMARK PROBLEMS

A media enterprise may encounter trademark issues in two ways: either by making
use of other companies' trademarks in the course of their work or when naming their
own products, services, and media properties.

USING OTHER COMPANIES' TRADEMARKS

Just like copyright, trademark protection is not absolute, and not every use of another
entity's trademark is necessarily an infringement. The law recognizes three situations
where a third party may make use of a trademark owner's mark without their permission: expressive use, classic fair use, and nominative fair use.[10]

EXPRESSIVE USE

Using a trademark in a manner that is not primarily intended to serve a commercial
purpose is known as an **expressive use**, and is generally not considered trademark
infringement. Examples include using a mark for artistic reasons, or for parody, criticism, or commentary.

The leading case on expressive use is *Rogers v. Grimaldi*,[11] in which Ginger Rogers,
famous for her performance duo with Fred Astaire, sued film producer Alberto
Grimaldi over his film *Ginger and Fred*. The central characters of the film were two
fictional cabaret performers that were evocative of Rogers and Astaire and had
become known in Italy as "Ginger and Fred."[12] Rogers sued, alleging that the title
of Grimaldi's film infringed on the trademark rights in her name because consumers
might be confused into thinking that the film was about her or that she was involved
with its production.

The Second Circuit disagreed and concluded that the use of trademarks in connection
with an expressive work is appropriate if the use of the mark is artistically relevant
and not explicitly misleading.

DESCRIPTIVE FAIR USE

Under the doctrine of **descriptive fair use**, which is sometimes also called **classic
fair use**, an entity may use another entity's trademark in a descriptive sense, so long
as it is done in good faith. For instance, the Seventh Circuit held that Ocean Spray's

---

10 Note that although two of the concepts discussed here use the phrase "fair use," they are very different
    than the copyright fair use doctrine discussed earlier in this chapter.
11 875 F.2d 994 (2d Cir. 1989).
12 *Id.* at 996–97.

use of the phrase "sweet-tart" to describe its cranberry juice did not infringe on the rights of the purveyor of SweeTarts brand fruit-flavored candy. The court determined that Ocean Spray did not use the phrase to identify the origin of its product, but rather its core characteristics, which the court agreed were properly identified as "sweet" and "tart."[13]

NOMINATIVE FAIR USE

Finally, **nominative fair use** occurs when someone uses a trademark for the purpose of identifying the product with which it is associated or its source. As one court described it, nominative use of a mark is "where the only word reasonably available to describe a particular thing is pressed into service."[14] Such use is acceptable, and therefore not a trademark infringement, if:

1. The product or service in question is not readily identifiable without the trademark;
2. Only as much of the mark or marks as necessary to effectively identify the goods or services; and
3. The user must not do anything that would, in conjunction with the mark, suggest sponsorship or endorsement by the trademark owner.

For instance, you need not say "the restaurant commonly identified by its famous golden arches" to avoid using the McDonald's trademark, assuming that you intend to identify McDonald's and do not do it in a way that suggests that McDonald's has sponsored or otherwise endorses the content around it.

Among the most active protectors of their trademarks are athletic teams and their leagues. The National Football League (NFL), for instance, is known to aggressively police the use of its "Super Bowl" mark. For that reason, broadcasters are often warned to avoid using the statement in promotional announcements and advertising.

For example, the NFL would likely object to an ad for a local car dealer's "Super Bowl sale" because it suggests a connection between the car dealer and the league, and because the NFL routinely licenses such uses to paid sponsors. As a result, many media enterprises advise their talent to refer to the annual event as "the big game."

Still, it is perfectly legal to refer to the "Super Bowl" in the context of news reporting or other non-trademark uses that are intended to refer to the Super Bowl event, provided it is done in a way that does not improperly suggest an association with or endorsement of the NFL. Similarly, it is entirely appropriate to refer to individual teams by their trademarked names – for example, the "Los Angeles Rams," as opposed to "the Los Angeles football team that moved to St. Louis then back to Los Angeles."

13 *See Sunmark v. Ocean Spray Cranberries*, 64 F.3d 1055 (7th Cir. 1995).
14 *New Kids on the Block v. News Am. Publ'g, Inc.*, 971 F.2d 302 (9th Cir. 1992).

Note that the first prong in the nominative fair use test is that the mark is necessary to identify the product or service and that the user takes no more than necessary to make the identification. That means that it is riskier to use logos than it is to use word marks without permission since it is harder to show that the use of the logo was necessary to identify the product or service. For example, the words "Los Angeles Rams" are sufficient to identify the team in question; you generally wouldn't need the logo. Indeed, the leading case on nominative fair use contains a footnote that explains "a soft drink competitor would be entitled to compare its product to Coca-Cola or Coke, but would not be entitled to use Coca-Cola's distinctive lettering."[15]

Still, it has become common for people to use logos when referring to other companies and their products or services, and one of the leading trademark scholars thinks that such uses probably do qualify as nominative fair use. He writes that

> most people would agree that a business magazine or web site illustration could properly use the logos of companies whose economic performance is being discussed. The same will be true with many parodies and expressive criticisms of the owner of a trademark. Whether logo use is more than necessary is a highly fact-intensive issue that must be determined on a case by case basis.[16]

One context in which a company might use the trademark of a competitor is **comparative advertising**, which compares the performance of one branded product to that of another – for example, a battery manufacturer might say its batteries last three times as long as a competing brand. Generally, comparative advertising is legal, so long as the comparisons being made are true, not deceptive, and are backed up with appropriate evidence, just like any other ad.

Note that merely characterizing a branded product, bearing a trademark, in an unflattering light is not likely to give rise to a trademark concern, but don't forget about other considerations, such as defamation. If a branded product or service is characterized in a way that suggests it could be harmful, or that it will malfunction, for instance, the company that manufacturers the product may be able to assert that the characterization is defamatory.

Also, there may be conflicting commercial objectives to consider. If a creative work prominently features a particular brand in a negative or unflattering light, it could jeopardize relationships with that brand, even if the reference does not rise

---

15 *Id.* at 308 n. 7 (citations omitted).
16 McCarthy on Trademarks § 23:11 (footnotes omitted).

to the level of being legally actionable. For instance, in 1990, there was a widely played song by hip-hop group Digital Underground that contained the lyric: "I once got busy in a Burger King bathroom." Although there is nothing legally objectionable about the statement, a number of radio stations "bleeped" the line for fear of antagonizing Burger King or its local franchisees, which were buyers of significant amounts of radio advertising time.

SELECTING YOUR OWN TRADEMARKS

The other circumstance where media enterprises must consider trademark issues is in the selection of their own names, logos, slogans, and the like. Typically, before selecting a mark, the user will want to undertake a comprehensive search and confirm that it is free for use – a process called **clearance**.

Although the U.S. Patent and Trademark Office's database is online and easily searched, it is often advisable to have a trademark professional conduct a formal clearance search. That's because doing it comprehensively requires not only a search of federal registrations, but also every state database, domain name registrations, and various other sources. It also sometimes requires some judgment to determine whether a particular third-party use of a similar mark is likely to be construed as infringing and thus block your intended use.

Note that titles of single works are generally not protectable, but titles to series or franchises are. For instance, *Harry Potter and the Philosopher's Stone*, the first in the popular series of Harry Potter books, would not have been protectable as a trademark when it existed as a single book, but upon the publication of the second book, "Harry Potter" would have become protectable. Of course, today Harry Potter is a powerful brand that stands for much more than books, including a blockbuster movie franchise, amusement park attractions, and myriad consumer products.

Because single titles cannot function as trademarks, it is generally not necessary to clear titles of a single book, podcast, television show, article, and the like. But names of series, platforms, streaming services, or other products or services may well be protectable, and therefore may also infringe on another party's rights if they are confusingly similar to marks already being used in the marketplace, and it is generally advisable to clear them.

CYBERSQUATTING

The internet has led to the development of a new form of trademark infringement called **cybersquatting**, which is when somebody registers a domain name for a well-known trademark (e.g., disney.com), with the intent of profiting by selling the domain back to the trademark owner at an exorbitant price. Cybersquatting was a particularly big problem in the early days of the commercial internet before major brands discovered the importance of owning the domain names for their brands, even if they had no intention of using them.

Congress gave trademark owners an avenue of redress when it passed the Anticybersquatting Consumer Protection Act (ACPA) in 1999. The ACPA allows trademark owners to sue cybersquatters who register, use, or traffic in domain names that are identical or confusingly similar to another entity's trademark or even dilutive of it. To determine whether an individual acted in bad faith under the ACPA, courts consider the person's association with the mark and the rights they may have had to use it, and their intent to deceive consumers by registering the domain name.

Note that the ACPA does not apply to **gripe sites** or the practice of **cybergriping**, which is where someone uses a trademark as part of a domain that is used primarily for the purpose of commenting on or criticizing the brand. Using the trademark in this way has been deemed to be protected by the First Amendment and does not meet the criteria for bad faith under the ACPA in any event. For example, someone dissatisfied with a company whose consumer brand is BrandCo, might register brandcosucks.com or worthlessbrandco.net on which they publish their anti-BrandCo screeds. Despite the fact those domain names both contain the BrandCo mark, the owner of the mark would not be able to stop the use under the ACPA.

Note, however, that just because the use of the trademark is acceptable under the ACPA does not mean that other legal doctrines don't apply. If brandcosucks.com were to publish articles that made false and misleading claims against BrandCo, the owner might be liable for defamation or various other causes of action.

IN THE NEWS: "LINKING" VERSUS "EMBEDDING"

In 2016, photographer Justin Goldman took a photograph of sports luminaries Tom Brady and Danny Ainge that he then posted to his Snapchat account. From there, various people took the image by taking a screenshot, and uploaded the resulting captured image to other platforms, including Twitter, all without Goldman's authorization. A number of news organizations saw the image on Twitter and embedded it into their own reports that appeared on their respective websites.[17]

---

17 *Goldman v. Breitbart News Network, LLC*, 302 F. Supp. 3d 585, 586–87 (S.D.N.Y. 2018).

"Embedding" is a practice that involves using a small portion of code that allows the author of a webpage to incorporate content from other sources, such as a post from a social media site, without making a copy of it. Embedded content is in contrast to "hosted" content, which is where the material that appears on the webpage is stored on the same server that hosts the other webpage content. To an average user viewing a webpage, the distinction between hosted and embedded content is indistinguishable. The embedded content appears seamlessly alongside the hosted content to create a unified web browsing experience.

Goldman sued several of the news organizations that featured his image claiming that they infringed his copyright in the photo by displaying it on their websites. The defendant news organizations responded by arguing that they could not have infringed his work because they never made a copy of it, rather, they merely embedded it from Twitter. In support of their position, the defendants pointed to a Ninth Circuit case that stands for the proposition that whether a publisher infringes on a copyright owner's work depends on whether that work is hosted on the alleged infringer's server, or on the copyright owner's server (or that of someone authorized by the copyright owner).[18] Note that the case was brought in the Southern District of New York, which is in the Second Circuit, so the judge had no obligation to follow the Ninth Circuit's precedent, but could have chosen to follow it if she had found it persuasive.

But the judge did not find the case, or the defendants' arguments persuasive, and declined to dismiss the case. Specifically, Judge Forrest observed that the Ninth Circuit appeared to have conflated the right of display and the right of reproduction, which are conferred separately to copyright owners under the Copyright Act.[19] In other words, the court suggested that even though the publishers did not reproduce Goldman's photo by copying it onto their own servers, they still might be liable for copyright infringement by publicly displaying it on their websites without his permission.

The court also recognized that the Ninth Circuit case involved the use of images in a search engine context, where the goal is to help users navigate to a particular webpage, which is "manifestly not the same as opening up a favorite blog or website to find a full color image awaiting the user" as in the *Goldman* case.[20]

Eventually, the news organizations settled with Goldman, but the issue continues to come up. In 2017, photographer Paul Nicklen posted a video of a starving polar bear to his Instagram and Facebook accounts. The video soon went "viral" and Sinclair Broadcast Group, which owns more than 100 local television stations, embedded it in

18 *See Perfect 10, Inc. v. Amazon.com, Inc.*, 508 F.3d 1146 (9th Cir. 2007).
19 *Goldman*, 302 F. Supp. 3d at 595.
20 *Id.*

an article that was published on many, if not all, of its local station websites.[21] Nicklen sued for copyright infringement in the Southern District of New York and, as in Goldman's case, the court rejected the defendant's argument that embedding was not an infringement of the display right.[22] The court also determined that Sinclair's use was likely not a "fair use" under the Copyright Act.[23]

Meanwhile, courts in the Ninth Circuit have continued to apply the "server test." In 2021, two photographers sued Instagram for offering a software tool by which website operators can easily embed copyrighted photos posted to the Instagram platform. The court dismissed the case because the embedding tool only allowed the display of images posted to Instagram without having to copy them, which, under Ninth Circuit precedent, did not constitute copyright infringement.[24]

While the case was pending, and under mounting pressure from the American Society of Media Photographers, the National Press Photographers Association, and other creator rights organizations, Instagram updated its embedding tool to allow those who post images on its platform to determine whether they can be embedded on third-party websites.[25]

Whether other platforms follow Instagram's lead remains to be seen. Regardless of how the platforms react, however, there remains a stark split in the way courts think about embedding images from social media. The Southern District of New York has rebuked the "server test" while it remains binding precedent in the Ninth Circuit. Eventually, the matter may get teed up for the Supreme Court to consider, which would provide some nationwide clarity. Until that happens, media enterprises must carefully evaluate the risk of embedding images from social media without first securing permission from the copyright owner.

KEY POINTS AND TAKEAWAYS

1. Intellectual property is a class of intangible property that can be divided into four categories: patents protect inventions and discoveries, trade secrets protect commercially valuable, confidential information, copyrights protect original creative works, while trademarks protect words, names, symbols, or devices that identify the source of a particular good or service.
2. A copyright is a "bundle" of rights that gives the author the exclusive right to reproduce, distribute, and prepare derivative works, and publicly perform or

---

21 *Nicklen v. Sinclair Broadcast Group, Inc.*, 2021 WL 3239510, *1-2 (S.D.N.Y. Jul. 30, 2021).
22 *Id.* at *4-5.
23 *Id.* at *7.
24 *Hunley v. Instagram, LLC*, 2022 WL 298570, *1 (N.D.Cal. Feb. 1, 2022).
25 Thomas Maddrey, *Instagram Users Can Now Prevent Embedding*, American Soc'y of Media Photogs., December 17, 2021, https://www.asmp.org/advocacy/instagram-now-prevents-embedding/.

display their work. Generally, the author of a work is the initial copyright owner, except where the work is created as part of an employer-employee relationship, in which case the copyright is owned by the employer. Generally, exploiting any one of the rights in the bundle without permission of the copyright owner is copyright infringement.

3. Copyright protection is not absolute. The law contains a number of limitations and exceptions that permit people to make certain limited, socially desirable, uses of copyrighted works without the permission of the owner.

4. The most widely known limitation is fair use, which allows for certain limited uses for purposes such as criticism, comment, news reporting, teaching, scholarship, or research. To determine whether fair use applies in a particular case, courts balance four factors, including the purpose and character of the use, the nature of the copyrighted work, the amount and substantiality of the portion used, and the effect of the use on the market for the work.

5. Generally, the safest way to use copyrighted content, when a limitation or exception to copyright law does not apply, is to secure the permission of the copyright owner, that is, get a license. Stock photography, footage, and production music libraries are good sources of such material. In recent years, media producers have also looked to content licensed under a Creative Commons license, which allows for certain free-of-charge uses in exchange for complying with certain conditions.

6. Trademarks protect words, names, symbols, or devices (such as colors or sounds) that have commercial significance in that they identify the source of a particular good or service. Trademark infringement occurs when someone other than the trademark owner uses the trademark in a way that is likely to cause confusion

7. As in copyright, trademark rights are not absolute. The media may refer to trademarks in certain ways that are not likely to cause consumer confusion or otherwise harm the effectiveness of the trademark as a source identifier.

QUESTIONS FOR DISCUSSION

1. A colleague at your multiplatform media company has asked you to help her create a podcast series that celebrates the life and music of pop star Michael Jackson. She intends to prominently feature Jackson's music, and portions of interviews he gave in the past to other media outlets. She also intends to create a companion website that features images and video footage from his last concerts, media appearances, and the like. What issues should you encourage her to consider?

2. Would your answer change if, instead of a podcast series celebrating Jackson's life and music, it was a documentary that would explore Jackson's legal issues that he experienced toward the end of his career.

3. A local bowling alley is hosting a "March Madness Bowl-a-Thon" party and is looking to buy a multiplatform ad campaign on your television station, streaming service, and website. What will you tell the bowling alley? Why? What are some ways you might alleviate any concerns you have?

4. The premise that underlies copyright law is that the period of time during which
    the author may exclusively exploit his or her works serves as an incentive for
    authors to create new works, which enrich the public good by existing in the first
    place, and then ultimately falling into the public domain where they are free for
    use by anyone. Some have argued, however, that given how easy it is to create
    new works today (cheaper to produce, easier to distribute), the incentives previ-
    ously thought to be offered by copyright are no longer relevant, and that the
    complexity of copyright law stifles more creativity than it incentives. Based on your
    understanding of copyright from this chapter, what do you think?

CHAPTER 12
INTELLECTUAL PROPERTY: MEDIA AS PRODUCER

Just as media enterprises are frequent users of others' intellectual property assets, they are in the business of creating them – namely, copyrighted content represented by trademarked brands. What issues do media enterprises face as owners of intellectual property and what approaches can they take to enforce their rights to protect their content and brands?

This chapter looks at the same substantive areas of law, but from the perspective of a media organization whose works may be infringed, which is a growing problem in the "digital first" distribution environment.

THE PIRACY LANDSCAPE

Unfortunately, one side effect of having popular brands and content is that there is typically no shortage of people looking to copy or imitate them. In media, the simplest type of infringement media enterprises must deal with is slavish, direct copying of a media property, such as an entire film, television show, book, and the like. Mass infringement is often referred to as **piracy**.

Just as the digital environment has made it easier for media enterprises to create and distribute content, it has never been easier to pirate content. What used to require sophisticated equipment to duplicate videocassettes, CDs, or DVDs, for instance, and an on-the-street distribution network, can now be done at the push of a button.

Broadly, piracy today takes two basic forms: enterprise piracy and platform piracy.

ENTERPRISE PIRACY

Just as some organized crime rings are involved in distributing drugs, weapons, and other illegal activities, recently there has been a growing number of criminal operations involved with the sale and distribution of illegal content. Such enterprise pirates engage in piracy as a business model, often creating elaborate websites and service offerings that closely mimic their legitimate counterparts with well-designed user interfaces, real logos and artwork for the featured content, and live tech support. A similar piracy business involves the distribution of media devices that look similar to familiar, legitimate products that facilitate streaming content, such as Apple TV, Roku, or Amazon's Fire devices. Unlike those legitimate devices, piracy devices

DOI: 10.4324/9781003197966-12

often come pre-loaded with unlicensed content, or apps that direct users to sources of pirated content. Just as a Roku user might click on the HBO Max app to watch HBO, a user of a pirate device might click on an app that loads an illegitimate, unlicensed streaming platform.

Because enterprise pirates typically charge for their products or services, and feature popular brands on their marketing materials, it can be difficult for a consumer's untrained eye to tell the difference between pirated offerings and legitimate ones.

One tell-tale sign is that the cost of an illegal service or device is often much lower than its legitimate counterparts. That's because unlike legitimate services, which either own or license the content that appears on their platforms, and pay license fees that ultimately make their way to the creative professionals that produced the content, the revenues from enterprise pirate services go straight into the pockets of criminals, and they do not have to cover the cost of their content since they simply steal it.

> Piracy used to be primarily about distributing or providing access to illegal copies or streams of copyrighted works. Today, a new form of piracy has emerged in the form of **credential** or **password sharing**. Of course, probably everyone reading this book has shared a password to a streaming service or two with their friends, roommates, or family members over the years, but enterprise pirates have developed elaborate schemes to buy, sell, and trade stolen credentials for popular streaming services. As a result, most streaming platforms have been forced to implement sophisticated tools to identify credential misuse. Looking at a constellation of data points, ranging from the number of users who have accessed a particular account, the location of each login, the time between each one, and various other factors, media enterprises attempt to separate the casual sharers from the criminal enterprises.

ENFORCEMENT

Enterprise pirates are most commonly dealt with through criminal charges or civil litigation.

For instance, in July of 2021, a Newport, Oregon, man was sentenced to a year in federal prison and ordered to pay just over $4 million in restitution after pleading guilty to criminal copyright infringement and tax evasion stemming from his operation of numerous websites that allowed paid subscribers to download and stream various movies and television shows.[1]

---

1 U.S. Department of Justice, Press Release, *Newport Man Sentenced to Federal Prison for Creating Illegal Video Streaming and Downloading Websites*, July 9, 2021, https://www.justice.gov/usao-or/pr/newport-man-sentenced-federal-prison-creating-illegal-video-streaming-and-downloading (accessed June 18, 2022).

Even if a piracy operation does not catch the attention of criminal prosecutors, rights owners may sue the operator, resulting in potentially significant financial exposure. In 2019, an alliance of studios and networks sued Omniverse, a purveyor of whole-sale pirated content and infrastructure that other pirates could re-sell to consumers. The outfit was ultimately ordered to pay $50 million in damages, and its operator is prohibited from operating a similar service in the future.[2]

One of the great frustrations of antipiracy professionals is that enterprise pirates are often difficult or impossible to reach because their operations are often headquartered overseas, in jurisdictions where copyright laws are lax, or where enforcing copyright laws is not a priority. One solution is a legal and technical procedure colloquially known as "site blocking." Under a site blocking regime, copyright owners whose works are being infringed on a website or other inter-net-based service that is outside the reach of normal legal process may apply for an injunction ordering internet service providers to stop providing access to the offending site or service. The mechanism works well in the UK and numerous other countries, but legislative attempts at establishing a site blocking regime in the United States have not been successful.

PLATFORM PIRACY

Platform piracy refers to unauthorized content that appears on otherwise lawful, legitimate platforms. YouTube, for instance, allows users to upload their own videos, but it can also be used just as easily to upload content that the uploader does not own or have any rights to.

Unlawfully posted content harms copyright owners in two ways. First, it serves as competition to the legitimate, lawful versions of the same content. If consumers can watch *The Simpsons* on YouTube, they probably are not going to watch it on regu-lar television, thus reducing the number of viewers, and in turn, the amount that advertisers are willing to pay for ads during the show. Similarly, if enough content is available through unauthorized sources, those sources will displace subscriptions to legitimate, paid-for streaming services.

Unlike enterprise pirates, which operate services that are designed for the specific purpose of engaging in or facilitating copyright infringement, platforms are generally built for some legitimate, non-infringing use, which means that the tools used to go after enterprise pirates are not appropriate.

2 Alliance for Creativity and Entertainment, Press Release, *ACE Secures Consent Judgment for $50 Million in Damages and Permanent Injunction Against Omniverse*, November 12, 2019, https://www.alliance4creativity .com/news/ace-secures-consent-judgment-for-50-million-in-damages-and-permanent-injunction-against -omniverse/ (accessed June 18, 2022).

THE DIGITAL MILLENNIUM COPYRIGHT ACT

Section 230 immunizes online service providers for actions arising out of material posted by users on their platforms, but it specifically carves out intellectual property-related claims. That's because the **Digital Millennium Copyright Act or DMCA** provides similar protections for claims of copyright infringement that take place on a service provider's platforms.

Unlike Section 230, however, which requires nothing of the service provider, the DMCA puts some obligations on the provider in exchange for which it receives immunity from claims of copyright infringement by its users. This portion of the DMCA is often called the "safe harbor" provision. To receive the protection of the safe harbor, a service provider must:

1. Not be aware that the service is being used for copyright infringement. This includes actual awareness of infringement, but also awareness of any "red flags" that would suggest that the platform is being used for infringement;
2. Not have any right or ability to control the actions of its users;
3. Establish a procedure by which copyright owners may provide notice of infringing copies of their works that appear on the platform and the service provider removes them "expeditiously." The platform must also have a procedure in place to receive "counter notifications" from the original poster in the event that they believe the request to remove the content was a mistake or otherwise incorrect. Collectively, this process is referred to as the **notice-and-takedown** procedure.
4. Have a policy for dealing with repeat infringers that provides for the termination of users' accounts in appropriate circumstances.[3]

The heart of the DMCA is the notice-and-takedown provision. A takedown notice is effective if it contains these six elements:

1. A physical or electronic signature of the copyright owner or a person authorized to act on the copyright owner's behalf;
2. Identification of the copyrighted work that has been infringed;
3. Identification of the material that is infringing;
4. The contact information for the person submitting the takedown notice;
5. A statement that the person submitting the takedown notice has a good faith belief that the use of the copyrighted work is not authorized; and
6. A statement that the information submitted in the takedown notice is accurate, and under penalty of perjury, that the person submitting the takedown notice is authorized to act on behalf of the copyright owner.[4]

3 17 U.S.C. § 512(c).
4 *Id.* at § 512(c)(3)(A).

Upon receipt of a valid notice, the service provider is obligated to remove the content "expeditiously," although neither the law nor the courts have defined the term, and some platforms are better than others at removing content quickly. The slow pace of the takedown processes of some platforms is particularly troublesome when it comes to live programming such as high-profile sports events, which are most valuable when they are first broadcast.

If the person whose content is removed believes that the takedown notice was issued by mistake or that their use of the copyrighted work was authorized, including under the fair use doctrine, they have the right to issue a counter notice, after which the platform is obligated to restore access to the removed material within 10–14 days.

The reason for the delay, which is written into the law, is to allow the copyright owner to file a suit against the uploader if they continue to believe its rights are being infringed. As a practical matter, few rights owners sue individual uploaders because of the time, expense, and potential for negative publicity. In practice, if a user issues a counter notice, the copyright owner typically has little recourse, and the content remains online.

Courts have interpreted the DMCA to require a separate notice for each instance of infringing work on a particular platform. That means that if a user uploads a piece of copyrighted content, and the copyright owner has it removed, but somebody uploads the same content, the platform is not obligated to remove it unless it receives another notice.

PLATFORM-SPECIFIC PROCEDURES

Under the law, it is sufficient to send a takedown notice to the service provider's designated agent as registered with the U.S. Copyright Office at http://dmca.copyright .gov, but most of the major platforms have their own web-based forms that ask for the information required by the DMCA and typically have checkboxes for the required certifications – that the person submitting the notice has a good faith belief that the use of the copyrighted work is unauthorized, and that the information submitted in the notice is accurate.

Many copyright owners believe that the DMCA is antiquated and largely ineffective at mitigating online piracy. Content owners have advocated for the development of a "take down/stay down" regime that would require platforms to prevent the re-uploading of content that was already the subject of a takedown notice. Critics argue that requiring service providers to scan everything uploaded by their users would be cost prohibitive, and that the financial burden would prevent new companies from entering the market. They also assert that upload filtering would lead to overbroad enforcement because it would likely catch fair uses and other permissible uses of copyrighted work without any human intervention.

BRAND PROTECTION

Just as there is no shortage of people willing to make unauthorized copies of your work, when a media brand becomes well known, there is usually no shortage of people looking to take advantage of the goodwill of that brand. Nefarious actors may, for example, create fake social media profiles, for instance, representing an association with a well-known media brand or impersonating a popular media personality.

Often those fake pages include links to websites that lead unsuspecting users to download malware or to scam sites that solicit personal information or credit card details. Because the pages are branded with the media enterprise logo, or photos of their popular talent, some consumers may falsely associate those negative experiences with the media brand.

Along similar lines, popular media properties that sell branded merchandise may find themselves victims of counterfeit or otherwise unauthorized products. Print-on-demand services allow users to upload their own artwork from which they can create various products.

Unfortunately, there is no DMCA-like procedure for trademark issues or other forms of brand impersonation, but virtually all the legitimate platforms have their own policies against such conduct and will terminate users caught doing it. Every platform has its own procedure for reporting trademark infringement or brand impersonation, often described in the same place as each site's DMCA procedures.

FAN FICTION

Another challenge that falls into the "a good problem to have" category is when a media property, usually a film, television series, or book, is so successful that it inspires fans to create their own versions or extensions of the underlying creative work. On the one hand, such versions are flattering and are a sign of success (you can't have fan fiction without any fans), but on the other hand, fan fiction can be challenging because it is essentially an unauthorized derivative of the original content.

Further, if the audience mistakes it as originating from the source of the original work, it could damage the reputation or image of the original, especially if the fan fiction involves themes or puts characters in situations that are considered "off brand" for the underlying property, such as criminal conduct or sexually explicit activity.

As a practical matter, most media enterprises don't worry too much about fan fiction, provided it is not released commercially, and it appears in a manner that does not suggest an affiliation with or endorsement by the original author. But when a project becomes more professional and consumers may confuse it as originating with the source of the original production, copyright owners may grow more concerned.

That's what happened in 2015 when Paramount Pictures and CBS Studios, owners of the *Star Trek* franchise, sued Axanar Productions, Inc., a small production company that had produced a short film titled *Prelude to Axanar*, and had announced plans to produce a new feature-length film called *Axanar*. Axanar raised the money for the first film, and was fundraising for the second, on the popular crowdfunding website Kickstarter, and intended to distribute the new production on YouTube, alongside its first production. According to one press account, the project generated $1.13 million.[5]

In their lawsuit, Paramount and CBS alleged that the films were infringing unauthorized derivative works of the original *Star Trek* series. While the case was pending, Paramount and CBS issued guidelines for fan works, promising not to object to or bring legal action against those who create films consistent with the guidelines.

Those guidelines require that films be no more than 15 minutes, may not include the name *Star Trek* in the title, but must include the subtitle "A *Star Trek* Fan Production," must be noncommercial (with a production budget of less than $50,000), and must use amateur cast and crew that are not being compensated for their work. The complete set of guidelines is available at www.startrek.com/fan-films.

Axanar ultimately settled with CBS and Paramount, which allowed the company to release its films commercial free on YouTube in 15-minute increments. The company also agreed to follow the fan film guidelines for all future projects. In a statement announcing the settlement, CBS and Paramount said that they "continue to be big believers in fan fiction and fan creativity," and that they "would like *Star Trek* fans, with their boundless creativity and passion, to 'Live Long and Prosper.'"[6]

UNSOLICITED SUBMISSIONS

A funny thing happens when you become a successful producer of content: everyone suddenly has ideas for a story you should write, a movie you should make, or an amazing idea they have for a podcast.

While those discussions are generally entirely benign when they arise among friends, family, and colleagues in informal settings, more formal attempts at pitching new ideas to media companies can often lead to legal difficulties down the road.

Mark Twain once said that there is no such thing as an original idea, and the California Supreme Court once observed that "ideas are as free as the air."[7] Taking these concepts together suggests that no matter how original one might believe their

---

5 Matt Pressberg, *Paramount, CBS Settle 'Star Trek' Fan Film Lawsuit*, The Wrap, January 20, 2107, https://www.thewrap.com/paramount-cbs-settle-star-trek-fan-film-lawsuit/ (accessed June 18, 2022).
6 *Id.*
7 *Desny v. Wilder*, 46 Cal.2d 715, 731 (1956).

idea is, there is a strong likelihood that there is something very similar already in development somewhere in the creative ecosystem.

For that reason, most major media enterprises will not accept unsolicited submissions of creative material, unless submitted through a recognized agent, out of concerns that should they already have a similar project in development, they may be accused of copyright infringement.

For example, Disney's unsolicited submissions policy states that:

> It is the long-standing policy of The Walt Disney Company not to accept unsolicited submissions of creative material.
>
> We hope you understand that it is the intent of this policy to avoid the possibility of future misunderstandings when projects developed by our professional staff might seem to others to be similar to their own creative work.[8]

Some companies will accept unsolicited submissions, but only if the material is accompanied by a submission release that expressly acknowledges that there may be similar projects in development, and that the submitter will not sue the company to which the material is submitted in the event that a similar project moves forward.

IN THE NEWS: RETRANSMISSION SERVICES

In addition to the enterprise and platform piracy discussed previously, there is an occasional third type of mass-scale infringement that emerges from time to time, advanced by people who believe they have identified yet undiscovered a loophole in the copyright law.

In 2012 a new online service called Aereo debuted in New York. The service took traditional over-the-air broadcast signals, which were composed of copyrighted programming, and redistributed those signals over the internet to users' computers and other connected devices.

The company claimed that the service was lawful because their re-distribution of the signals did not constitute a "public performance" as contemplated by the Copyright Act. That's because rather than take signals from a central antenna and distribute them to each customer when they logged in, the service purported to assign to each user a small antenna, located in a distant warehouse, that could be tuned remotely by the user. Because of that technical arrangement, said Aereo, its distribution of the

---

8 The Walt Disney Company, *How Can I Submit My Ideas for Disney to Use in New Productions?*, https://support
   .disney.com/hc/en-gb/articles/115005422606-How-can-I-submit-my-ideas-for-Disney-to-use-in-new
   -productions- (accessed June 18, 2022).

copyrighted programming was not a public performance, but rather, a private transmission, which was outside the bounds of copyright law.

The Supreme Court disagreed, and Aereo ultimately ceased operations in 2014.[9] In a lower court decision, one judge described Aereo's multiple-antenna scheme as a "Rube Goldberg-like contrivance, over-engineered in an attempt to avoid the reach of the Copyright Act and to take advantage of a perceived loophole in the law."[10]

Four years later, a new service called Locast tried its own attempt at retransmitting television signals without authorization from the broadcasters. The service launched initially in New York and by May 2021, it was accessible in 32 U.S. markets. Locast was free to use, but it featured periodic interruptions with announcements encouraging users to make a donation to support the service.

Locast asserted that its service was lawful by virtue of a narrow exception in copyright law that applies to not-for-profit organizations that operate "translator" or "booster" stations. Such stations amplify existing broadcast signals in areas where terrain or atmospheric conditions make it difficult to receive signals otherwise; they are usually operated by municipalities as a service to their communities.

The four major U.S. broadcast networks sued Locast in July of 2019 arguing that the relevant exception did not apply to internet retransmission services such as Locast, and that Locast was collecting more money than necessary to defray its operating costs and was therefore not a nonprofit as contemplated by the law.

The court agreed with the broadcasters' position and held that Locast was not covered by the exception.[11] Locast suspended operations as a result, and shortly thereafter, the court entered an injunction, requiring Locast to shut down the service permanently.[12] Locast also agreed to pay the broadcasters statutory damages of $32 million.[13]

KEY POINTS AND TAKEAWAYS

1. The production and distribution of infringing copies of media properties are often referred to as "piracy." Just as the methods of legitimate content distribution have evolved over time, the methods of piracy have evolved with them, from selling

---

9 *American Broadcasting Companies v. Aereo*, 573 U.S. 431, 451 (2014).
10 *WNET, Thirteen v. Aereo*, 712 F.3d 676, 697 (2d Cir. 2013) (Chin, J., dissenting).
11 *American Broadcasting Companies v. Goodfriend*, 2021 WL 3887592 (S.D.N.Y. Aug. 31, 2021).
12 Jon Brodkin, *Locast's Free TV Service Ordered to Shut Down Permanently After Copyright Loss*, Ars Technica, September 16, 2021, https://arstechnica.com/tech-policy/2021/09/locasts-free-tv-service-ordered-to-shut -down-permanently-after-copyright-loss/ (accessed June 18, 2022).
13 Blake Brittain, *Locast Agrees to Pay $32 Million to Resolve Dispute with Major TV Networks*, October 28, 2021, https://www.reuters.com/legal/transactional/locast-agrees-pay-32-million-resolve-dispute-with-major-tv -networks-2021-10-28/ (accessed June 18, 2022).

bootleg VHS tapes or DVDs in unsavory parts of town to sophisticated streaming services that look and feel like their legitimate counterparts.

2. Today's pirates are often sophisticated criminal operators operating illegal businesses that traffic in unauthorized content. Often these rogue companies operate outside the reach of effective copyright laws or law enforcement and are therefore difficult to shut down.

3. Another form of piracy happens on otherwise legitimate platforms such as Facebook and YouTube. The Digital Millennium Copyright Act provides a mechanism by which copyright owners can have infringing material removed from such platforms. In exchange for complying with the notice-and-takedown provisions of the DMCA (among other things), platforms are granted immunity from the infringing conduct of their users.

4. Brand protection is another important part of a media enterprise's intellectual property program. As media enterprises and their properties become more popular, they may become misappropriated or otherwise misused, requiring trademark owners to take action where appropriate.

QUESTIONS FOR DISCUSSION

1. You are the publisher of a popular young adult book series called "The Misadventures of Johnny Wishbone" that features a young detective and a group of friends who help the local police solve crimes. Some of the books have been turned into movies. As a middle school class assignment, a teacher asked each student to write their own short-story version of a Johnny Wishbone tale. What legal issues do you see, if any, and what would be an effective way to deal with them?

2. How would your answer change, if at all, if the teacher sets up a class website, hosted by the school district, on which all of the student stories are publicly posted? What if the website were instead hosted outside of the school district's server and its web address was wishbonetales.net?

3. The teacher subsequently creates a printed volume comprising all the students' stories and gives one to each student at the end of the year as a memento. As the publisher of the original, official series, do you have any concerns? What additional information, if any, would you want before making a decision about how to respond, if at all?

4. What if the teacher sells the book from the wishbonetales.net website? What if the teacher sells the book on Amazon's marketplace?

5. One of the student's parents is a famous Hollywood producer and wants to turn his daughter's Johnny Wishbone story into a film. What issues does he need to consider before doing so?

CASE

Mountain One Media

What follows is a hypothetical case study from the fictitious Mountain 1 ("M1") television station located in the midsize city of Two Rivers. The region's top source for news and public affairs programming, M1 boasts over 14 hours of local news each day, which it distributes on its traditional television station, as well as over various streaming services and its own app that is compatible with all major mobile operating systems. The station also operates a popular website that offers live streams of its newscasts, written articles, and additional in-depth material, as well as archives versions of its broadcast stories.

The case study gives you an opportunity to explore the concepts discussed throughout this book and apply your learning to the type of scenario that might well arise in a real media enterprise. As you cover the material in this book, periodically revisit the facts in the pages that follow and see how the legal principles you have learned might apply in a scenario that mimics a situation in which you might find yourself during your career.

Note that this case was developed solely for teaching and training purposes and to serve as the basis for class discussion. It is not intended to serve as an illustration of effective or ineffective management or legal decisions. The story, all names, characters, and incidents portrayed in this book are entirely fictitious. No identification with actual persons (living or deceased), places, buildings, and products or services, is intended or should be inferred, and any similarities are purely coincidental.

Recently, a devastating fire broke out at the Mountain Metro Fashion Center, a massive regional mall located on the outskirts of town. With nearly 200 stores, two dozen restaurants, a movie theater, and an indoor amusement park, "the Metro" as it was known among locals, had become a de facto town square. M1 was among the first news organizations on the scene with live, breaking news coverage – six reporters on the ground, two anchors in the studio, and an aerial reporter in a helicopter – each of whom stayed on the air covering the story for nearly eight straight hours (the helicopter reporter took a few breaks to refuel throughout the day).

Several hours after the fire broke out, one of the reporters on the ground, Nancy Hildegard, a longtime investigative journalist, tweets that she has a tip from "a source close to the police department" that investigators are beginning to believe that the fire was the work of an arsonist. Several minutes later, she appears on camera holding an envelope that she claims to contain a search warrant, "This is an M1 exclusive," she says, tearing open the envelope on live television. "No other station in

Two Rivers has this. This was given to me by a confidential source inside the police department. This document has been sealed by the court. Nobody has seen this except the judge, the prosecutor, and the investigators."

Still live on television, she aimlessly banters with the anchor back at the studio while she sifts through the papers. "Okay, okay. Here. Here it is," she says with a progressively increasing sense of excitement. "Jeremy Stevens! It's Jeremy Stevens! Jeremy Stevens is the subject of the search warrant." She calms down slightly. "Jeremy Stevens is the man that police believe set the Fashion Center – our community gathering place, the center of so many lives here in Two Rivers – on fire here today. It's just such a tragedy, for our community, and for Jeremy Stevens and his family."

Hildegard and the anchor continue their banter when the control room abruptly switches to the helicopter, which is tracking a man who has abruptly leaped out of the smoldering embers of the mall into a heavily wooded area. When the anchor realizes what's happening, he cuts off Hildegard: "Wow! Did you see that? I mean, wow. We certainly don't want to speculate, but that guy ... wow, it's hard to imagine why he would just run off into the woods like that unless he was running from something. Perhaps trying to get away from the scene quickly. Again, we don't know for sure, but it is certainly possible that the gentlemen we just saw dart off into the woods could be Jeremy Stevens that is now wanted for arson as Nancy was just explaining to us."

While all this was going on, production assistants in M1's newsroom were gathering up all they could find about Jeremy Stevens. A few minutes later, a graphic appears on the screen with a photograph of a gentleman identified as Jeremy Stevens and the caption "Wanted for Arson." The photo was credited to a popular social media service. Using various other social media services, M1's producers were able to determine where Mr. Stevens lived and worked. They sent a reporter and camera crew to each location.

Mr. Stevens lives in an apartment building in downtown Two Rivers, where the reporter and accompanying photojournalist tried to gain entry but the door is locked. After waiting for about ten minutes, they encounter a departing resident who lets them in the building; he was skeptical at first but allowed them in after they said they were there to shoot some footage of the cityscape from the roof of the building.

Once inside, they proceed to Mr. Stevens's apartment where they are greeted by a woman who politely but firmly asks them to leave. Just as they're about to walk away a child – about seven or eight years old – comes to the door. The reporter immediately asks the child: "Where's your dad? Has he been acting strange lately? When did you last see him?" The door slams shut.

The crew dispatched to Mr. Stevens's workplace – an industrial complex just west of the city – was similarly turned away without comment, so the reporter and his photojournalist retreated to the public sidewalk from where they launched a drone to fly over the building and gated grounds. The resulting footage showed several employees, some of whose faces were clearly identifiable. M1 featured the footage on its website alongside a caption: "Suspected Arsonist's Coworkers."

Shortly thereafter, an M1 producer decides to do a live-shot standup with the reporter, on the air, to show and discuss the video footage. Just as the reporter goes live, a security guard for the employer comes running up, screaming "Get the [expletive] out of here. [Expletive] off, man." The reporter replies "[Expletive], Man. You could have just asked." The entire exchange made it to air before the control room had time to cut back to the studio.

As the day wore on, Hildegard's continued reporting revealed that the name on the search warrant was erroneous. The proper target was not Jeremy Stevens as first reported, but in fact, Jeremiah Stephenson. A clerical error somewhere between the investigators and the judge's chambers resulted in the name being wrong on the final paperwork. As soon as M1 learned of the error, it immediately stopped reporting on Jeremy Stevens.

A routine criminal background investigation into Jeremiah Stevenson revealed that he was convicted of possessing child pornography in 1998, but a miscommunication in the newsroom resulted in M1 reporting the prior charge as "sexual abuse by a person in a position of trust." The error persisted throughout M1's online and on-air reporting for several hours before it was corrected.

While all this was going on, the M1 promotions department was busy preparing "proof of performance" promos – short commercial-length vignettes that air during commercial breaks and describe how M1 was first on the scene, or the first to break certain aspects of the story – to amplify M1's position in the market as a leader in covering breaking news. The promos primarily comprise clips of M1's own reporters and anchors covering the fire, but one of the promos features footage of Two Rivers' police, fire, and paramedics at the scene of the fire, over which a voiceover says: "When you need to know, turn to the station that Two Rivers' first responders turn to first. M1 News." In addition to the footage of the first responders, the promo also features various images of different places around Two Rivers. The producer took a couple of the pictures herself, but she isn't sure where the others come from. The musical underscore for the promo came from Spotify.

Several days after the fire and the search warrant fiasco, the chief of police for Two Rivers holds a press conference updating the community on the status of the arson investigation. In the course of the conference, he calls out M1's Nancy Hildegard for her "abhorrent behavior" by "illegally using a sealed search warrant" in the course of her "reckless, irresponsible reporting." Hildegard responds by producing a three-part expose into the chief's history of domestic abuse. Although she gets some of the dates and details wrong, the reports are mostly accurate. The public demands that the chief resign, but he refuses; the mayor subsequently fires him for cause because he had misrepresented his criminal history when he applied for the Two Rivers job. As a result, the chief will not be eligible for his pension.

Separately, the Two Rivers District Attorney sends Hildegard a letter demanding that M1 supply the police department with "all footage, whether broadcast or not, of or pertaining to the fire and all related activities" and all of Hildegard's notes, e-mail, cell phone records, text messages, and any other records she may have "pertaining to her reporting" of the recent fire. He also demands that Hildegard "immediately disclose the source of the search warrant upon which she reported last Saturday."

The DA also caught wind of an upcoming story that Hildegard is working on that suggests the police and DA's arson investigation has gone off the rails. Specifically, she has identified two anonymous sources from within the police department who explained how gross mismanagement within the department has led to a disastrous investigation that is unlikely to ever result in an arrest. Concerned that it will jeopardize the investigation, the DA sues M1 and Hildegard seeking an injunction to stop the report from airing.

INDEX

Note: Page numbers in *italics* indicate figures and page numbers in **bold** indicate tables in the text

ABC News 78, 85, 119–120
absolute privileges 74
the Administration 16
administrative appeal 144
administrative law 18–19
adversarial press 40
advertising 7, 159, 218; advertising-supported streaming services 193; comparative 240; drug prices 41; endorsements and social media influencers 169–171; evidence-based requirement 165; false or deceptive 163–166; Ford's advertising agency 97; FTC enforcement tools 165–166; "green" products and services 167; special categories 166–167; targeted at children 166; unfair business practices 165; weight loss, dietary supplements, and related products 167
Aereo (online service) 256–257
Amazon 5–6, 215; Fire devices 249; Kindle line of devices 4; Prime Video 1
Americans with Disabilities Act (ADA) 183
Animal Planet 193
Anticybersquatting Consumer Protection Act (ACPA) 242
appellant 26
appellee 26
Apple 9, 194, 236; Apple Music 5; Apple TV 249
appropriation 96–102
arbitrary marks 236
arraignment 22
arrest 22, 64, 139, 262
articles 84, 100, 101
artificial intelligence (AI) 205, 209
ASCAP 233
aspirin 236
Association of National Advertisers (ANA) 172
Astaire, F. 238
AT&T 193
Audacy (radio broadcaster) 5, 9, **186**
audio description 182–183
authenticated viewing 190
Axanar Productions, Inc. 255

Bartnicki, G. 121
Bartnicki v. Vopper case 121
Beef Products, Inc. (BPI) 78

Bento Box Entertainment 214
Bethel School District No. 403 v. Fraser case 53
Biden, H. 206
Biden, J. 19, 203, 206
bill 16, 129
Billboard Music Awards 181
Bill of Rights 15, 89
Blackburn, M. 206
Black, J. 40
black letter law 20
blockchain 213, 214; Blockchain Creative Labs 216; ecosystem 215
Bloomberg Law 31
blurring 237
BN.com 5
Boal, M. 101
Bolton, J. 52–53
Brady, T. 214
Branzburg v. Hays case 126
Brennan, J. 126
Breyer, J. 54–55
broadcast content regulation 180; candidate access rule 184; children's programming 182; closed captioning and audio description 182–183; equal-time rule 184; fairness doctrine 184–185; false information, hoaxes, and news distortion 183–184; indecent and profane material 180–182; loud commercials 183
broadcasting 189; broadcast-cable spectrum of protection 189–190, *191*; and First Amendment protection 177–179; industries 3; radio 5, 12
Bundy, T. 151
burden of proof 24–25
Bureau of Alcohol, Tobacco, and Firearms 16

California Business and Professions Code 18
California Consumer Privacy Act (CCPA) 216
California law 127–128, 210
California Legislative Information website 30
California Penal Code 18
California Privacy Rights Act (CPRA) 216
California Public Records Act 147
California Regulations, Code of 30
California statute 127, 209

cameras: body 146; cell phone 137; in courtroom
    151–155; for filming movie 3; hidden 116;
    "lipstick" 119
candidate access rule 184
case law 20, 30–31
CBS Studios 85, 255
*Central Hudson Gas & Electric v. Public Service
    Commission* case 161
Central Hudson test 162
change of venue 149
Chauvin, D. 153
Child Online Protection Act (COPA) 201
Children's Online Privacy Protection Act
    (COPPA) 106, 166
children's programming 182
Children's Television Act 182
chilling effect 51
circuit courts of appeal 26–27, 29
circuit split 28
cite/citations 31; federal cases 32; state cases
    32–33; statutes and regulations 31
civil claims 21, 24
civil contempt 125
civil laws 21
civil litigation 21, 23–24, 250
claims 21, 83, 92, 96, 167; civil 21, 24; defamation
    64, 65, 74, 77, 78, 81, 82, 83; health or safety
    165; intellectual property related 252;
    intrusion 104; legal 81; of libel 61; minimizing
    threat of 65–66; patent 224; personal injury 83
clearance 241
Clinton, B. 179
closed captioning 182–183
CNN 6, 84–85, 188
codes 18
Colorado Open Records Act 146
Colorado Sunshine Act 146
Comcast + Disney **191**
Comcast 188, **191**, 198
Comcast Xfinity 3
Comey, J. 130
Commercial Advertisement Loudness Mitigation
    Act (CALM Act) 183
commercial licensing 230–231
commercial speech 159; compelled 162;
    for constitutional purposes 160; federal
    regulation 162–163; levels of First
    Amendment protection *161*; regulating
    161–162; spectrum of First Amendment
    protection 160; sponsorship identification
    rules for broadcasters 167–168; state
    regulation 163
common law system 19–20

communication 10, 55, 68, 71, 177; law 17,
    18; mass 61; platforms 57; private 115;
    privileged 143; radio and wireline 19; social
    media 11
Communications Act 19, 179–180
Communications Decency Act (CDA) 200–201
community antenna television system (CATV
    system) 187
comparative advertising 240
compelled commercial speech 162
compelled disclosure 125–126
compelled speech 41–42, 206
complaint 23, 43, 63, 165, 205
Computer Fraud and Abuse Act 21, 217
Congress 19, 38, 82–83, 179, 182, 204–205,
    210, 242
consent 74, 99–100, 115–116, 154, 211
contempt of court 125, 153
content-based restrictions 43–44
content-neutral restrictions 43, 44–45
cookies 216
copyright(s) 225; damages 227–228; duration
    226; infringement 21, 227–228; law 228;
    licensing 230; limitations and exceptions 226;
    registration 228
Copyright Act 25, 31, 243–244, 256, 257; *see also*
    Digital Millennium Copyright Act
cord cutters 191
cord nevers 191
Cosko, J. 217
cost of media technologies 7–8
Court of Appeals for Third Circuit 138
courts/courtroom 15, 23, 39, 40, 42, 46, 71, 147;
    access to judicial information 148; cameras
    in 151–152; change of venue 149; changing
    technology and changing attitudes 152–153;
    circuit court of appeal 26–27; district courts
    26; ensuring impartiality 148–149; gag orders
    150–151; judicial appointments 28–29; jury
    selection 149; sequestration 149; state
    courts 29
COVID-19 pandemic 43, 107, 152, 172–173, 203
Crawford, J. 108
Creative Commons (CC) 232–233
credentials 10, 138, 250
criminal: contempt 125; criminal 24, 118, 250;
    laws 20–21; prosecution process 22–23
criticism 76–77, 228, 238
"cross-ownership" rules 187
Cumulus Media (radio broadcaster) **186**
Curry, S. 214
cybergriping 242
cybersquatting 241–242

damages 72–73
data security 215–218
Davis, B. 108
de-platforming 205–207
deceptive advertising 163–164, 166, 168
deepfakes 209–211
defamatory/defamation 50, 61–62; anti-
    SLAPP statutes 79; defamation-proof
    plaintiff 67; defenses and privileges 74–78;
    elements 62–63; falsity 63; fault 68–72; food
    disparagement 78; harm 72–73; identification
    63–66; law 62; libel, and slander 61–62;
    litigation and procedural considerations
    80–83; *per quod* 67; *per se* 66–67; publication
    67–68; related causes of action 83; *Sandmann
    v. the media* case 83–85; speech 50, 61
defendant 20–24; advantage 98–99; civil 25;
    consent from plaintiff 74; constitutional right
    154; copyright infringement 25; criminal 25,
    52, 148, 151; and IIED 83; misappropriation
    and right of publicity 97; and NIED 83;
    nominal damages to punish 73; punitive
    damages to punish 73; viable claim against
    62, 63
defenses: affirmative 25; to disclosure claim 96;
    expressive work 100–101; in false light claims
    92; to intrusion claims 104–106; for plaintiff
    74–78
de Havilland, Olivia 108–110
De Havilland v. FX Networks, LLC case 108; false
    light 109–110; misappropriation and right of
    publicity 108–109
deliberative process 22; privilege 143
Delta Air Lines, Inc. 235
depositions 23
derivative works 226, 255
descriptive fair use 238–239
descriptive marks 235
digital media 1; characteristics 3–6; enterprise
    8; feature of 11; gatekeepers 8–10; law of 12,
    177; *see also* traditional media
Digital Media Law 12, 64
Digital Millennium Copyright Act (DMCA) 200,
    252–253
DIRECTV 187
disclosure 170; compelled 125–126; of personally
    identifiable information 107; proactive 140;
    see also public disclosure of private facts
Discovery Channel 6, 193
Discovery Communications 6
Discovery+, 5
discrete elements 24
discretionary jurisdiction 28

Dish Network 187
Disney 9, **191**
Disney+, 4, 6
disorderly conduct 116–117
distinctive trademark 235
district courts 26, 29
Dominion Voting Systems 62
Dorsey, J. 215
Douglas, William O. 89
doxing 216
Drone Journalism Code of Ethics 124
drones, newsgathering with 122; federal
    licensing considerations 122–123;
    professional considerations 124; state
    considerations 123
Drug Enforcement Administration 16
duopoly 186
duty of care 69
duty of loyalty 119–120

"educational and informative" programming
    (E/I programming) 182
Educational Media Foundation (radio
    broadcaster) **186**
Electronic Communications Privacy Act 115, 121
electronic reading room 140
electronic voting systems 62
Ellsberg, D. 52
embedding 242–244
en banc hearing 27
endorsers/endorsements 168, 169–171
enterprise piracy 249–251
equal-time rule 184–185
Esquire company 219
evidence-based requirement 165
exceptions: for copyrights issue 226; to First
    Amendment protection 50–51; to Section 230
    202; for social media 231; to wiretapping
    laws 116
executive orders 19, 30
exemptions 142–144
explicit claim 165
expressive conduct 38
expressive use 238
expressive work defense 100–101
extrinsic evidence 67

Facebook 1, 10–11, 43, 57, 204, 205–206, 213
fair comment 76–77
Fair Credit Reporting Act (FCRA) 106
fairness doctrine 184–185
fair report privilege 77
fair use 228–229, **230**

false information 183–184
false light invasion of privacy 90, 109–110;
    defenses 92; falsity 90–91; highly offensive
    to reasonable person 91; identification 91;
    known falsity or reckless disregard 92; public
    disclosure 90
falsity 63, 90–91, 92
Family Educational Rights and Privacy Act
    (FERPA) 89, 106–108
famous mark 237–239
fanciful marks 235
fan fiction 254–255
fault 68; actual malice 68–69; general-purpose
    public figures 70–71; involuntary limited-
    purpose public figures 71–72; limited-
    purpose public figures 71; negligence
    69–70; private figures 72; public and private
    figures 70; standards 68
FCC v. Pacifica Foundation case 178, 180
Federal Aviation Administration (FAA) 122–123
Federal Bureau of Investigation 16
federal cases 32
Federal Communications Commission (FCC) 19,
    179–180, 199
federal constitution 18, 29, 43, 89
federal courts structure 25; circuit courts of
    appeal 26–27; district courts 26; geographic
    boundaries 27; judicial appointments 28–29;
    Supreme Court 28
federal regulations 19, 162–163
Federal Reporter 31, 32; privilege 128–129
federal separation of powers 15–16, 17
Federal Supplement 31–32
Federal Trade Commission (FTC) 162, 172;
    enforcement tools 165–166; regulations 167
fees for FOIA request 141
Feud: Bette and Joan television miniseries 108
Fields v. City of Philadelphia case 138
fighting words 48–49
Filter Bubble Transparency Act 205
First Amendment of U.S. Constitution 37, 147,
    177; compelled speech 41–42; degrees of
    protection 51; fundamental freedoms 37–38;
    internet and 55–58; levels of judicial scrutiny
    for constitutional questions 46; press 39–40;
    protections 109, 208; regulating speech
    42–43; regulation 43–45; prior restraint 51–53;
    right to receive information 40–41; spectrum
    of protection 50–51; spectrum of scrutiny
    45; speech 38–39; student speech 53–55;
    time, place, and manner regulations 45–48;
    unprotected speech 48–50; vagueness and
    overbreadth 51

Florida trial of serial killer Ted Bundy 151
Floyd, G. 130, 131
food advertising and labeling 163, 164
Food and Drug Administration 143, 163, 172
Food Lion v. ABC case 119–120
Forrest, J. 243
Fortas, J. 53
Fourteenth Amendment of U.S. Constitution 38
Fourth Amendment of U.S. Constitution 103
fourth estate 39, 125, 137
Fox Corporation 191
Fox television network 102; Fox Entertainment
    214
Freedom of Information Act (FOIA) 139, 146, 148;
    exemptions 142–144; fees 141; Improvement
    Act 140; library 140; open meetings
    145; proactive disclosures 140; refusals
    and appeals 144; request 140–141, 144;
    turnaround time 141
Free Flow of Information Act 128

gag orders 150–151
Garland, M. 130
General Data Protection Regulation
    (GDPR) 216
Gitlow v. New York case 38
Goldman, J. 242
Google Drive 213
Gramm-Leach-Bliley Act (GLBA) 106
Gray (television group) 186
Gray, E. 154
Greyhound 236
Grimaldi, A. 238
group defamation 65
guilty of charges 22–23

harassment: and hate speech 49; and stalking
    117–118
hate speech 49, 57
Haugen, F. 203–204
Hauptmann, B. 151
HBO 6–7, 188; HBO Go 190–191, 198; HBO Max
    5, 191
Health Insurance Portability and Accountability
    Act (HIPAA) 89, 106–107
HGTV 5, 6
highly offensive to reasonable person 91,
    94, 104
Hildegard, N. 259–262
hoaxes 183–184
Holder, E. 130
Holmes, P. 132–133
House of Representatives 16

Hulu 1, 6, 198
hung jury 22
The Hurt Locker 101, 108–109

identification 63, 91, 93–94, 98; direct 64; group
     defamation 65; indirect 64; of real people
     in fictitious works 65–66; sponsorship
     identification rules 167–168; as sword and
     shield 64–65
iFOIA project 146
iHeartMedia (radio broadcaster) 5, 9, 177, **186**
Illinois Supreme Court 212
implicit claim 165
incitement 48, 49, 52
incremental harm 75
indecency 50, 181
indecent and profane material 180–182
indirect identification 64
individual freedom of mind 42
information: compilation for law enforcement
     143; content provider 201; false 183–184;
     information gatherings 120–121; privacy
     215–218; right to receive 40–41; services 200
initial court appearance 22
injunctive relief 21, 24
Instagram 213, 244
intellectual property (IP) 223; avoiding
     trademark problems 238–241; brand
     protection 254; copyrights 225–228;
     cybersquatting 241–242; enterprise piracy
     249–251; fair use 228–229; fan fiction
     254–255; "linking" *vs.* "embedding" 242–244;
     music licensing 233–235; patents 223–224;
     permission 229–233; piracy landscape 249;
     platform piracy 251–253; retransmission
     services 256–257; trademarks 225, 235–238;
     trade secrets 225; unsolicited submissions
     255–256
intentional infliction of emotional distress
     (IIED) 83
intentional intrusion 103–104
interactive computer services 201
intermediate scrutiny 45
internet 199; CDA 200–201; de-platforming
     205–207; deepfakes 209–211; and First
     Amendment 55–58; frustrations with online
     platforms 202–205; information privacy and
     data security 215–218; network neutrality
     197–200; NFTs 213–215; nonconsensual
     pornography 211–213; *Nunes v. Lizza, et al.*
     case 218–220; Section 230 201–202; violent
     content in video games 207–209
internet protocol address (IP address) 198

internet service provider (ISP) 197–198
intrusion upon seclusion 103; defenses 104–106;
     highly offensive to reasonable person 104;
     intentional intrusion upon the solitude or
     seclusion of another 103–104
involuntary limited-purpose public figures 71–72

Jackson, J. 181
James, L. 214
Jefferson, T. 39
Jewel-Osco case 101, 102
Jordan, M. 101
journalists 121; compelled disclosure 125–126;
     protecting sources of 124–130; reporter's
     privilege 126, 128–129; shield laws 126–128;
     third-party subpoenas 130
judge-made law 20
judicial appointments 28–29
jury: hung 22; selection 149
Justice Against Malicious Algorithms Act 204

Kavanaugh, B. 217
"KidVid" rules 182
"killing people" platforms 203
Kindle Direct Publishing 8
King, Jr., Martin Luther 69

Lange, J. 108
law enforcement 250–251; agencies 16, 116, 139;
     files 137; FTC enforcement tools 165–166;
     information compilation for 143
law(s) 18; administrative 18–19; black letter
     20; Bloomberg 31; California 127–128, 212;
     case 20, 30–31; civil 21; common 19–20;
     communication 17, 18; copyrights 230;
     criminal 20–21; defamation 62; of digital
     media 12, 177; finding and researching
     30–33; food disparagement 78, 79; judge-
     made 20; media 11–13; regulation 45; shield
     127–128; sources 18–20; state 89; state open
     government 146–147; types 20–21
legal privilege 125
legislative branch 15–16, 18, 19, 28
LexisNexis 31
liable defendant 21
libel 61–62; claims of 61; tourism 82–83
license 229; CC 232, 233; Creative Commons
     245; FCC 180; master recording 233; NFL
     239; PRO 233; publishers 230; remote
     pilot 122
likeness 96, 97, 98, 100, 103, 109, 210
limited-purpose public figures 71
Lindbergh, C. 151

LinkedIn 10
linking 242–244
litigation and procedural considerations 80;
  libel tourism 82–83; republication rule
  81–82; single publication rule 82; statute of
  limitations 80–81; Streisand Effect 80
Lizza, R. 219
Locast 257
Los Angeles International Airport (LAX) 114;
  Media Guide *114*
Los Angeles Police Department 147
Los Angeles Rams 239–240
loud commercials 183

machine learning 209–210
Mad Cow Disease 78
Mahanoy Area School District v. Levy case 54
Make America Great Again 84
Maloney v. T3Media, Inc. case 32
Marshall, J. 126
master recording license 233
McBride, K. 106
McCain, J. 40
McCann, M. 12
McDonald's 235, 237, 239
media 1, 113–114, 217–218; applying shield laws
  to 127–128; building audience 7; circus 151,
  153; costs money to make 7–8; online 168;
  property 1, 249, 254
media enterprise 1, 3, 7, 11, 63, 83, 139, **191**,
  218, 231, 244, 254, 256; for defamation 65;
  defamation claim against 64, 80; digital 8,
  11; encountering trademark issues 238; fraud
  allegations for 118; infringement 249; modern
  12; policies against naming individuals 105;
  traditional 2, 6, 8, 12, 217
media law 11–13, 27; defamation role in 50;
  digital 12; traditional 12
media organizations 61, 69, 78, 83, 89, 132,
  153–154, 230; consortium of 108; traditional
  9, 127, 214
media product 1, 3, 8; cost of digital 4;
  traditional 2
Midler, B. 97, 98
Midler v. Ford Motor Co. case 97
Miller, J. 125
Miller test 50
Miller v. California case 209
Minnesota v. Chauvin case 153–155
"minor and moderate" annoyances 94
misappropriation 97, 98, 108–109, 160, 225
mistrial 22
money damages 21, 24, 227

motion: to dismiss 23, 84, 219, 227; for summary
  judgment 23
Mountain Metro Fashion Center 259
Mountain One Media 259–262
MuckRock 146
Muhammad Ali Enterprises 102
multichannel video programming distributors
  (MVPDs) 187, 190–191
multi-party consent 115–116
music licensing 233–235; for musical works *234*;
  for sound recordings *234*

National Basketball Association 214
National Football League (NFL) 239
National Freedom of Information Coalition 146
National Public Radio (NPR) 9
national reporters 31
NBA Top Shot 214
NCAA v. Alston case 103
Near v. Minnesota case 52
Nebraska Press Association v. Stuart case 150
negative option arrangements 165
negligence 63, 68, 69–70
negligent infliction of emotional distress
  (NIED) 83
Netflix 1, 4, 6, 192–193, 198–199, 217, 236
network neutrality 197; IP address discrimination
  198; peering 199; private network
  acceleration 198; protocol discrimination
  197–198; in United States 199–200
neutral reportage privilege 77
Nevada Supreme Court 128
new privacy regulations 216–217
news distortion 183–184
newsgathering 113; with drones 122–124; *Food
  Lion v. ABC* case 119–120; information
  120–121; interfering with police or failing
  to follow instructions *116*; limits 113–118;
  protecting journalists' sources 124–130;
  *Seattle Metropolitan Police v. Seattle Times,
  et al.* case 130–133
newspapers 2, 3, 127, 128, 149
newsstands 2, 3
newsworthy event 77, 82, 95–96, 100, 105
The New York Times 2, 9, 52, 69, 85; New York
  Times malice 68; *New York Times v. Sullivan*
  case 68
Nexstar (television group) **186**
Nicklen, P. 243
Nielsen 154
Ninth Circuit 98, 243–244
"no fly" provisions 123
nominal damages 73

nominative fair use 239–241
non-public forums 47–48; *see also* public forums
nonconsensual pornography 211; punishing
      perpetrators 211–212; removing offensive
      material 212–213
nonfungible tokens (NFTs) 213–215
not fair uses 229, **230**
"not for attribution" conversation 129
notice and retraction statutes 77–78
notice-and-takedown procedure 252
not liable defendant 21
Nunes, D. 218
Nunes v. Lizza, et al. case 218–220

Obama, B. 199
obscenity 37, 49–50, 52, 160, 180
"of and concerning" requirement 63, 65
"off the record" conversation 129
O.J. Simpson trial 151
Ollman test 76
Ollman v. Evans case 75
Omniverse 251
on background" conversation 129
OneDrive (Microsoft) 213
online media 168
"on the record" conversation 129
open meetings 145, 146
opinion, statements of 75–76
overbreadth 51
overbroad restriction 51
over the top services (OTT services) 190
ownership limits 185; "cross-ownership" rules
      187; radio 186; radio ownership caps **187**;
      television 186; U.S. radio groups **186**; U.S.
      television groups **186**
Oxenford, D. 183

PACER 148
Pai, A. 200
pamphleteers 56
Pappalardo, J. 123
paradox of choice 8
Paramount Global **191**
Paramount Pictures 255
Paramount+, 5, 6
Pareto principle 2–3
Parsons, E. 154–155
password sharing 250
patents 223–224; infringement 224; U.S. patent
      granted to Netflix *224*
pay-per-view movies 188
pay tv: evolution of 190–191; providers 187;
      regulation 187–188

Peacock (broadcasting company) 5
peering 199
Pelosi, N. 203, 209
Pentagon Papers 52
*The People of the State of California v. Orenthal
      James Simpson* case 20
performance rights organizations (PROs)
      233–234
permission 229; commercial licensing 230–231;
      Creative Commons 232–233; social media
      231–232
persuasive authority 26, 27
pervasive presence 178, 192
petitioner 28
petition for writ of certiorari 28
Phillipi v. CIA case 144
Phillips, N. 84
*Pico v. Board of Education, Island Trees Union
      Free School District No. 26* case 41
pin citation 32
piracy landscape 249
plaintiff 21, 23–24, 45, 63; attorney's fees
      and costs 227; without consent of 99–100;
      defamation 68; defamation-proof 67;
      establishing elements of defamation 74–78;
      false light 92; falsity and 90–91; identity 91,
      97–98; injury to 100; no fly provisions 124;
      public and private 92; showing publicized
      statement 93
Plame, V. 125
platform piracy 251; DMCA 252–253; platform-
      specific procedures 253
Playboy magazine 101
plea agreement 22
podcasts/podcasting 1, 5, 9, 12, 61, 168
police: misconduct 147; reporting on 137–139
political speech 160
pooling 154
pornography 50; child 50, 160; deepfake 210;
      nonconsensual 211–213
postmortem right of publicity 102–103
Powell, J. 126
preponderance of evidence 25
press 39–40
presumed damages 73
presumptive renewal 180
pre-trial release 22
Primetime Live news magazine program 119
prior restraint 51–53
privacy 89; false light invasion of 90–92; intrusion
      upon seclusion 103–106; public disclosure
      of private facts 92–96; statutory privacy
      protections 106–108

private: facts 93; figures 70, 72; network
     acceleration 198; parties 42
privileges 74, 125; absolute 74; attorney-
     client 125, 143; attorney work product 143;
     deliberative process 143; fair report 77;
     Federal Reporter 128–129; legal 125; neutral
     reportage 77; reporter's 126
proactive disclosures 140
product integration 167
product placement 167
profanity 50, 54, 181
"professional malpractice" model 69
professional news media 137
"proof of performance" promos 261
prosecution 20, 24; criminal 21, 22–23, 139
Protect Reporters from Exploitative State Spying
     Act (PRESS Act) 128, 130
protocol discrimination 197–198
public accommodation 183
publication 67–68; periodical 127; single
     publication rule 82
public disclosure of private facts 90, 92;
     defenses 96; highly offensive to reasonable
     person 94; identification 93–94; not of
     legitimate public concern 94–96; "private"
     facts 93; publicity 92–93
public domain 226
public figures 70, 95, 100; deepfakes
     among 210; general-purpose 70–71;
     involuntary limited-purpose 71–72, 95;
     limited-purpose 71
public forums 46–47, 56, 207; see also non-public
     forums
public inspection and copying 140
publicity 92–93; see also right of publicity
public library 47
public official 70
public performance 226, 230, 256
punitive damages 21, 73

quash 125, 132

Radio Act 179
radio and television: broadcast-cable spectrum
     of protection 189–190; broadcast content
     regulation 180–185; broadcasting 12;
     FCC and Communications Act 179–180;
     frequencies 178; new technologies
     190–192; ownership limits 185–187; pay tv
     regulation 187–188; streaming wars 192–194;
     traditional bases for regulation 177–179;
     viewers 183
Raskin, J. 128

rational basis review 45
R.A.V. v. St. Paul case 49
reading rooms 140
reasonable care 69
reasonable doubt 24
reasonable expectation of privacy 103
Reddit 57, 205, 213
Red Lion Broadcasting v. FCC case 177–178,
     179, 190
Reed, C. 64
refusals 144; to comply with lawful orders and
     disorderly conduct 116–117; to provide
     documents to citizens 146; to remove or
     moderate content 205
regional reporters 32–33
regulations 18–19, 30, 31, 43; content-based
     restrictions 43–44; content-neutral
     restrictions 43–45; federal 19, 162–163;
     FTC 167; laws 45; pay tv 187–188; privacy
     218–219; promulgated 19; regulating speech
     42–43; state 163; time, place, and manner
     45–48; traditional bases for 177–179; see also
     broadcast content regulation
remittitur 120
Reno v. ACLU case 55, 201
Reporters Committee for Freedom of the Press
     79, 146
reporter's privilege 126
reporting 137; covering courts 147–153; FOIA
     139–145; Minnesota v. Chauvin case 153–155;
     on police 137–139; state open government
     laws 146–147
republication rule 81–82, 93, 220
respondent 28
Restatement of Torts 62, 92
restatements 20
retransmission services 256–257
revenge porn(ography) see nonconsensual
     pornography
rhetorical hyperbole 76, 92
right of publicity: appropriation and 96–102;
     misappropriation and 108–109; postmortem
     102–103
Right to Know Law 108, 146
right to receive information 40–41
Roberts, J. 41
Rogers, G. 238
Rogers v. Grimaldi case 238
Roku 249, 250
Rolling Stone magazine 85, 145
routing reporting techniques 105
Rumsfeld v. Forum for Academic and Institutional
     Rights case 41

Sagdyev, B. 117
Sandmann, N. 84
Sandmann v. the media case 83–85
Sarandon, S. 108
Sarver, J. 101
Schafer, M. 152
Scripps (television group) **186**
seal documents 148
Seattle Metropolitan Police v. Seattle Times, et al. case 130–133
The Seattle Times 131
Section 230 201; attempts to change 204–205; exceptions 202
Securing the Protection of our Enduring and Established Constitutional Heritage Act (SPEECH Act) 82–83
Senate 16, 28, 74, 179
sentencing hearing 22–23
sequestration 149
serious crimes 21
serve defendant 23
server test 244
Seventh Circuit 101, 238
Shell 236
shield laws 126–128
shopping mall 43
Showtime 188
The Simple Life show 181
Simpson, O. J. 20
The Simpsons show 251
Sinclair (television group) **186**
Sinclair Broadcast Group 243–244
single-party consent 115
single publication rule 82
"sit-in"-style protests 39
site blocking 251
Sixth Amendment of U.S. Constitution 147
Skype 198
slander 61–62
smart contracts 214
Smartmatic 62
smartphone 4, 5, 8, 198
Smith, J. 64
Snapchat 55, 205
social media 10–11, 231–232; Facebook 1, 10–11, 43, 57, 204, 205–206, 213; fake profiles in 254; influencers 169–171; Instagram 213, 244; personality 70–71; platforms 43, 57, 201, 203, 205, 206, 207; Reddit 57, 205, 213; services 56, 203, 204; TikTok 1, 10; Tumblr 213; Twitter 1, 43, 213, 242
Soundcloud 4, 8–9
Souter, D. 152

special damages 73
special harm 63, 73
spectrum 3, 187; of First Amendment protection 50–51, 160; scarcity 177–178, 188, 189, 192; of scrutiny 45
speech 38–39; commercial 159–168; compelled 41–42, 206; compelled commercial 162; defamatory 50, 61; expressive 160; free 57, 89; hate 49, 57; political 160; student 53–55; symbolic 38; unprotected 48–50
Spence v. State of Washington case 38
sponsorship identification rules for broadcasters 167–168
sporting events 188
Spotify 5
Stahl, E. 133
stalking 117–118
standard of proof 24
Stanley v. Georgia case 40, 41
Star Trek series 255
State of Minnesota v. Derek Michael Chauvin case 20
statutes 18, 30, 31; anti-SLAPP 79, 108; California 127, 209; of limitations 80–81; retraction 77–78
statutory privacy protections 106–108
"Stay Home, Stay Safe" order 172
Stevens, J. 260
Stevenson, J. 261
Stewart, J. 126
Stewart, P. 159
strategic lawsuits against public participation suits (SLAPP suits) 79
streaming: services 61, 168; steaming wars 192–194
Streisand Effect 80
strict scrutiny test 44
student speech 53–55
subject matter restrictions 44
subpoena 125, 132; third-party 130
substantial injury 165
substantial truth 75
suggestive marks 236
Sullivan, L. B. 68–69
Sunshine Act 145–146
Super Bowl (2021) 96, 239
supremacy 18, 43; clause 17, 29
Supreme Court Reporter 30
surveillance 117, 123, 124
symbolic speech 38, 39
synchronization license 233

tarnishment 237
TEGNA (television group) **186**

Telecommunications Act 179, 184, 200
telecommunication services 200
Texas Beef Group v. Winfrey case 78
Texas False Disparagement of Perishable Food Products Act 78
Texas v. Johnson case 39
third-party subpoenas 130
Thomas, J. C. 57, 207
Tidal 5
TikTok 1, 10
titles 18
Todd, C. 40
Too Much and Never Enough: How My Family Created the World's Most Dangerous Man (Trump) 53
town criers 55, 56
Townsquare Media (radio broadcaster) **186**
Trade Commission Act 163
trademarks 225, 235; avoiding trademark problems 238–241; descriptive fair use 238–239; dilution 237–238; expressive use 238; infringement 237; losing trademark protection 236; nominative fair use 239–241; using other companies 238; protection 235–236; registration 236–237; selection 241
trade secrets 143, 145, 225, 244
traditional media 1, 177; characteristics 2–3; companies 4; enterprises 6
traditional radio broadcasting 5
trespassing 105, 113–115
trial 22; bench 26; impartial 143, 148
true threats 48–49
Truman, Harry 19
Trump, D. 52–53, 56–57, 130, 200, 205–206
Trump, M. 52–53
Trump, R. 52–53
truth 75
Tumblr 213
turnaround time 141
Turner Broadcasting System v. FCC case 188
Twain, M. 255
Twitch 205
Twitter 1, 43, 213, 242

undocumented labor 218
unfair business practices 165
United States Code (USC) 18
United States, network neutrality in 199–200
Universal Production Music 234
unprotected speech 48; defamation 50; fighting words and true threats 48–49; harassment and hate speech 49; incitement 48; obscenity 49–50

unsolicited submissions 255–256
U.S. Constitution 15, 18, 19, 30; executive branch 16; federalism and state governments 17; Fourteenth Amendment of 38; Fourth Amendment of 103; judicial branch 16; legislative branch 15–16; separation of powers 15–16; Sixth Amendment of 147; *see also* First Amendment of U.S. Constitution
U.S. Department of Justice 16, 130
U.S. legal system 15; burden of proof 24–25; civil litigation process 23–24; constitution of United States 15–17; criminal prosecution process 22–23; federal courts structure 25–29; hierarchy of U.S. court system 25; state courts structure 29

vagueness 51
verdict 22–23
veto 16, 19, 211
viewpoint restrictions 44
Viktoria, R. A. 49
violations 123; of criminal law 20; of right of publicity 100, 102; of state's food disparagement law 79
violent content in video games 207–209
Virginia Board of Pharmacy 161
Virginia State Board of Pharmacy v. Virginia Citizens Consumer Council, Inc. case 41, 159, 160
virtual MVPD 187
voir dire 149, 150
Vopper, F. 121

Walker, L. 154–155
walled garden 190
The Wall Street Journal 2
Walt Disney Company 6
wardrobe malfunction 181
Ward v. Rock Against Racism case 47
Warner Bros. Discovery **191**
Warner/Chappell Production Music 234
WarnerMedia 6, 193, 194
The Washington Post 2, 84–85
Washington's shield law 132
websites 168, 215, 233
weight loss 167
Westlaw 31
West Reporters 31
West Virginia State Board of Education v. Barnette case 41–42
Wheeler, T. 199
The White House 16

White, V. 98
White v. Samsung Electronics America, Inc.
   case 98
Whitmer, G. 172
wiretapping 115–116; laws 211
WordPress 8

Yahoo 213
Yocum, J. 121
YouTube 4, 8–9, 57, 205

Zacchini, H. 100–102
Zeta-Jones, C. 108

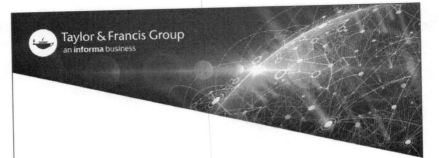

Made in the USA
Coppell, TX
18 January 2024

27867446R00160